The Professional Chef's®
ART OF
GARDE MANGER

The Professional Chef's®
ART OF
GARDE MANGER

Fifth Edition

FREDERIC SONNENSCHMIDT, C.M.C.

JOHN F. NICOLAS

 Van Nostrand Reinhold
New York

Copyright © 1973, 1976, 1982, 1988, 1993 by The Culinary Institute of America

Library of Congress Catalog Card Number 92-23801
ISBN 0-442-01153-9

I(T)P   Van Nostrand Reinhold is an International Thomson Publishing company.
         ITP logo is a trademark under license.

Printed in the United States of America

Van Nostrand Reinhold   International Thomson Publishing GmbH
115 Fifth Avenue   Königswinterer Str. 418
New York, NY 10003   53227 Bonn
                                         Germany

International Thomson Publishing   International Thomson Publishing Asia
Berkshire House,168-173   221 Henderson Bldg. #05-10
High Holborn, London WC1V 7AA   Singapore 0315
England

Thomas Nelson Australia   International Thomson Publishing Japan
102 Dodds Street   Kyowa Building, 3F
South Melbourne 3205   2-2-1 Hirakawacho
Victoria, Australia   Chiyoda-Ku, Tokyo 102
                                         Japan

Nelson Canada
1120 Birchmount Road
Scarborough, Ontario
M1K 5G4, Canada

16 15 14 13 12 11 10 9 8 7 6 5 4

Library of Congress Cataloging-in-Publication Data

Sonnenschmidt, Frederic H.
    The professional chef's art of garde manger / Frederic Sonnenschmidt,
  John F. Nicolas.—5th ed.
        p.   cm.
    Includes index.
    ISBN 0-442-01153-9
    1. Quantity cookery. 2. Cookery (Cold dishes). 3. Garnishes
  (Cookery) 4. Buffets (Cookery) I. Nicolas, John F. II. Title.
  III. Title: Art of garde manger.
  TX820.S64   1992
  641.7'9—dc20   92-23801
                                                CIP

*To the student and apprentice of
culinary arts and the future chefs*

Contents

Foreword

Over the years, *The Professional Chef's Art of Garde Manger* has established itself as one of the most complete and best-researched works focusing on practical application of cold food presentation, combining the necessary elements of artistry, creativity, and cooking sensitivity.

In realizing the dynamic changes that occur in the foodservice industry, the authors have very wisely updated *The Professional Chef's Art of Garde Manger* without changing its many desirable characteristics or its common sense approach, which made it so appealing to thousands of readers. They have included new culinary concepts, emphasized important aspects of buffet preparation, and addressed certain trends, particularly those that influence cold food presentation. This new revision includes a section of hot hors d'oeuvre, an update on various ingredients, and the development of low-fat forcemeats. The authors apply the international criteria developed by the American Culinary Federation, the standards by which buffet platters are being evaluated all over the world. *The Professional Chef's Art of Garde Manger* thus provides the interested culinarian with the fundamentals necessary to build

and perfect garde manger skills.

A new chapter on charcuterie (focusing on the preparation of various sausages and specialty items), a chapter on healthful cold foods, a chapter on cold foods for a la carte service, and an update of color photographs all represent a comprehensive and meaningful revision of this book. While many things have changed, the emphasis and recognition of basic culinary principles have remained untouched. The authors recognize that comprehension of the basic fundamentals is absolutely necessary for progress in a career as a cook and future chef.

Furthermore, the authors attempt to focus the attention of the reader on the fact that simplicity, combined with a feeling of elegance, is not a contradiction but, indeed, a desirable combination to achieve. Such an approach does not allow room for errors. The individual must be fully skilled in all elementary techniques and must have developed an eye for attractive and appetizing food presentations.

As a former Olympic Gold Medal winner and one of the few certified Master Chefs, Mr. Sonnenschmidt is uniquely qualified and brings to this book the necessary experience and professional perspective which he has passed on to the many graduates of the Culinary Institute, as well as to all serious readers of *The Professional Chef's Art of Garde Manger*. The recipes in this volume were developed and tested in the instructional kitchens of The Culinary Institute of America, where *The Professional Chef's Art of Garde Manger* is now used as a text for buffet catering courses. As such, *The Professional Chef's Art of Garde Manger* has established itself as one of the most desirable additions to any culinary library.

Ferdinand E. Metz
President
The Culinary Institute of America

Foreword

For almost two decades, *The Professional Chef's Art of Garde Manger,* a unique and most comprehensive text book, has evolved into a crucial and extremely beneficial professional working tool.

The authors' efforts to continuously seek perfection and excellence through updated revisions is exemplary of their commitment to the profession. Close attention has been focused on the ever changing food service industry and its growing demands. New interpretation of culinary concepts and new culinary equipment technology are discussed without ever losing sight of the fact that the young culinarian of today, first and foremost, must fully comprehend the complex, solid foundation of good cooking. And that, with the consistent adherence to basic culinary principles as the foundation, the young culinarian can further develop into the artist that he or she aspires to be.

Ultimately nothing is more rewarding to the young professional than experiencing growth, emotionally as well as intellectually.

Food continues to play an important role in our lives. As we accept the continuous learning experience, we begin to realize that we must have a passion for food. We must be sensitive to the food's origin and be aware not to adulterate the food product.

We also develop our sensitivity toward flavors, textures, colors, different taste sensations, and all the important elements that make up the food product. In other words, we are in the pursuit of perfecting our skills and craftsmanship, which is a lifetime commitment.

The authors of *The Professional Chef's Art of Garde Manger* have brought about all these feelings to the text. It is a "must read" for any aspiring culinarian. The book also provides the advanced professional with a fresh and renewed interest in refining and updating his or her garde manger skills. Therefore, it is sure to find a much-deserved home in many serious culinary libraries.

Mr. Sonnenschmidt is a pioneer and authority in his field and, as Culinary Dean of The Culinary Institute of America, his contributions will have a lifetime effect on the culinarians of tomorrow.

Victor A. L. Gielisse, C.M.C.
Chef-Owner/Actuelle Restaurant—Dallas

Preface

For many years, *The Professional Chef's Art of Garde Manger* has taught the preparation and presentation of cold food. This book is written to emphasize the standards, principles, and techniques required to produce quality food that is both nutritious and aesthetically pleasing. It is written for chefs, teachers, apprentices, students, and novices and is intended to function as a teaching aid as well as a working manual. Young chefs who are just starting out will find this book helpful for immediate problems in food production. They will still find it useful as they advance in their careers and their responsibilities become less involved with the actual production of food. This book should remain a constant source of reference for ideas, techniques, and easily understood recipes.

The operation of today's modern kitchen, especially garde manger, cannot be learned from books alone. It is essential for the apprentice-student to work with the required food in order to learn to apply the basic fundamentals of good food production. *The Professional Chef's Art of Garde Manger* not only covers the basic fundamentals of emulsion, roasting, poaching, sauteing, and baking, but also addresses new concepts of nutrition, preparation, and presentation. As a text, the book's material should be related to lectures, demonstrations, and actual work experience for professionals and hobby chefs.

New color photos of foods have been added for practical purposes as well as for culinary food displays. Hopefully, the combination of the textual materials, lectures, demonstrations, and kitchen experiences will improve learning and interest as well as allow apprentices/students to study more on their own.

Many colleagues have assisted in the development of this new edition. Our special thanks are due to The Culinary Institute of America; the New York Culinary Team; Henry Woods, Director of Learning Resources; Bill Reynolds, Director of Continuing Education; John Grubell, Photographer; and Lorna Smith, Assistant Photographer.

This book is dedicated to our students and colleagues, who have inspired us to write and revise *The Professional Chef's Art of Garde Manger*.

Acknowledgments

The authors would like to express their appreciation to the following people who helped in the preparation of this book:

J. B. Prince Company Inc.

The New York Regional Culinary Team 1992, especially Edward G. Leonard, Team Captain.

Timothy Ryan, C.M.C.

Lyde Buchtenkirch, C.M.C.

Bill Reynolds

David Kellaway, C.M.C.

Henry Rapp

Romanoff Caviar Company

Rougie and Cie, Souillac, France

Mark Erikson, C.M.C.

Fred Von Husen

Charles Koegler

Helmut Loibl

John Thomas Grubell, black-and-white and color photographs

and the many helpful students of the Culinary Institute of America and apprentices of the American Culinary Federation.

Also special thanks to David Kellaway, C.M.C., for his advice on chapter 15.

A final word of thanks to John O'Haire for his assistance with the design and preparation of the food platters.

The Professional Chef's®
ART OF
GARDE MANGER

The Art of Garde Manger

Reputations for fine food in many eating places depend on the performance of the garde manger department. In smaller operations that have no formal garde manger department, the same food specialties must nevertheless be prepared using the techniques that have been developed over centuries by masters of garde manger work. These are the methods and techniques presented in this book. However, the garde manger work shown and described here has been updated, incorporating modern methods that are adapted to today's menu requirements, food products, and equipment.

Garde manger tasks were so-called because in French the term *garde manger* meant food storage space; the work that was done in that location also was described by the term *garde manger*. In France, the garde manger area was located next to the kitchen and it was here that foods required for preparation of meals were stored. All preparatory work on meat, poultry, game, and other provisions also took place in this area. Since the area was located in a cool, airy spot that usually had some kind of food chilling facilities, cold food specialties were also prepared, decorated, and arranged for service there. This is how the work known as garde manger developed.

Since the basis of fine cuisine continues to include the preparation of specialties using aspic, chaud-froid, forcemeat, pâté, mousse, marinades, sauces, and dressings, the art of garde manger work is essential to culinary expertise.

The work done in the garde manger department starts with the preparation of basic ingredients—meat, poultry, fish and seafood, fruits, and vegetables. Barding, trussing, and the creation of fruit and vegetable decorations are among the skills to be learned.

The creation of a display piece such as a roast turkey is a process involving many steps. The turkey must be properly prepared for roasting; when roasted, the breast must be properly carved out; a mousse or salad must be prepared to fill the cavity; the breast must be sliced and arranged over the mousse or salad. The decorative touches needed must be selected, created, and put in place both on the bird and on the platter used in its presentation. All of these tasks require skills and methods learned in the garde manger department.

Garde manger output is also the foundation of such showcase items as hot and cold canapés, hors d'oeuvre, salads, galantines, and all of the cold food presentations that highlight the buffet, à la carte presentation, and reception food. Knowledge of the use of the ingredients essential to these presentations is indispensable.

An operation does not have to be large, formal, or committed to high food costs to profit from the art of garde manger. Preparation of a sizable number of specialties is not necessary; actually, it takes only one or two unique presentations to gain extra attention for a buffet or a special menu. Because garde manger specialties can be tailored to match menu requirements, the mastery of garde manger skills is an invaluable asset in food preparation for foodservice operations of every size and style.

Buffet Presentation

In a period of changing foodservice requirements, the buffet has proved to be a device for pleasing the public that can be used twenty-four hours a day. It can be styled as a formal presentation of elaborate food displays or it can offer a choice of favorite foods in casual array for the speedy service of roadside travelers or for weekly luncheons scheduled to meet the minimum time requirements of service club members.

Whatever the level of presentation, it is important that buffet foods be planned and necessary preparations completed well in advance so that the presentation for final service can be done speedily and without difficulty.

To plan a buffet effectively the following information should be obtained well in advance:

1. Number of covers (persons to be served)
2. Price per cover
3. Time of serving
4. Location for display buffet tables
5. Menu and zoning arrangement (see discussion that follows)
6. Number of serving lines (based on the number of covers and zones)
7. Number, sizes, and shapes of sectional tables available
8. Type and color of cloth desired

9. Nonedible pieces (such as ice or tallow carving) that will be needed, based on the theme, or as requested by the guests
10. Other elements that might be needed to enhance the theme or atmosphere, or that are requested by the guests.

TABLES

A buffet table in the desired size and shape can be constructed by assembling collapsible sectional tables that have been specially designed for this use. These sectional tables come in six basic shapes:

- Oblong (6 feet by 30 inches, 6 feet by 36 inches, 8 feet by 30 inches, or 8 feet by 36 inches)
- Round (60 or 72 inches in diameter)
- Half-round (60 inches across)
  Quarter-round (30-inch radius)
  Serpentine (built to fit with the above dimensions: inner arc, 2½-foot radius, outer arc, 5-foot radius)
- Trapezoid (built to fit with the above dimensions and measuring 5 feet at the base and 30 inches on each side of the three remaining sides)

The most popular shapes for buffet tables are oblong, round, half-round, and quarter-round. Serpentine and trapezoidal tables are used for buffets that require their special shapes to enhance presentation.

The shape of the buffet table will be determined by one or more of the following factors:

- Number of serving lines
- Size and shape of the room
- Seating arrangement
- Occasion
- Preferences of the guests

Before any decision can be made about shape, however, the required size must be calculated. Allow 1 linear foot of table per piece or arrangement of food (bowl or platter) to be displayed. Thus, a buffet menu having thirty-six pieces on display would require a table at least 36 feet long for an effective presentation.

When counting the number of pieces to be included in the display, do not forget to include the number of pieces that are not edible—centerpieces, stacks of plates, pepper mills, floral arrangements, and similar items.

Before the tables are to be assembled, a sketch should be made by the chef indicating the number of zones and courses. Each

Basic table shapes:

a. oblong;   b. round;

c. half-round;   d. serpentine;

e. trapezoid.

zone, or table area, contains a complete selection of the buffet items being offered. The number of times the selection is repeated depends on the number of persons to be served. This must be determined before the number, size, and shape of the buffet tables can be settled. In the accompanying illustration only two zones were needed.

The zoning must be correlated with the number of serving lines, and the number of serving lines will depend on the number of covers to be served. If there is more than one serving line, the guests will be served more efficiently and quickly.

Each zone should be divided into course areas; these will be duplicated in each zone. For example, the type of food displayed in Course Area No. 4 in Zone 1 should be identical to that displayed in Course Area No. 4 in Zone II.

In an à la carte dining room (as differentiated from a banquet room), the buffet table is preferably placed in the center of the dining room; this is often done in restaurants that feature a smorgasbord. Such a centrally located table will discourage guests from forming a line, and the operation will benefit from increased turnover. When a centrally located buffet table is not possible, the table can be built against a wall in a zigzag fashion (like teeth on a saw). This will generate a "scrambled" serving line that will speed and ensure the proper turnover.

BUFFET FOR FIFTY COVERS

The following lists suggest buffet items that may be arranged as in the illustration for a fifty-cover buffet.

1. Roast beef platter, Texas style (rib of beef as centerpiece and roast beef roulades)
2. Roast capon with Canadian bacon and asparagus
3. Poached salmon cut into slices with stuffed eggs and cucumbers

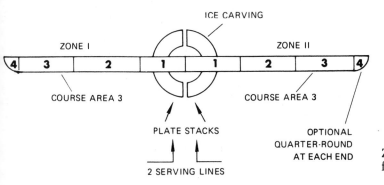

Zoning and course area for forty-eight pieces (6 by 8 feet).

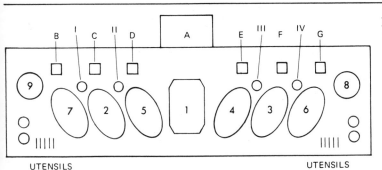

Buffet for 50 covers.

4. Stuffed eggs spring style
5. Pâtés de Foi de Volaille (garnish of poached apple rings; chopped pineapple flavored with Kirschwasser)
6. Medallions of veal with liver pâté and black cherries
7. Roulades of beef tongue with creamed horseradish (garnish of artichoke bottoms stuffed with ham mousse)
   A. Ice carving
   B. German potato salad
   C. String bean salad
   D. Vegetable salad
   E. Italian salad
   F. Fish salad
   G. Prosciutto ham and melon
   H. Prosciutto ham and pears
   I. Creamed Horseradish Sauce
   II. Sauce Verte
   III. Sauce Chantilly
   IV. Sauce Cumberland

Note: Hot foods and desserts should be on separate tables.

BUFFET FOR 100 TO 150 COVERS

The following lists suggest buffet items that may be arranged as shown in the illustration for a 100- to 150-cover buffet.

1. Prawn salad or langostino salad
2. Smoked salmon, smoked eel, and brisling sardines
3. Tea sandwiches and canapés
4. Stuffed eggs and watercress and stuffed tomatoes
5. Rooster baked in a crust (see Pâté)
6. Boiled ham with bone in and ham roulades
7. Roast sirloin roulade (slice roast beef and spread sweet relish mixed with mayonnaise over slices, then roll slice around a piece of celery)
8. Stuffed roast chicken in madeira aspic jelly
9. Saddle of venison stuffed with liver pâté and decorated with grapes
   A. Tomato salad

FLORAL ARRANGEMENT
(6" TIER)

ICE CARVING
(10" TIER)

TALLOW CARVING
(6" TIER)

Buffet for 100 to 150 covers.

Buffet for 200 covers.

ZONE IV   ZONE III

ZONE I   ZONE II

SERVING LINE

B. Swiss salad
C. Asparagus Vinaigrette
D. Cucumber salad, English style
I. Sauce Cumberland
II. Creamed Horseradish Sauce
III. Green Peppercorn Sauce with Honey Mustard

Note: For this buffet extra platters of food should be ready to make speedy replacements. Hot food should be set on separate tables.

BUFFET FOR 200 COVERS

The following lists suggest buffet items that may be arranged as shown in the illustration for a 200-cover buffet.

1. Roast turkey with pineapples and truffles
2. Westphalian ham and canned ham with pickled vegetables
3. Pâté of pheasant with orange salad in port wine
4. Smoked fresh trout
5. Roast duck with bananas
6. Roast veal with tuna-fish sauce
7. Stuffed Dover sole with lobster mousse and stuffed eggs
   A. Sauce Cumberland
   B. Sauce Raifort (horseradish)
   C. String bean salad, beet salad, coleslaw, Waldorf salad, salad Niçoise, mousse of salmon garnished with cucumbers, parfait of chicken liver in port aspic

Note: Hot foods and desserts should be on separate tables.

The remainder of this chapter provides examples of buffet menus and recipes for their preparation.

French Modern Buffet

HORS D'OEUVRE

Cocktail de Tomates	Tomato Cocktail
Asperges Mimosa	Asparagus Mimosa
Tomatoes Farcies Antiboise	Stuffed Tomatoes Antiboise
Roulades de Saumon Fumé aux Oeufs	Smoked Salmon Roulades

POISSONS

Billi Bi Froide	Cold Mussel Soup
Homard à l'Armoricaine	Lobster Armoricaine
Mousse de Saumon Fumé	Smoked Salmon Mousse
Coquilles St. Jacques Rémoulade	Scallops Rémoulade

ENTRÉES

Galantine de Volaille	Chicken Galantine
Terrine aux Légumes	Vegetable Terrine
Pâté d'Artichauts	Artichoke Pâté
Rôti de Boeuf Bouquetière	Cold Roast Beef Bouquetière
Mousse de Poulet en Gelée	Mousse of Chicken in Aspic
Dinde et Canard Fumé	Smoked Turkey and Duck
Jambon Persillé	Parsleyed Ham

SALADES

Céleris Rémoulade	Celeriac Rémoulade
Artichauts à la Parisienne	Artichokes à la Parisienne
Salade Lorette	Salad Lorette
Salade Russe	Russian Salad

DESSERTS

Crème Brûlée	Crème Brûlée
Gateau Moka	Moka Cake
Patisseries Françaises	French Pastries
Tartes aux Fruits	Fruit Tarts
Sorbet aux Framboises et Ananas	Raspberry and Pineapple Sorbet

FROMAGES DE FRANCE

Fromages de Chèvre Variés	Assorted Goat Cheeses
Mousse de Roquefort	Roquefort Mousse
Boursin à l'Ail	Boursin with Garlic
Brie aux Herbes	Brie Cheese with Herbs

TOMATO COCKTAIL

Yield: 6 portions

Ingredients

Tomatoes	3 large
Ketchup	¼ cup
Tomato paste	2 T
Salt	½ tsp.
Cayenne pepper	⅛ tsp.
Unflavored gelatin	1½ T
Chicken broth	⅓ cup
Heavy cream	½ cup
Aspic	1 cup
Lettuce leaves	to garnish

Method

Peel, seed, and dice the tomatoes. Stir in the ketchup, tomato paste, salt, and cayenne.

Dissolve the gelatin in the hot chicken broth. Whisk into the tomato mixture.

Whip the cream until stiff. Fold into the tomato mixture. Spoon the tomato mousse into individual molds lined with aspic jelly. Smooth the tops. Set in refrigerator. Cover with some more aspic jelly. Refrigerate until firm. Unmold the mousse on individual plates lined with lettuce leaves.

ASPARAGUS MIMOSA

Yield: 4 portions

Ingredients

Asparagus	16 stalks
Vinaigrette	½ cup
Dijon mustard	1 T
Tarragon, chopped	1 tsp.
Eggs, hard-cooked	2
Parsley, chopped	2 T

Method

Peel and cook asparagus in boiling water. Drain and cool. Cut into 2- to 3-inch lengths.

Combine the vinaigrette, mustard, and tarragon. Pour over asparagus and marinate for 30 minutes. Arrange asparagus on serv-ing platter or individual plates. Sprinkle with grated egg and chopped parsley.

STUFFED TOMATOES ANTIBOISE

Cut 1½-inch diameter openings at the top of twelve medium-sized, ripe tomatoes. Using a small spoon, remove all seeds. Marinate tomatoes for 1 hour in French dressing. Remove tomatoes from marinade; dry on absorbent paper. Fill tomatoes with following mixture: 1 cup tuna, two diced hard-cooked eggs, 1 tablespoon capers, and a little finely chopped parsley, chervil, and tarragon. Blend with mayonnaise to which mashed anchovy has been added. Refrigerate for 1 hour and serve.

SMOKED SALMON ROULADES

Stuff slices of smoked salmon with egg salad. Chill and glaze with some aspic. Arrange on a platter covered with a chiffonade of lettuce. Garnish with marinated tomato wedges and sliced hard-cooked eggs.

COLD MUSSEL SOUP

Yield: 4 portions

Ingredients

Fresh mussels in shells	3 lb.
Butter	1 oz.
Flour	1 oz.
White wine, dry	1 cup
Shallots, chopped	2 large
Parsley, chopped	½ cup
Heavy cream	1 qt.
Salt and pepper	to taste

Method

Clean, scrub, and debeard the mussels. Melt the butter in a saucepan. Add the flour. Stir over low heat until roux is light brown. Set aside. Combine wine, shallots, and parsley in a large kettle and bring to a boil. Add the mussels, cover, and steam until mussels are opened. Remove the mussels and discard those that did not open. Strain the cooking liquid, reduce to 2 cups, and blend in the roux. Add the cream and cook over low heat for about 30 minutes. Meanwhile, remove the mussels from shells. Season the soup to taste, then strain. Refrigerate. To serve, ladle the cold soup over the mussels.

Note: If too thick, thin with milk or heavy cream.

LOBSTER ARMORICAINE

Yield: 10 servings
Ingredients

Parsley, chopped	½ cup
Watercress, chopped	1 cup
Dill, chopped	¼ cup
Mayonnaise	½ cup
Aspic jelly	½ cup
Butter, softened	4 oz.
Smoked salmon, sliced	8 oz.
Lobster chunks	2 lb.
Salt	½ tsp.
White pepper, ground	¼ tsp.
Lemon juice	1 T
Seafood seasoning	¼ tsp.

Method
Combine the three green herbs. In a bowl, mix the mayonnaise with liquid aspic jelly and butter. Place a sheet of wax paper or plastic wrap on a flat surface. Lay the smoked salmon over the surface of paper or wrap.

Combine the herbs with the mayonnaise and aspic. Fold in the lobster chunks. Season to taste with the remaining ingredients.

Spoon the lobster mix over the center of salmon. Shape into a log. Lift the paper or film so that the smoked salmon seals the lobster mix. Twist both ends of lobster roll and refrigerate for 2 to 3 hours. Slice chilled lobster roll and serve with mayonnaise or other cold sauce.

SMOKED SALMON MOUSSE

Follow recipe (p. 133).

SCALLOPS RÉMOULADE

Poach bay or sea scallops in fish stock and dry white wine. Season to taste and cool. Marinate in Rémoulade Sauce (see p. 171) for an hour. Arrange in a bowl over a bed of lettuce.

CHICKEN GALANTINE

Follow recipe (p. 123).

VEGETABLE TERRINE

Follow recipe (p. 243).

ARTICHOKE PÂTÉ

Yield: 12 portions
Ingredients

Pork fatback	5 oz.
Veal, boneless	8 oz.
Pork, boneless	8 oz.
Oil	2 T
Onions, diced	½ cup
Salt	1 tsp.
Pâté spice	1 tsp.
Basil	1 tsp.
Cream	1½ cup
Egg whites	2
Artichoke hearts	12
White wine, dry	1 cup
Brandy	1½ T
Pistachios, chopped	½ cup
Ham, diced	⅔ cup
Pastry dough	16 oz.
Egg yolk	1 to glaze
Sherry wine aspic	to fill chimney

Method
Dice and freeze fatback. Dice the veal and pork. Heat oil in skillet and sauté the onions. Combine meat, onion, and seasonings in a bowl. Combine the cream and egg whites and pour over the meat. Refrigerate

for a few hours. Marinate artichokes in wine and brandy. Season with salt and pepper.

Grind the meat with the fatback. Blend in a food processor until smooth. Fold in pistachios and ham.

Grease a 5-cup mold and line side and bottom with pastry dough. Alternate forcemeat and artichokes, ending with forcemeat.

Cover pâté with dough. Brush with egg yolk and cut an opening in the center. Bake at 350°F for about an hour. When cold, fill the pâté with sherry wine aspic.

COLD ROAST BEEF BOUQUETIÈRE

Trim a sirloin of beef and season with salt and pepper. Roast to medium doneness. Allow the roast to cool completely, then slice three-quarters of the sirloin into thin slices. Reserve the remaining meat to garnish. Glaze slices with aspic. Arrange on large platter or over a mirror. Garnish with remaining meat and bouquets of marinated cooked vegetables such as small carrots, French string beans, cherry tomatoes, asparagus tips, and stuffed green olives. Serve with prepared mustard.

MOUSSE OF CHICKEN IN ASPIC

Follow recipe (p. 131). For best results, use a large mold in the shape of a chicken. Garnish with chopped aspic, stuffed cherry tomatoes, and tomato roses.

SMOKED TURKEY AND DUCK

Remove smoked turkey and duck breasts from their carcasses and carve into thin slices. Fill the resulting cavity with chicken liver or duck liver mousse (see recipe p. 134) and arrange sliced meats over the mousse so that the meat extends down the

serving platter or mirror (see page 149). Glaze with aspic. Garnish with Waldorf salad.

JAMBON PERSILLÉ

Jambon Persillé is a country-style dish, native to Burgundy, an area renowned for its subtle white and red wines.

Yield: 12 to 15 portions
Ingredients

Onion	1 large
Cloves, whole	2
Pigs' knuckles	5
Chicken stock	3 cups
Water	3 cups
Bay leaves	2
Thyme	1 tsp.
Unflavored gelatin	1 envelope
Ham, cooked, in 1-inch cubes	3 lb.
Red wine vinegar	¼ cup
Parsley, coarsely chopped	1½ cups
Salt and pepper	to taste
Cornichons, Dijon mustard	for garnish

Method

Stud the onion with cloves. Combine in a kettle the pigs' knuckles, 2½ cups chicken stock, water, onion, bay leaves, and thyme. Bring to a boil, cover, and simmer for an hour.

Dissolve the gelatin with the remaining ½ cup of chicken stock. Add to the kettle, along with the cubed ham. Return to a boil and simmer uncovered for an hour.

Discard the bay leaves. Remove the pigs' knuckles and take the meat from the bones. Chop the meat and skin coarsely and return it to the kettle. Continue cooking for 15 more minutes, then remove from the heat and add the vinegar, parsley, and seasonings. Pour the mixture into a terrine or a mold and refrigerate until set. Serve with cornichons and Dijon mustard on the side.

CELERIAC RÉMOULADE

Yield: 6 to 8 portions
Ingredients

Celery roots	2 medium
Lemon juice	1 T
Basic French dressing	½ cup
Mayonnaise	½ cup
Dijon mustard	1 T
Parsley, chopped	2 T

Method
Peel the celery roots, cut into cubes, and quickly grate in a food processor. Stir in the lemon juice immediately to avoid discoloration. Mix in the French dressing, mayonnaise and mustard.

Spoon into an oiled ring mold. Chill for 1 hour. Unmold over a round platter and sprinkle with parsley. Serve cold.

ARTICHOKES À LA PARISIENNE

Remove center from small cooked artichokes and fill with diced vegetable salad blended with mayonnaise.

SALAD LORETTE

Yield: 9 oz.
Ingredients

Beets, cooked	4 oz.
Celery, blanched	4 oz.
Basic French dressing	½ cup
Boston lettuce	3 leaves

Method
Cut beets and celery into julienne strips. Toss with dressing. Place lettuce leaves on serving plate and top with salad.

RUSSIAN SALAD

Yield: 1 lb. 7 oz.
Ingredients

Beets, cooked, drained, diced	2 oz.
Potato, cooked, diced	2 oz.
Carrots, cooked, diced	2 oz.
Peas, cooked	2 oz.
Beans, cooked, diced	2 oz.
Mayonnaise, well seasoned	½ cup
Asparagus tips, cooked	5 oz.

Method
Combine all vegetables except asparagus tips with mayonnaise. Arrange salad on plate and top with asparagus. *Note:* To give additional flavor, grated onion can be added to this salad.

CRÈME BRÛLÉE

Yield: 10 portions
Ingredients

Whipping cream	1 quart
Sugar	4 oz.
Egg yolks	10
Vanilla	1 T
Sugar, dark brown	¾ cup

Method
Preheat oven to 300°F. Bring the cream to a boil. Combine sugar and egg yolks. Stir until creamy. Gradually pour the cream over the egg mixture and stir well. Stir in the vanilla.

Pour mixture into individual ramekins or a shallow casserole. Place in a pan and add hot water to come halfway up custard container. Bake custard for 20 to 30 minutes, making sure center remains soft. Remove from water and refrigerate until cold.

Sift brown sugar evenly to depth of ¼ inch over the top of the custard. Place custard under a hot broiler, 6 to 8 inches from heat until browned lightly. Watch carefully as sugar will melt rapidly. Refrigerate and serve very cold.

MOKA CAKE

Yield: 16 portions
Ingredients

Chocolate sponge	2 thin slices
Vanilla sponge	2 thin slices
Kahlua syrup	as needed
Coffee buttercream	as needed
Marzipan coffee beans	for garnish
Chocolate cake crumbs	for garnish

Method
Split sponges and sprinkle in kahlua syrup. Spread buttercream on first layer of sponge and top it with a second layer.

Ice cake with buttercream and mark for 16 portions. Pipe a plain dollop of buttercream on each slice, and top each dollop with a marzipan coffee bean.

Trim the bottom edge of the cake with chocolate cake crumbs.

FRENCH PASTRIES

One of the most striking dessert displays for the French buffet can be an arrangement of French pastries with a centerpiece such as the Arc de Triomphe made of pastillage (gum paste) or decorations made of pulled sugar. A large variety of French pastries can be prepared. With puff paste make napoléons, cream horns, and turnovers. With cream puff paste make cream puffs, chocolate éclairs, coffee éclairs, and profiteroles. Tartlets with many different fillings can be part of a display for a French buffet although they would not be appropriate for this French buffet as two different tarts have been planned for it.

FRUIT TARTS

For a buffet presentation the tarts may be individualized tartlets or 8- or 9-inch tarts.

Prepare a sweet piecrust dough. Bake.

Garnish with custard cream. Arrange assorted fruits, such as strawberries, kiwi slices, raspberries, and cherries, on top of cream. Glaze with apricot jelly.

RASPBERRY AND PINEAPPLE SORBET

Yield: 10 to 12 portions
Ingredients
Pineapple Sorbet

Water	1 cup
Sugar	6 oz.
Pineapple pulp, puréed fresh	2 cups
Lemon juice	1 oz.

Method
Boil water and sugar. Stir to dissolve. Mix syrup with pineapple and lemon juice. Freeze in an ice cream freezer. The sorbet should be white and creamy.

To prepare raspberry sorbet, purée 2 cups of raspberries. Strain to remove seeds and follow the same method of preparation using the same amount of water, sugar, and lemon juice.

Arrange the sorbet in a mold, alternating layers of pineapple and raspberry. Serve with petits fours.

FROMAGES DE FRANCE

France produces over 400 varieties of cheese, each as distinctive as a fingerprint. It is best to serve cheese at room temperature. Take out of the refrigerator an hour or two before serving. Serve with thinly sliced French bread or crackers.

If a large assortment of cheeses is to be presented on a buffet table, arrange them on a board or a platter decorated with a few green and red grapes and grape leaves.

Use cheese markers to identify the cheeses so that the guests can be more knowledgeable about what they are eating or tasting.

Pastry Display. From left to right: Cold Orange Soufflé, Marzipan Figures; Crème Brûlée in Chocolate Cups; Wine Cream; French Pastries.

ROQUEFORT MOUSSE

Yield: 10 portions
Ingredients

Roquefort cheese	1 lb.
Cream cheese	8 oz.
Walnuts, chopped	1 cup
Heavy cream	1½ cups
Sherry aspic jelly	enough to line mold

Method

Allow the two cheeses to soften at room temperature. Mix in a food processor. Blend in the walnuts. Whip the cream until thick. Fold into the cheese mixture. Line a mold with the aspic jelly. Set in refrigerator. Fill the mold with the cheese mixture and refrigerate for 2 hours or more. Unmold and garnish with whole walnuts.

WURST SALAD, BAVARIAN STYLE

Yield: 2½ lb.
Ingredients
Marinade

Water	12 oz.
Vinegar, white	4 oz.
Olive oil	2 oz.
Prepared mustard	1 tsp.
Black pepper, ground	½ tsp.
Knockwurst, peeled, thinly sliced	2 lb.
Onion, thinly sliced	½ lb.
Parsley	for garnish

Method

Combine marinade ingredients and mix well. Combine with sliced knockwurst and onion, reserving some onion rings for garnish. Arrange mixture in salad bowl. Garnish around edge of bowl with sliced onion rings and parsley.

German Buffet

SALATE/SALADS

Wurst Salad, Bavarian Style	Wurstsalat Auf Bayrische Art
Cucumber Salad with Sour Cream	Gurkensalat mit Saurer Sahne
Potato Salad with Apple	Kartoffelsalat mit Apfeln
Celeriac Salad	Selerie Salat

VORSPEISEN/APPETIZERS

Bif Steak Tartare with Schinken Haeger	Steak Tartar mit Schinken Haeger
Smoked Eel with Horseradish and Pumpernickel	Geräucherter Aal mit Meerrettich und Pumpernickle
Herring in Mustard Sauce	Herring in Senf Sauce
Marinated Ox Tongue Bavarian Style	Ochsen Maulsalat

KALTE PLATTEN/COLD PLATTER

Saddle of Fallow Deer Seefeld	Rehrücken Seefeld
German Cold Cuts with Pumpernickel, Callenberger Style	Kalter Auf Schnitt Callenberger Stiel
Parfait of Chicken Livers, Bayerischer Hof	Parfait von Hühnerlebern Bayrischer Hof

HEISSE PLATTEN/HOT PLATTER

German Bratwurst with Sweet Mustard	Münchner Bratwurst mit Süssen Senf
Smoked Pork Loin with Wine Kraut	Kassler Rippchen mit Wein Kraut
Spaetzle with Brown Butter	Spaetzle in Brauner Butter
Venison Sausage	Hirschwürstchen

NACHSPEISSEN/DESSERTS

Zuger Kirsch Torte	Zuger Kirsch Torte
Bavarian Cream Bombe	Bayrische Bombe
Puff Pastry	Blatterteig Gebäck
Fruit Compote	Obst Compote

CUCUMBER SALAD WITH SOUR CREAM

Yield: 4 lb.
Ingredients

Cucumbers, 10 to 11 oz. each	6
Coarse salt	2 T
Vinegar, white, distilled	1 tsp. plus ½ cup
Onion, diced	1 medium
Dill, finely chopped	4 T
Sugar	1 tsp.
Sour cream	1½ cups
Oil	½ cup

Method
Peel cucumbers and slice thinly; mix with salt and 1 tsp. vinegar. Marinate for 30 minutes, drain through sieve, and dry thoroughly.

Combine the remaining vinegar with the onion, dill, sugar, and sour cream. Add cucumbers, mix well, taste, and add more salt if needed. Then add oil and toss. Marinate for 2 to 3 hours or overnight.

POTATO SALAD WITH APPLE

Yield: about 2 lb.
Ingredients

Potatoes	2 lb.
Vinegar, white	¼ cup
Chicken stock, hot	⅓ cup
Onion, medium, sliced or diced	½ cup
Salt	1 tsp.
Pepper	½ tsp.
Sugar	⅓ tsp.
Oil	¼ cup
Apple, peeled and diced	1

Method
Wash potatoes and cook in jackets. When done, let potatoes cool to room temperature and peel while still warm. Dice or slice, as preferred. Combine vinegar, chicken stock, onions, salt, pepper, and sugar in a saucepan and bring to a boil. Remove from heat and add oil and apples. Pour over potatoes and toss lightly. Marinate for 2 hours. Serve at room temperature.

CELERIAC (CELERY ROOT) SALAD

Yield: 5 lb.
Ingredients

Celeriac	6 lb.
Onions, medium	2
Water or chicken stock	2 qt.
Vinegar	1½ cups
Lemon juice	1½ cups
Sugar	6 T
Salt	2 T
Olive oil	1 to 2 oz.

Method
Peel celeriac, halve, and slice into ¼-inch-thick slices. Shingle into a stainless steel pan.

Slice onions thinly and sprinkle over celeriac.

Combine water, vinegar, lemon juice, and sugar; add salt and pour over vegetables. Make sure all slices are covered well. Bring to a boil and simmer al dente. Remove and chill in the liquid. To serve, add olive oil.

BIF STEAK TARTARE WITH SCHINKEN HAEGER

(Steak Tartare German Style)
Yield: 2 portions
Ingredients

Lean boneless beef, from fillet, top or eye round	½ lb.
Egg, whole	1
Salt, coarse	to taste
Black pepper, Malabar, crushed (see note)	to taste
Schinken Haeger (gin)	½ oz.
Onion, chopped	2 T
Pickles, chopped	2 T
Anchovy fillets, flat	3

Vinegar, white, distilled	½ tsp.
Hungarian paprika, sweet	½ tsp.
Prepared mustard	½ tsp.

Method

Blend all ingredients thoroughly; serve on pumpernickel.

Note: Malabar black pepper, which comes from the southwestern Malabar Coast of India, has excellent aroma, flavor, and pungency and adds a unique touch to this version of Steak Tartare.

SMOKED EEL WITH HORSERADISH AND PUMPERNICKEL

Remove skin and bones from smoked eel; cut into ½- to 1-inch pieces. Serve with Frozen Horseradish Sauce (p. 174).

HERRING IN MUSTARD SAUCE

Yield: 4 lb. 5 oz.

Ingredients

Schmaltz herring	10
Marinade	
Vinegar, white, distilled	1 qt.
Sugar	8 oz.
Dill stalks	15
Pickling spices	1 T
Carrots	4 oz.
Horseradish, fresh	1 oz.
Onion, medium	1
Juniper berries	10
Cloves	2
Peppercorns	20
Mustard seeds	1 tsp.
Mustard Sauce	
White wine	½ cup
Shallots, chopped	1 tsp.
Mustard seeds	1 T
Mayonnaise	1 cup
Dijon or Dusseldorf mustard	1 to 2 tsp.
Dill, fresh	for garnish
Pimentos	for garnish

Method

Fillet Schmaltz herrings and soak in water overnight. Combine all ingredients for marinade and boil for 5 minutes. Let cool.

Place fillets in a crock and pour cold marinade over them. Marinate for 4 to 5 days.

Remove herring fillets from marinade and cut into one-inch pieces. Drain well and mix with mustard sauce. Garnish serving dish with fresh dill and pimentos.

To make *mustard sauce*, combine wine, shallots, and mustard seeds and heat to boiling. Reduce liquid by three-quarters and cool. When cool, mix into mayonnaise. Add mustard; after 5 to 10 minutes, strain through cheesecloth.

Note: Herring can also be used for Her-

Saddle of Fallow Deer Seefeld.

ring Salad, Bismarck Herring, Rollmops, and similar dishes.

MARINATED OX TONGUE BAVARIAN STYLE

Yield: 2½ to 3 lb.
Ingredients
Smoked ox tongue	1

Marinade
Vinegar, white	¾ pt.
Stock, from tongue	1 pint
Onion, finely diced	8 oz.
Bay leaf	1
Black pepper, crushed	to taste
Mustard	to taste
Oil	2 oz.

Method
Cover ox tongue with water and simmer for 2 to 3 hours. Cool overnight; slice paper thin. Bring marinade ingredients to a boil; remove from heat, and while still warm, pour over sliced tongue. After marinating for several hours, drain and season with coarsely crushed black pepper, mustard, and oil. Garnish serving dish with thinly cut raw onion rings.

SADDLE OF FALLOW DEER SEEFELD

Yield: 6 to 8 portions
Ingredients
Saddle of fallow deer	3½ lb.
Oil	⅓ oz.
Liver mousse	16 oz.
Oranges	to garnish
Grapes	to garnish
Walnuts	to garnish
Aspic	to coat

Garnish
Pears, small size	6
Poaching Liquid (see recipe, p. 26)	
Red currant jelly	4 oz.
Raspberry brandy	½ oz.
Barquettes	to garnish
Peaches, diced	16 oz.
Champagne	4 oz.
Strawberries	8

Method
Trim venison saddle well. Remove loins and fillet from carcass. Trim carcass bone evenly with a meat saw. Season loins and fillet. Sear in oil for 5 to 8 minutes on all sides (should be pink) and chill.

Prepare a liver mousse and fill carcass. Shingle with thinly sliced loin of venison.

Decorate with oranges, grapes, and walnuts. Coat with aspic.

Garnish with chilled poached pears filled with red currant jelly flavored with raspberry brandy and barquettes filled with diced peaches and strawberries marinated in champagne.

GERMAN COLD CUTS WITH PUMPERNICKEL, CALLENBERGER STYLE

Usually six or seven different kinds of sausage and meats are offered in this buffet item. The sausage or *wurst* (the German word for sausage) can be made in an operation's own kitchen and requires neither extra equipment nor expense. Create the garnish for this display with pickle, radishes, and small pumpernickel sandwiches filled with cream cheese. (See recipe, p. 218.)

CHICKEN LIVER ORTRERER

Yield: 1 lb. 10 oz.
Ingredients
Fresh pork fat, chopped	8 oz.
Chicken livers	1 lb.
Shallots, finely chopped	2
Mushroom trimmings, chopped	½ cup
Salt	to taste
Pepper	to taste

Cold Cuts Callenberger Style. Left: boiled ham, roast beef, smoked cheese; center: roast turkey; right: Cheddar cheese, roast beef, sliced bologna; garnish: pickles, olives, red peppers.

Pâté spice	⅓ tsp.
Thyme	⅓ tsp.
Bay leaf	1

Method

Melt pork fat in sauté pan and use the fat to sauté the chicken livers. Do not overcook chicken livers; they should be pink. Remove the livers and sauté shallots and mushrooms in same pan; add seasonings and herbs. Combine all ingredients and cool. Blend in blender until smooth. Chill before serving.

PARFAIT OF CHICKEN LIVERS, BAYERISCHER HOF

Yield: 2 lb.
Ingredients

Chicken Liver Ortrerer	22 oz.

Brandy	1 oz.
Aspic	6 to 8 oz.
Heavy cream	4 to 5 oz.
Truffles, diced	as desired

Method

Mix the chicken liver, the brandy, aspic, and cream in a blender. Press through a fine sieve. Pour into a pie mold or timbale and chill. Garnish with truffles.

SMOKED PORK LOIN WITH WINE KRAUT

Yield: 20 4-oz. portions of meat; 20 2.5-oz. portions of sauerkraut
Ingredients

Onion, diced	4 oz.
Oil	2 oz.
Sauerkraut	3 lb.
White wine	1 pt.

Stock	1 pt.
Caraway seeds	2 T
Applesauce	4 oz.
Salt	to taste
Pepper	to taste
Juniper berries	2 T
Loin of smoked pork, 6 lb.	1
Potato, raw, grated	4 oz.

Method

Sauté onion in the oil until transparent. Combine onion, sauerkraut, wine, and stock, caraway seeds, applesauce, salt, and pepper; add juniper berries in sachet bag. Place in bottom of large roasting pan or brazier. Place smoked loin of pork on top of sauerkraut. Cover pan and cook in preheated oven at 350°F for 1½ hours, or until meat is tender.

Remove loin of pork. Stir grated raw potato into sauerkraut and heat well. Slice pork loin and arrange on top of sauerkraut to serve.

SPAETZLE WITH BROWN BUTTER

Yield: 1½ to 2 lb.

Ingredients

Flour, all-purpose	8½ oz.
Manitowa flour	9 oz.
Eggs	4
Water (tempered)	7 oz.
Salt	to taste
Butter	2 oz.

Method

Combine two flours. Make a well and break in the eggs. Mix with flour. Add tempered water and salt. Mix into a dough. Bring a large pot of water to a boil. Use either a pastry bag or a spaetzle machine to shape the dumplings and drop them into the boiling water. As soon as spaetzle float on top of water, remove to cold water. Drain well. Heat the butter until brown and use it to sauté the noodles before service.

ZUGER KIRSCH TORTE

Yield: 1 torte

Ingredients

Eggs	5
Egg yolks	2
Sugar	¾ cup
Cake flour	1 cup
Cornstarch	¼ cup
Butter, melted	5 T
Kirschwasser	6 T
Buttercream	2½ cups
Japonaise layers (see recipe below)	2
Cake crumbs, toasted	5 T
Powdered sugar	to dust
Candied cherries	12

Method

Whip eggs, egg yolks, and sugar over a double boiler to a thick consistency. Remove from double boiler and beat until cool. Fold in flour and cornstarch. Mix well. Gradually fold in warm melted butter. The mixture should be smooth. Pour into a cake mold, smooth the surface, and bake in preheated oven (375 to 400°F) for 30 minutes. Rest for 10 minutes in mold.

Fold 3 tablespoons Kirschwasser into buttercream and spread some on one japonaise layer. Remove top crust from cake and top cake with japonaise layer. Turn upside down and sprinkle 3 tablespoons Kirschwasser over cake. Spread some of the buttercream over it and top with the second japonaise layer. Cover entire cake with buttercream. Press cake crumbs into side of cake. Chill for one hour, dust with powdered sugar, and decorate with cherries.

JAPONAISE

Yield: 2 10-inch disks

Ingredients

Egg white	1 cup
Sugar	2 cups
Hazelnuts, ground	1 cup

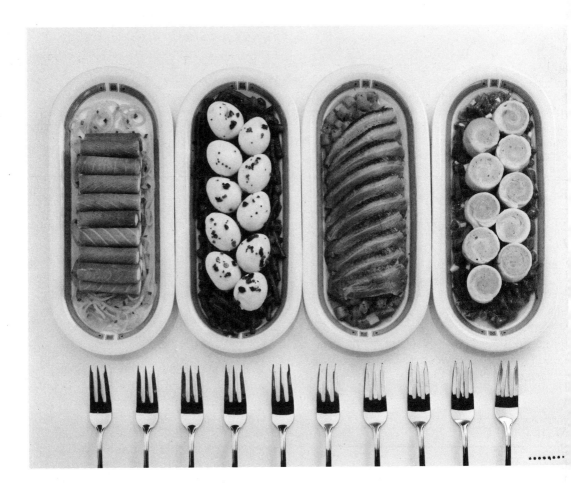

Method

Whip egg whites to soft peaks. Fold in sugar and hazelnuts. Pipe onto parchment paper to form 2 10-inch disks and bake in a preheated 250°F oven for 30 minutes or until dry.

BAVARIAN CREAM BOMBE

Yield: 8 to 10 portions

Ingredients

Strawberries	1 qt.
Orange or cherry liqueur	1 cup
Water	½ cup
Ladyfingers, split	16
Sweet butter, soft	½ lb.
Superfine sugar	1 cup
Almond extract	¼ cup
Almonds, finely ground	1¼ cups
Heavy cream, for whipping	2 cups
Whipped cream	for garnish

Method

Select ripe strawberries and wash and dry them with a paper towel. In a bowl, combine ½ cup liqueur with water. Dip ladyfingers into the mixture and drain on a wire rack. Line the bottom and sides of a 7-inch mold with about half of the ladyfingers. Cream butter and sugar until light and fluffy. Beat in the remaining liqueur and the almond extract. Stir in the almonds, whip the cream, and fold it into the butter mixture. Spread one-third of the mixture in the lined mold. Cover with half the strawberries, then add a layer of ladyfingers. Repeat the layers of the whipped cream mixture, berries, and ladyfingers. Then finish off with a layer of the whipped cream mixture and ladyfingers. Cover the top with a piece of parchment paper and weight down with a small plate. Chill overnight, then carefully unmold. Serve with additional whipped cream.

PICKLED MUSHROOMS

Yield: 3 lb.

Ingredients

Oil	2 oz.
Mushrooms, sliced	3 lb.
Carrots, cut into julienne	1 lb.
Marinated roasted peppers (see recipe, p. 23) or pimentos, cut in julienne	12 oz.
Oregano	1 tsp.
Garlic, minced	1 tsp.
Vinegar, cider	½ cup
Salt	to taste
Pepper	to taste

Method

Heat oil. Sauté mushrooms over high heat until tender. Cook carrots in water until tender. Add to mushrooms and cook for 3 minutes. Add prepared roasted pepper or pimento, oregano, garlic, cider vinegar, salt, and pepper. Bring to a boil, remove from heat, and refrigerate for 24 hours. Serve.

MARINATED ONIONS

Yield: 1 lb.

Ingredients

Marinade

White wine, dry	¾ cup
Vinegar, white	¾ cup
Water	4 cups
Oil	6 T
Garlic cloves	2
Parsley	small bunch
Sugar	1 tsp.
Salt	1 tsp.
Cayenne pepper	pinch
Basil, finely chopped	1 tsp.
Prepared Dijon mustard	1 tsp.
Pearl onions, peeled	1 lb.
Parsley, chopped	for garnish

Method

Combine marinade ingredients and heat. When the marinade comes to a boil, remove

American Buffet

RELISHES AND SALADS

Pickled Mushrooms, Onions, Carrots,
Roasted Peppers, Green Beans
Eggplant and Tuna Salad
Wild Turkey Salad Teddy Roosevelt
Black Beans with Ham
Known in the south as "Hopping John."
Succotash
*The Indians called it Misiquatash and
Henry Hudson never had it this good!*

APPETIZERS

Stuffed Cucumber, "Trapper Style"
*Early settlers found many ways to pre-
pare simple garden vegetables. This
one is stuffed with eggs and smoked
trout.*
Dried Beef with Pears
*The Indians smoked dried meat and
called it "jerky." Served with plump,
ripe pears, its called delicious.*
Pork Loaf with Eggs
*Woodsmen often took a repast of cold pies
with them as they set off for a day's
logging in the mountains.*
Hudson Valley Apples
*Red and ripe and stuffed with the river-
man's delight—crawfish.*
Celery, Carrots, Olives
*Served on a clean, icy floe of Mountain
River ice.*

MAIN COURSE

Marinated Duck Cornelius Vanderbilt
Deftly seasoned with local herbs.
Beef Stew "Settlers Style"
*Headed west in the wagon trains, buffalo
was used for this dish.*
Whole Smoked Pheasant
Preserved game of local hunters.
Barbecued Fresh Ham
*Innkeepers usually had a whole fresh ham
ready on the spit for travelers coming
by coach up the old Albany Post
Road.*

DESSERTS

Dutch Apple Crumb Pie
*The Pennsylvania Dutch housewife
turned the simple apple into an All-
American dessert.*
Peg Leg Peter Stuyvesant's Poundcake
Beaten with an old wooden spoon.
Strawberry Shortcake
*Wild strawberries, small and sweet, grew
in the meadows of New York. With
dollops of freshly whipped cream it's
as traditional as a picnic on the 4th
of July!*
Baskets of *Bearfoot Bread* will be on each
table.
*Made with cornmeal, or maize, it repre-
sents the American Indians' gift to the
first white settlers.*

from heat and pour over onions. Cool. Refrigerate for 48 hours. When ready to serve, sprinkle with chopped parsley.

MARINATED CARROTS

Yield: 2 lb. 10 oz.
Ingredients
Marinade

White wine, dry	¾ cup
Vinegar, white	¾ cup
Water	4 cups
Oil	6 T
Garlic cloves	2
Parsley	small bunch
Sugar	1 tsp.
Salt	1 tsp.
Cayenne pepper	pinch
Basil, finely chopped	1 tsp.
Prepared Dijon mustard	1 tsp.
Carrots, tender, young	1 No. 10 can
Parsley, chopped	for garnish

Method
Combine marinade ingredients and heat. When marinade comes to a boil, remove from heat and pour over carrots. Cool. Refrigerate for 48 hours. When ready to serve, sprinkle with chopped parsley.

MARINATED ROASTED PEPPERS

Yield: 2 lb.
Ingredients

Green peppers	2 lb.
Red peppers	2 lb.
Olive oil	2 cups
Vinegar, cider	½ cup
Garlic cloves, chopped	2
Oregano	1 tsp.
Salt	to taste
Pepper	to taste

Method
Hold the peppers over a flame and char well on all sides. Rinse charred peppers under running water. Remove cores and seeds, and slice lengthwise into one-half-inch strips. Place into mixture of olive oil, vinegar, garlic, oregano, salt, and pepper, and marinate for 24 hours.

Note: If fresh red peppers are not available, use pimento instead.

MARINATED CUT GREEN BEANS (HARICOTS VERTS)

Yield: 2 lb. 4 oz.
Ingredients

Green beans, cut	2½ lb.
Italian Dressing (see below)	1 cup

Method
Cook green beans only until crisp; drain, but do not cool. Pour Italian Dressing over green beans and marinate for ½ hour.

ITALIAN DRESSING

Yield: 1 qt.
Ingredients

Salad oil	2 cups
Chicken stock	1 cup
Vinegar, cider	1 cup
Garlic, finely chopped	2 cloves
Oregano, fresh, finely chopped	2 T
Salt	to taste
Pepper	to taste

Method
Put all the ingredients in a bowl or jar and beat or shake until they are well combined.

EGGPLANT AND TUNA SALAD

Yield: ½ gal.
Ingredients

Eggplant	2 medium
Tuna fish	1 13-oz. can
Marinara Sauce (see p. 24)	1 qt.
Ripe olives, sliced	1 small can
Green olives	1 small jar

Method
Slice eggplant lengthwise, ¾ inch thick, then cut into ¾-inch cubes. Sauté in oil

until tender, remove from heat, drain, and cool. When cool combine with the tuna fish, sauce, and olives and refrigerate for 24 hours. Serve in a plain white porcelain bowl.

MARINARA SAUCE

Ingredients

Oil	1 cup
Garlic, chopped	4 cloves
Tomato purée	1 No. 10 can
Crushed tomatoes	1 No. 10 can
Oregano	1 T
Salt	to taste
Pepper	to taste

Method

Heat oil in sauce pot, add garlic, and cook until garlic starts to brown. Add tomato purée and cook for 20 minutes. Add crushed tomatoes and cook for another 20 minutes. Add oregano, salt, and pepper to taste, and remove from fire.

Note: Only half of the sauce is needed for the above recipe.

WILD TURKEY SALAD TEDDY ROOSEVELT

Yield: 9 to 10 lb.

Ingredients

Smoked turkey, whole, 9 to 10 lb.	1
Pecans	16 oz.
Celery, diced	1 to 2 lb.
Lemon	juice of 1
Mayonnaise	3 to 4 cups
Worcestershire sauce	1 tsp.
Ripe olives	for garnish
Tomato rose	1

Method

Debone turkey. Dice all dark meat and one turkey breast. Save the other breast for use in salad presentation. Mix diced turkey, pecans, celery, and lemon juice. Add mayonnaise and Worcestershire sauce and mix well. Slice remaining turkey breast.

Set turkey salad in a bowl and shape the mound into a dome. Fan slices of turkey breast over dome of salad. Decorate with ripe olives and a tomato rose.

American Platter. Center: New England corn mousse, Parma ham, zucchini terrine, sugarsquash with lobster, and pressed wild mushroom terrine; garnish: smoked pheasant with cured breast of quail, mashed carrots on carrot croutons garnished with dill, roast loin of fallow deer, and whole wheat dough fish spoons topped with shrimp rounds rolled in poppy seeds.

BLACK BEANS WITH HAM

Yield: 8 lb.

Ingredients

Black beans	2 lb.
Ham hocks (or a 2-lb. ham)	4
Bouquet garni of carrots, celery, and leeks	1
Onion	1 large
Scallions	1 bunch
Vinegar, white	1 to 2 cups
Salt, coarse	to taste
Pepper	to taste
Oil	2 cups
Eggs, hard-cooked	3

Method

Soak beans in cold water for 24 hours. Pour off water and cover beans with warm water. Add ham hocks and the bouquet garni. Boil until beans are soft, then drain the beans and remove the bouquet garni. Remove ham hocks, cool, and chill.

Dice ham hocks, onion, and scallions, and mix with black beans. Add 1 cup of vinegar, taste, and add more vinegar gradually if needed. Add salt, starting with 1 tablespoon of coarse salt and 1 teaspoon of pepper; add more if needed. Mix well and add oil. Marinate for 2 to 3 hours at room temperature, then put in a bowl. Shape bean-ham mixture into a dome and decorate with sliced eggs. Serve immediately.

SUCCOTASH

Yield: 5 lb.

Ingredients

Lima beans, frozen	2½ lb.
Baby corn, frozen	2½ lb.
Red onion, diced	1 large
Scallions, diced	1 bunch
Vinegar, white	1 to 1½ cups
Coarse salt	1 to 1½ T
Black pepper	½ tsp.
Sugar	½ tsp.
Oil	1 to 1½ cups
Red peppers, chopped	2

Method

Cook lima beans and corn just to crispness. Sauté diced onion and scallions and mix with lima beans and corn. Add 1 cup of vinegar; if needed, add more gradually. Then season with salt, black pepper, and sugar. When seasoned to taste, add oil. Marinate for 24 hours. Put in a bowl, shape into a dome, and decorate with chopped red peppers.

STUFFED CUCUMBER, "TRAPPER STYLE"

Yield: 16 Cucumber Baskets

Ingredients

Cucumbers, medium	4
Coarse salt	2 oz.

Filling	
Smoked trout fillet	12 oz.
Eggs, hard-cooked, chopped	2
Horseradish, fresh or frozen	1 to 2 oz.
Mayonnaise	2 T
Green olives	for garnish
Dill sprigs	for garnish

Method

Peel cucumbers and cut into 1- to 2-inch pieces. Remove centers and sprinkle with salt. Let stand one hour. Rinse well and dry.

To make filling, prepare trout as described on p. 154. Fillet trout and remove skin. Purée and add chopped eggs, horseradish, and mayonnaise. Adjust seasoning. Use mixture to fill cucumber baskets, and top filled pieces of cucumber with a ripe green olive and a sprig of dill.

Note: If ready-made horseradish is used, be sure to remove some of its moisture before adding to recipe.

DRIED BEEF WITH PEARS

Yield: 4 lb. 5 oz.

Ingredients

Cure	
Salt	1¼ lb.
Sugar (dextrose)	7 oz.
Curing salt	2 oz.
Juniper berries, crushed	1 oz.
Beef, eye of round	6 lb.
Pears	8
Vegetable centerpiece	for decoration

Method

Combine all cure ingredients. Rub cure into beef on all sides. Cure for 7 days, turning daily. Then smoke at 190°F for 14 hours or to a 150°F internal temperature. Chill and slice paper thin. Cut pears into wedges and alternate one slice of beef with one wedge of pear around the edge of a round tray. Decorate center with a vegetable centerpiece.

Note: Prosciutto ham or bundnerfleisch can be substituted for beef in this recipe. If no smokehouse is available, sprinkle the meat with smoked powder and roast to an internal temperature of 150°F.

PORK LOAF WITH EGGS

(Jacques de Chanteloup)

Yield: 6 lb. 8 oz.

Ingredients

Pork liver	1 lb.
Pork, boneless, not too lean	5 lb.
Garlic, small	2 cloves
Onion	½ lb.
Parsley	5 or 6 sprigs
Flour	5 oz.
Eggs, whole	4
Table salt	1½ oz.
Curing salt	pinch
Pepper, white, ground	½ tsp.
Brandy	2 oz.
Heavy cream	½ pt.
Pork fat	to line molds
Aspic	to replace fat
Eggs, hard-cooked	to garnish

Method

Grind liver, 1 lb. of the pork, garlic, onion, and parsley through a fine plate. Grind the remainder of the meat through a coarse plate. Mix coarse and fine ground meat in mixing bowl, very slowly adding flour, eggs, seasonings, brandy, and heavy cream. Place mixture in molds or terrines lined with thinly sliced pork fat. Refrigerate for 24 hours.

Bake molds or terrines in a 350°F oven to an internal temperature of 160°F. Fifteen minutes before baking is complete, remove the hot fat from molds or terrines and replace with a strong, hot aspic. Bake for 15 more minutes. Cool overnight. Unmold the loaf, slice, and decorate with sliced hard-cooked eggs.

HUDSON VALLEY APPLES

Yield: 3 lb. 4 oz.

Ingredients

Poaching liquid for apples	
Water	2 qt.
Salt	1 oz.
Vinegar	¾ oz.
Cooking apples	10
Langostino or titi shrimp	2 lb.
Apples, peeled, cored, and diced	1 lb.
Dill, chopped	2 T
Sugar	½ tsp.
Lemon	juice of 1
Mayonnaise	1 to 1½ cups
Salt	if needed

Method

Bring poaching liquid to a boil. Peel and halve apples and remove cores with a parisian scoop. Simmer apples in poaching liquid at a temperature of 170 to 180°F for 5 to 8 minutes. Remove apples from liquid while still crisp and plunge at once into ice water to cool. Dry before using.

Mix langostino or shrimp, diced apple, dill, sugar, lemon juice, and mayonnaise well. Let mixture stand for 1 hour, then use it to fill poached apple halves. Place remaining salad in a small bowl and arrange apple halves around it.

Note: Frozen langostino should be defrosted slowly overnight. When defrosted, squeeze them slightly to remove some of the liquid.

MARINATED DUCK CORNELIUS VANDERBILT

Yield: 2 to 2½ lb.
Ingredients
Marinade
Water, cold	1 gal.
Coarse salt	½ lb.
Honey	1 cup
Saltpeter or curing salt	½ oz.
Madeira wine	2½ cups
Pickling spice—thyme, bay leaf, black pepper, juniper berries, sage	1 pinch
Domestic duck, whole, 3 to 4 lb.	1
Dill, fresh, chopped	4 T
Parsley, fresh, chopped	3 T
Black pepper, whole, crushed	½ tsp.
Cardamom powder	1 tsp.
Egg white powder (albumen) or plain gelatin	½ tsp.
Duck stock	to poach

Method
Mix marinade ingredients thoroughly in a saucepan. Heat to a boil, boil for 2 minutes, remove from heat, and cool.

Debone duck as for galantine (see p. 127). Remove as much fat as possible. Place duck on moist cheesecloth, skin side down, and sprinkle with dill, parsley, pepper, cardamom, and egg white powder or gelatin. Roll duck into cheesecloth tightly and tie cloth

at 1-inch intervals. Place in marinade and marinate for 2 to 3 days.

Place duck in duck stock and simmer, 20 minutes per pound, or until the duck reaches an internal temperature of 160° F. Remove and place in stainless steel or porcelain dish. Pour stock over duck, place a heavy weight on duck to press it, and cool overnight. When ready to serve, remove cheesecloth and slice duck paper thin.

Note: If duck becomes loose in cheesecloth after cooking, open cloth and reroll contents tightly before pressing.

DUTCH APPLE CRUMB PIE

Yield: 6 to 8 slices
Ingredients
Butter	2½ oz.
Sugar	5 oz.
Egg yolks	3
Orange peel, grated	1 oz.
Vanilla	1 drop
Salt	⅛ tsp.
Flour	8 oz.
Baking powder	⅕ oz.
Milk	¼ pt.
Currants	1¾ oz.
Raisins	1¾ oz.
Egg whites	3
Apple wedges	18 oz.
Cake crumbs	2 to 3 oz.
Powdered sugar	enough to dust pie

Method
Whip butter, sugar, egg yolks, grated orange peel, vanilla, and salt until creamy. Add flour, baking powder, milk, currants, and raisins. Whip the egg whites until stiff, and fold into the mixture. Line a well-greased cake mold with parchment paper. Fill with mixture. Arrange apple wedges over mixture and top with cake crumbs. Bake in a preheated oven at 375°F for 40 minutes. Remove, cool, and dust with powdered sugar.

POUNDCAKE

Yield: 2 lb. of cake batter

Ingredients

Egg whites	4
Sugar	1 cup
Butter or shortening	1 cup
Egg yolks	4
Flour	1 cup
Cream of tartar	½ tsp.
Baking soda	½ tsp.
Salt	1 tsp.
Milk	1 cup
Vanilla	1 tsp.

Method

Beat egg whites until stiff and set aside. Blend sugar and shortening with egg yolks. Add flour, cream of tartar, baking soda, and salt. Add milk and mix well. Flavor with vanilla and fold in egg whites. Line a large tube pan with parchment paper and pour mixture into it. Bake in preheated oven at 350°F for 1 hour and 30 minutes.

Note: ½ tsp. baking powder can be substituted for the combined cream of tartar and baking soda.

STRAWBERRY SHORTCAKE

Yield: 6½ lb.

Ingredients

Cake flour	1½ cups
Sugar	½ lb.
Salt	¾ oz.
Baking powder	¾ oz.
Emulsified shortening	10 oz.
Skim milk	2 cups
Eggs	7
Heavy cream, for whipping	1 qt.
Sugar	2 oz.
Strawberries	2 lb.

Method

In the bowl of an electric mixer, combine the flour, sugar, salt, baking powder, shortening, and 1 cup of the milk. Mix at slow speed for 5 to 7 minutes. Blend the eggs and the remaining cup of milk and add to first mixture in three parts. Mix 3 to 5 minutes at slow speed. Pour into a cake mold and bake in preheated oven at 375°F for 18 minutes. Cool and cut into three layers.

To assemble the cake, whip cream with sugar, blend with strawberries, reserving the necessary amount for decoration. Place whipped cream and strawberry mixture between layers. Decorate with whipped cream and reserved strawberries.

3

Garde Manger Area Planning

LAYOUT

Planning the layout for a garde manger department can be a complex task. Unlike other departments that can depend on a basic menu and a basic workload, the garde manger department is unique in its operation. It is often a complete foodservice facility within a larger foodservice facility. On a daily basis, the garde manger department may handle its own butchering; its own baking; its own sauce making; its own frying; its own smoking of fish, meat, and poultry; all the decorating, perhaps including tallow and ice carvings; plus a complete line of charcuterie products (sausages, galantines, pâtés, and terrines).

How does this department relate to the entire operation?

Knowing exactly how this department relates to the whole foodservice facility makes it easier to select the proper layout. The garde manger department can relate to a foodservice operation in three ways:

1. On a "pick-up" basis
2. On a "distribution" basis
3. On a combination of the two bases

What do "pick-up" and "distribution" basis mean?

When a garde manger department executes food orders from the waiters on an à la carte basis, this is known as "pick-up," since the waiters first place their orders, then later pick them up. This system of necessity operates in an unpredictable fashion, since the timing for the orders and the number of guests in the party cannot be known in advance. This method of operation is often found in "à la carte" restaurants. Where pick-up is the system used, the workloads of the garde manger department will be set on the basis of a predetermined number of dishes that are listed on the menu. Because the menu is approximately the same each day, the "mise en place," or arrangement of the space for preparing the dishes, can be determined, and the layout can be worked out properly.

When a garde manger department executes food orders in advance, for a known quantity, to be delivered to a given location at a definite time (for group feeding, for example), this is known as the "distribution" basis. This situation is often found in hotels, where the garde manger department always knows about banquets, private functions, and room service requests in advance. The main problem is that the work-

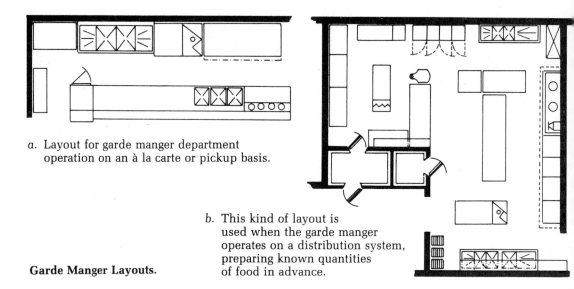

a. Layout for garde manger department
   operation on an à la carte or pickup basis.

b. This kind of layout is
   used when the garde manger
   operates on a distribution system,
   preparing known quantities
   of food in advance.

Garde Manger Layouts.

c. This layout is needed when an operation
   uses both the pickup and distribution systems.
 1. Walk-in cooler
 2. Walk-in freezer
 3. Sinks for foodstuffs
 4. Clam and oyster sinks
 5. Cooling sink
 6. Pot sinks
 7. Work benches
 8. Chopper–bench–mixer
 9. Meat saw
10. Electric blender–work bench
11. Slicer
12. Reach-in refrigerator
13. Salad center, including dressing and
    bain-marie
14. Dry-food storage cabinets
15. Special-equipment cabinets (terrines,
    molds, etc.)
16. Ice machine–ice maker
17. Iced bain-marie
18. Steam center with floor curb and hood

19. Ranges with overhead hood
20. Overhead shelving
21. Reach-in refrigerator-freezer
22. Egg-timing machine
23. Waiter pickup area, with plate shelves
24. Mobile rackshelves

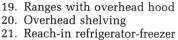

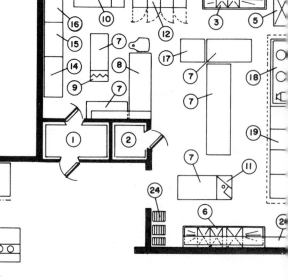

loads will be different each day because function and room service requests will vary as to kind and amounts of food to be prepared. For this reason, it is difficult to establish an appropriate mise en place. The layout for this kind of operation should be planned with basic preparations in mind, rather than for specific dishes.

How are "pick-up" and "distribution" combined?

The type of layout needed when pick-up and distribution are both in use in the same operation represents a combination of the two described above. This layout is appropriate when the garde manger department is located between an "à la carte" dining room and banquet rooms, but on the same floor. When the banquet rooms are located on a different floor, the garde manger department can be located by itself or in conjunction with a separate banquet kitchen on the same floor as the banquet room. When it fills a combined pick-up and distribution function, the garde manger department can become a part of, or be located close to, the main kitchen on the same floor as the à la carte dining room.

REFRIGERATION

After finding out how a garde manger department relates to the whole operation (pick-up basis, distribution basis, or combination of the two), attention can be directed to the equipment needed.

Refrigeration equipment is of prime importance since without refrigeration (refrigerators, freezers, cold bain-marie, refrigerated counter tops, etc.) the output of the garde manger department and the type of dishes prepared would be very limited in variety and easily contaminated.

The problems of food preparation in the garde manger department are complicated by the fact that in no other department is food manipulated as often as it is there. Frequent manipulation of foodstuffs accelerates deterioration, detracts from the appearance, odor, and taste of the finished product, and can lead to contamination. To prevent these developments, it is not enough for workers to be knowledgeable about keeping hands, tools, and garments immaculately clean. There must also be proper refrigeration equipment and the worker must make proper use of it.

Anyone working on food preparation should have a good basic understanding of what refrigeration is all about and how it works. When this is understood, it will be easy to select the appropriate refrigeration or freezing unit for the food to be held and to know how to use and maintain such a unit. The table on pp. 37–38 gives freezing, storing, and defrosting information for basic foods.

There is one basic principle of refrigeration that must be understood: cold is not created; cold is obtained by removing heat. Therefore, all refrigerators, freezers, and air-conditioning units are equipped with machinery designed for heat removal.

Basically, heat is removed from a refrigerator via the three methods of heat transfer: conduction, radiation, and convection. However, because conduction and radiation occur in a negligible percentage of equipment, it can be stated that the convection method is responsible almost exclusively for removing the heat.

How does heat get into a refrigerator?

Heat enters a refrigerator in three ways:

1. Because a refrigerator has doors, it cannot be completely insulated; therefore, heat keeps seeping in around the doors. Although the amount of heat that gets in is not large, it seeps in steadily.
2. When food is placed in a refrigerator, the food itself introduces a certain

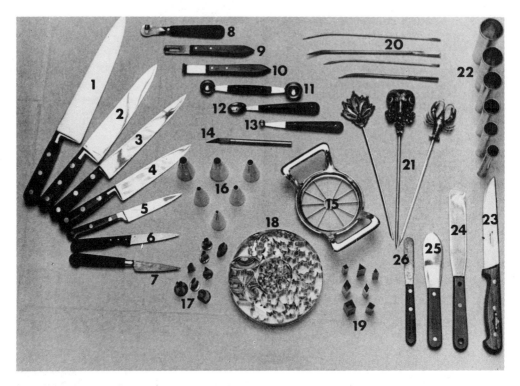

Special Tools and Equipment. In every industry today workers depend on special tools. Such tools have long been important in foodservice. For each item made by the chef or a helper, a tool is needed, and having the proper tool will not only make it easier to work, but actually is essential to proper preparation. For example, to create the various food decorations, a small paring knife is necessary; for chopping parsley, a French knife; when working with melon, a melon ball cutter. Pictured here is a collection of some of the most important tools. After collecting them, you must protect them as you would your hands. The experienced chef follows the rule: "Respect your working tools as you would respect yourself." The chef knows that the tool that is not properly cared for soon becomes worthless, making work harder rather than easier.

1. French knife (10 in.)
2. French knife (8 in.)
3. Chef's slicer (8 in.)
4. French knife (6 in.)
5. Paring knife, stainless (4½ in.)
6. Paring knife (3½ in.)
7. Paring knife (2½ in.)
8. Zesteur or cester for fruit carving
9. Zesteur or cester for melon carving
10. Zesteur or cester for butter decoration and lemon or orange peeler
11. Parisian scoop (2 sizes)
12. Olivette cutter
13. Tiny parisienne scoop for decorative work
14. Scalpel to cut leeks or carrots
15. Apple cutter, can be used for radishes
16. Set of pastry tubes, can be used as round cutters and for truffles
17, 18, 19. Fancy aspic cutters, miniature, medium, large
20. Larding and curved sewing needle
21. Hatelets or decorative silver skewers
22. Column cutters
23. Boning knife
24. Spatula (6 in.)
25. Sandwich spreader with flexible blade
26. Spatula (2½ in.), for pâtés and small timbales

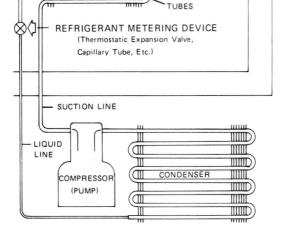

1. *Inside Air*

2. *Evaporator*

3. *Refrigerant*

4. *Compressor*

5. *Condenser*

6. *Outside Air*

Interior of insulated enclosure.

amount of heat, especially if the food has been stored at temperatures above 72°F.

3. Heat also "walks into" the refrigerator each time the doors are opened.

The Refrigeration Cycle

Heat is removed from a refrigerator through a series of heat transfers known as the refrigeration cycle. Specifically, there are four elements involved in the process of heat transfer:

1. The evaporator
2. The refrigerant
3. The compressor
4. The condenser

The refrigeration cycle goes through the following phases:

1. Heat present in a refrigerator is dis-

persed throughout the air in the unit.

2. As it rises, the air transfers the heat to the evaporator, which is made out of tubing surrounded by fins. The fins have many surfaces which collect the heat and transfer it to the refrigerant flowing in the tubing.

3. The refrigerant carries the heat to the compressor. The refrigerant is a gas that expands as it collects the heat.

4. The compressor (which is a pump) removes the heat from the refrigerant by compressing it back to its original volume and, in turn, transfers the heat to a condenser.

5. The condenser collects the heat in its tubing and transfers the heat to the numerous surfaces of the fins surrounding the tubing. At that point, a fan blows the heat out of the refrigerator.

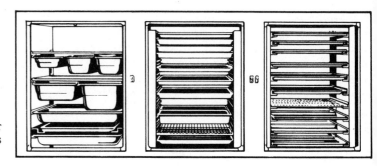

Refrigerator storage space: for pans (left); for bakery products (center); for varied foods (right).

6. The now compressed, cold refrigerant returns to the evaporator to collect more heat, and the cycle takes place again and again.

Depending on the type of refrigerator, various engineering methods are used to complete the refrigeration cycle. Some condensors are water-cooled. In this case, heat is transferred to the water which carries the heat along to a drain or, again, back to the evaporator where it evaporates.

What makes a good refrigerator?

A good refrigerator is one that is engineered to keep a:

1. Constant appropriate temperature
2. Constant relative humidity
3. Constant air flow

Constant appropriate temperature is achieved through:

1. Insulation
2. Door gasket or lining
3. Door "hardware," mainly the lock and/or hinges

Providing proper humidity in a refrigerator depends on the following process. Like a sponge holding water, air holds water vapor, or moisture. The warmer the air in a refrigerator, the more moisture it will hold, with absolute humidity at 100 per-

cent. However, the cold air in a refrigerator only holds a certain percentage of moisture and most food will respond well to an 80 percent to 85 percent relative humidity. When the relative humidity is too low (below 80 percent), the dry cold air will begin to absorb humidity from the moisture contained in certain foods, causing these foodstuffs to discolor, dry up, and crack. When the relative humidity is too high (above 80 percent), the air in the refrigerator will release some of its moisture, and dry foodstuffs will become soggy or shiny or covered with "sweat" (condensation).

Unless a refrigerator is designated to contain only one type of food, it is difficult to control the relative humidity. Heterogeneous foods (some dry and some moist) stored in the same refrigerator will be affected differently by the relative humidity. This is why some refrigerators are designed to contain homogeneous foods (all dry or all moist items).

Air flow is important because foodstuffs do not respond well to a stagnant climate. Natural air movement exists inside a refrigerator but, depending on how the food is being stored, some containers may block air movement and prevent other foods from getting proper air circulation. For this reason, modern refrigerators use forced air circulation, produced by a fan located in the vicinity of the evaporator. Well-designed air circulation is also found in refrigerators equipped with a louvered vertical shaft that can distribute the air through all of the shelves, no matter how the food is stored.

Because there are so many refrigerator designs on the market, only a few basic designs and their suggested purposes can be listed here.

Walk-ins are excellent for storing food in bulk (usually found in main storage areas).

Roll-ins are similar to "walk-ins," but are equipped with a small ramp at the door to the area to allow hand trucks and mobile shelves to be wheeled in. These are excellent for quantity storage of pre-portioned food (especially for high-volume operations).

When used for such storage, there should be three compartments (three doors), one for dairy, one for meat, one for vegetables; dairy and vegetable products can be combined, as these products usually are kept at the same temperature.

Reach-ins with full-length doors are excellent for storage in small operations, or as "hold" refrigerators for foods to be held in temporary storage awaiting further preparation steps.

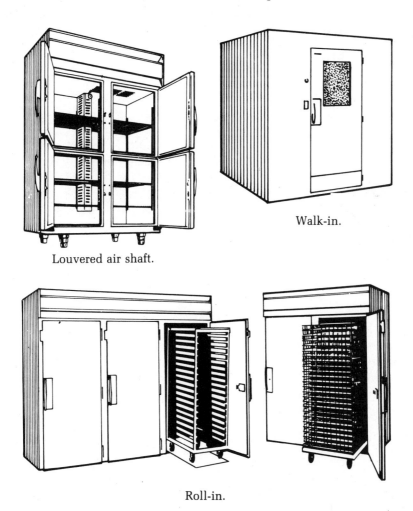

Louvered air shaft.

Walk-in.

Roll-in.

Half-length door.

Reach-in, full-length door.

Pull-out.

Reach-ins with half-length doors are excellent when heterogeneous foods are used within the same preparation area and when heterogeneous portions of prepared foods have to be located in the immediate vicinity of cooking appliances for processing "to order."

Pass-throughs with full- or half-length doors are excellent when located between preparation and service areas.

Pull-outs are excellent when refrigerators must have mobility from one area to another. This design prevents spillage while in motion as these units are usually portable and travel from the production area to a service area.

All the above-mentioned refrigerators are designed with swinging doors (right- or left-hinged) or sliding doors. Sliding doors, also available in a solid- or glazed-type glass door, make it easy to locate a specific food without having to open the doors unnecessarily.

STORING AND THAWING FROZEN FOODS

Foodstuffs	*For Freezing*	*Storage*	*Defrosting*
Bakery			
Bread	Very good	2–4 months	300°F oven
Rolls	Very good		Heat in oven (low temperature)
Beef			
Cuts not listed below	Very good	Up to 12 months	In refrigerator
Bones	Good	6–8 months	Use frozen
Chopped beef	Good	4–6 months	In refrigerator
Liver	Good	3–6 months	Do not defrost; cook frozen
Stew meat	Good	4–6 months	In refrigerator
Dairy Products			
Butter	Very good	8–10 months	Refrigerator
Egg without shell	Good	8–10 months	In refrigerator
Egg yolk	Good	8–10 months	In refrigerator
Egg white	Very good	10–12 months	In refrigerator
Fish			
Fat fish (mackerel, herring, or salmon)	Good	1–3 months	Whole frozen fish should be defrosted in cold water
Fillet of fish (sole or haddock)	Very good	3–4 months	Do not defrost, just wash and cook
Lean fish (trout or cod)	Very good	4–6 months	Defrost in cold water
Smoked fish		1–2 months	In refrigerator
Game			
Birds	Very good	8–10 months	In refrigerator
Meat	Very good	Up to 12 months	Put frozen in marinade
Herbs (in an aluminum pouch)			
Fresh	Very good	8–10 months	Use frozen
Pâté (Maison)	Good	2–3 months	In refrigerator
Pork			
Cuts not listed below	Very good	6–8 months (if very fat, not over 4 months)	In refrigerator
Fatback	Good	4–6 months	In refrigerator
Sausages	Good	4–6 months (if strongly seasoned, not over 3 months)	In refrigerator

STORING AND THAWING FROZEN FOODS

Foodstuffs	For Freezing	Storage	Defrosting
Poultry			
Broilers	Very good	8–10 months	Remove from wrappings
Capon	Very good	8–10 months	In refrigerator
Duck	Good	4–6 months	In refrigerator
Other	Very good	8–10 months	In refrigerator
Veal	Good	6–8 months	In refrigerator
Vegetables			
Asparagus	Very good	10–12 months	In boiling water
Button mushrooms	Good	6–8 months	While cooking
Cabbage (Savoy)	Good	10–12 months	While cooking
Carrots (sliced)	Very good	10–12 months	While cooking
Cauliflower	Good	8–10 months	In boiling water
Corn	Very good	10–12 months	While cooking
Cucumber (sliced)	Very good	6–8 months	Defrost in marinade
Green pepper	Very good	6–8 months	Defrost in marinade
Peas	Excellent	10–12 months	In boiling water
Spinach	Excellent	10–12 months	While cooking
String beans	Excellent	10–12 months	In boiling water

4

Aspic—Gelée—Chaud-Froid

Aspic and gelée play an important part in the preparation of many of the cold dishes created in the garde manger department. The glistening coating or sparkling bases supplied by aspic and gelée highlight the ingredients being presented. Proper preparation and application of aspic and gelée are essential to assure maximum impact for a large piece of meat or fish or a whole fowl or fish.

ASPIC AND GELÉE

In American cuisine there is usually no distinction between aspic and gelée. In continental cuisine, however, a gelée, or jelly, is a gelatinous meat or fish stock. A gelée becomes an aspic gelée or aspic jelly when it is clarified. The word *aspic* is used to refer to a combination of cold meat, fish, vegetables, eggs, etc., placed in a mold to form a decorative arrangement that is then covered with aspic jelly. When thoroughly chilled, the arrangement is unmolded on a silver platter and surrounded with aspic jelly croutons.

The aspic jelly must always be crystal clear and of a light, golden color. The quantity of gelatin used in the aspic jelly should be well proportioned so that the jelly, when set, is neither too firm nor too light in consistency. The aspic jelly provides special protection for cold dishes. A display of poultry, fish, game, or other ingredients when covered with aspic jelly will keep its original flavor and freshness for a longer period.

The making of a fresh aspic jelly is elaborate and in modern kitchens is often considered very time consuming. However, aspic jelly can be bought commercially in powdered form and can be used with acceptable results when time does not allow the preparation of fresh aspic jelly.

How do you prepare aspic jelly?

The preparation of aspic jelly consists of several steps:

1. A stock must be made using gelatinous products such as veal bones, calves' feet, or pork skin.
2. The stock must be reduced and clarified with the addition of aromatic products such as vegetables, wines, and seasonings.
3. Finally, the jelly must be tested to determine its consistency when cold.

Note: Today's modern chef may use well-known savory jelly brands.

Using Aspic and Aspic Jelly.

For practical and production purposes, brush aspic on cold food products to enhance presentation and flavor.

For show purposes, dip cold food slices into aspic. Place on a sheet pan, refrigerate, and chill. Trim excess aspic for display. This dipping technique coats both sides of the food with aspic, improving presentation and preserving appearance and flavor.

CLEAR ASPIC JELLY (CLASSICAL)

Yield: 1 gal.

Ingredients

Veal bones, cut into small pieces	3 lb.
Calves' feet, split in half lengthwise	2
Pork skin	8 oz.
Veal shank	1
Beef chuck	2 lb.
Water	6 qt.
Carrots	3 to 4
Onions	2 medium
Leeks, white portion	2
Celery	2 stalks
Salt, pepper, sachet bag	

Method

Blanch the bones, calves' feet, and pork skin. Rinse well in cold water. Place in a pot and add veal shank and beef. Cover with water and bring to a boil.

Skim boiling liquid, then add all the vegetables and seasonings. Cook for 5 to 6 hours on low heat. Pour stock through a strainer, cool, and remove all fat. Reduce stock to 1 gallon.

CLARIFICATION FOR ONE GALLON STOCK

Ingredients

Beef, lean ground	1 lb.
Leeks, celery, onion, finely diced	1 cup
Egg whites	4
Cold stock	1 gal.
Madeira, port, or sherry	1½ cups

Method

Mix beef, vegetables, and egg whites well in a large pot, then add one gallon of the cold stock. Bring to a boil, stirring occasionally with a wooden spoon.

Simmer for ½ to 1 hour and strain through a cheesecloth. Add 1½ cups of Madeira, port, or sherry wine. In order to know the consistency of natural gelatin contained in the gelée, refrigerate a sample. If it sets to desired consistency, the aspic jelly is ready to be used. If the jelly is to be used to make aspic molds, it is necessary to reduce the stock by half in order to achieve the necessary strength.

Variations

The above recipe produces clear aspic jelly with practically no color. A light to dark golden aspic jelly can be obtained by using a brown stock. For this stock, brown the bones, meat, and vegetables and proceed in the same manner described for clear aspic jelly.

For poultry aspic jelly, substitute chicken or other fowl bones for veal bones and shank. A game aspic jelly can be obtained by using veal bones with game bones added for special flavor.

Whatever the aspic to be produced, it is only necessary to brown the appropriate bones and then follow the recipe for clear aspic jelly.

ASPIC OR MEAT JELLY

(Commercial)

Yield: 1 gal.

Ingredients

Beef, lean, chopped	16 oz.
Celery, onion, leeks, finely diced	1 cup
Parsley stems	2 to 3
Chervil sprigs (fresh or dried) (If chervil is not available, use tarragon)	2
Black peppercorns	1 tsp.
Salt	1 to 2 tsp.
Egg whites	5 to 6
Gelatin	12 oz.
Meat stock (chicken, veal, beef, or fish fond)	5 qt.

Method

To clarify aspic, place the beef and mirepoix of celery, onions, and leeks in a large pot together with parsley, chervil, peppercorns, salt, egg whites, and the gelatin. Mix well. Add cold stock and fold into the mixture. Heat slowly just to the point of simmering. Agitate the pot gently, either by shaking or by stirring slowly with a wooden spoon, so that the ingredients will be thoroughly mixed with the liquid. Simmer 30 to 40 minutes.

Remove from heat and let rest for 5 to 10 minutes so the raft can settle to the bottom of the pot. Carefully ladle aspic through a fine sieve or a strainer lined with cheesecloth. At this time adjust the seasoning.

Cool in the refrigerator, remove fat, and melt aspic before using.

Note: If fish stock is used, use herbs and whipped egg whites only for clarification. If a golden color is desired, add 1 cup of finely diced carrots.

How to Prepare Aspic Croutons

Pour some of the clarified, cooled liquid aspic into a sheetpan, filling it approximately ½ inch thick. Let it set. This aspic sheet has to be very cold and firm (hard) before it can be used.

Note: Make sure there are no air bubbles present in the liquid aspic. For garnitures, cut the hard aspic sheet into large squares, triangles, serrated half-moons, stars, diamonds, or plain half-moons. The aspic can also be finely or coarsely diced.

How to Make Aspic Color Sheets

For decoration, or as background for various food presentations, aspic color sheets

This bouquet of flowers was created from pieces of egg yolk, pimentos, radish skins, truffle-colored aspic, and leeks.

Pieces of aspic that have been colored with pimento were arranged to make this striking red lobster.

Using Aspic Decoratively.

The designs can be created by cutting the elements shown from sheets of colored aspic and combining them. Use different sizes. Stems for floral sprays can be made of leek leaves.

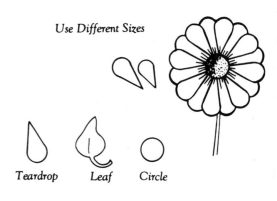

Use Different Sizes

Teardrop   *Leaf*   *Circle*

are very effective. The recipe that follows is considered a basic formula and can, therefore, be used for all kinds of color sheets. A list of the colors that can be created follows the recipe.

ORANGE ASPIC SHEETS

Size of Sheet: 14 to 17 inches
Ingredients

Pimento, canned	3½ oz.
Water or stock	¾ cup
Salt	pinch
Unflavored gelatin	1 oz.

Method
Combine pimento and warm water or stock in blender; purée to a fine paste. Slowly add salt and plain gelatin and mix together well. Remove from blender into a small pot and place in hot water bath for 2 or 3 minutes to remove the air bubbles. Then pour a thin layer onto a slightly oiled, half-size sheetpan and cool.

Variations
For other colors, use the above recipe, sub-

stituting one of the following for the pimento.

> For red aspic, use ½ pimento, ½ tomato paste.
>
> For yellow aspic, use boiled egg yolks.
>
> For white aspic, use boiled egg whites.
>
> For green aspic, use blanched or frozen spinach or asparagus.
>
> For light green aspic, use fresh watercress or Boston lettuce.
>
> For black aspic, use truffle peelings or roland truffle.
>
> For brown aspic, use a mixture of half glace de viande and half aspic.

Note: If the mixture is too thick, add aspic jelly or wine until desired texture is achieved.

Why True Blue Is Not Suitable

In working out color formulas for aspic sheets, one color is not used; "true blue" is not considered suitable for edible foods because blue is not found in natural products; therefore, artificial color would have to be used. Artificial colors may run into other colors and, therefore, are avoided by professionals. Moreover, even if blue were found in natural products, it would not be used because of its adverse psychological effect on diners. (Can you imagine eating blue potato salad or blue egg salad?)

Fish Aspic Jelly

Fish aspic jelly is obtained by first clarifying a reduced gelatin-enforced fish fumet (a reduced fish stock) and adding either white or red wine to it, the choice depending on the use to be made of the jelly.

CHAUD-FROID

One of the cold sauces used most frequently in the garde manger is the chaud-froid sauce. The French word *chaud-froid*

means "hot-cold," as the sauce is prepared hot but used cold.

There are several types of chaud-froid and their uses are different:

1. Classical chaud-froid, red or green
2. Cream sauce chaud-froid
3. Mayonnaise chaud-froid
4. Brown chaud-froid

CLASSICAL CHAUD-FROID SAUCE

This chaud-froid is used to coat meats, especially poultry, galantines, or terrines, but mostly pieces of white meat. If well prepared, this chaud-froid will enhance the flavor and the presentation of the displays.

Yield: 1½ qt.

Ingredients

Veal stock (see below)	1 qt.
Heavy cream or crème fraîche	1¼ pt.
Unflavored gelatin	2 to 2½ oz.
Salt	⅓ tsp.
Hot pepper sauce	3 drops
Egg yolks	3

Veal Stock

Veal joint bones	6 lb.
Oil	to brown
Carrots	2
Celery	3 stalks
Parsley stems	4
Wine, white	½ bottle
Salt	½ to 1 oz.
Peppercorns	2 tsp.
Lemon	juice of 2
Garlic	2 cloves
Water	to cover

Method

To make veal stock for chaud-froid, cut 6 lb. of veal bones into small pieces, blanch, and wash in cold water.

Lightly brown bones in oil with carrots, celery, and parsley stems. Deglaze with the white wine and add salt, peppercorns, lemon juice, and garlic. Place mixture in a stock pot and cover with water. Simmer for 4 hours, then strain stock through cheesecloth.

Reduce the veal stock to 1 quart.

Add 1 pint of heavy cream in which gelatin powder has been dissolved. Season with salt and hot pepper sauce. Simmer sauce 5 to 10 minutes.

Make a liaison with the remaining cream and egg yolks. Add to the chaud-froid sauce. Bring to a boil. Strain sauce through cheesecloth, and cool to the desired consistency.

CHAUD-FROID NUMBER 2

Due to the shortage of personnel in most kitchens, and in order to save time, the following recipe is a good substitute for Classical Chaud-Froid.

Yield: 3 qt.
Ingredients

Butter	4 oz.
Flour	4 oz.
Aspic jelly	2 qt.
Heavy cream	20 oz.
Salt	1/3 tsp.

Method
Prepare a roux with butter and flour. Add aspic, mix well, and stir until the sauce comes to a boil. Simmer for 15 minutes on low fire.

Add cream and reduce sauce for 5 minutes on low flame. Season with salt, if needed, and strain through cheesecloth.

Note: If this chaud-froid is used for ham, add 1/3 cup of sherry wine. When cooling the sauce, be sure to stir occasionally to prevent formation of skin.

CHAUD-FROID TOMATE

(Red Chaud-Froid)
Yield: 1 qt.

Ingredients

Tomato paste	2 T
Chaud-froid sauce	1 qt.
Hungarian paprika	1/2 T
Heavy cream	1 oz.

Method
Add tomato paste to ready-made chaud-froid sauce. Mix paprika with cream and add to the sauce.

CHAUD-FROID VERTE

(Green Chaud-Froid)

Yield: 1 qt.
Ingredients

Fresh spinach leaves or green asparagus, blanched	7 oz.
Classical chaud-froid sauce	1 qt.

Method
In a blender, purée spinach or asparagus with a little chaud-froid and bring to a fast boil. Strain through cheesecloth and add to remaining chaud-froid. It is important to cool this sauce rapidly as it may lose its green color and turn grayish.

SAUCE CHAUD-FROID

(For Display Foods and Chaud-Froid Mirrors)

Yield: 5 qt.
Ingredients

Shortening	8 oz.
Flour	8 oz.
Milk, boiling	1 gal.
Unflavored gelatin	1 cup

Method
Make a roux with shortening and flour. Add boiling milk and mix until thick and smooth. Cook sauce for 5 minutes and slowly pour in 1 cup of high-bloom unflavored gelatin powder that has been soaked in water.

Working with Chaud-Froid Sauce.

Melt sauce chaud-froid and set into an ice-filled bowl to cool. Chaud-froid must be stirred frequently while it cools to prevent lumps from forming.

Place the object to be coated (here, a chicken) on a wire rack, with a clean pan beneath to catch the overflow of coating. Using a ladle, coat the object swiftly and evenly, being careful not to let the ladle touch its surface. Cool in the refrigerator until coating sets. Repeat as often as needed.

After coating has set, decorate and cover with a coat of clean aspic jelly.

Note: The cream sauce chaud-froid is a white sauce, generally used on nonedible displays for exhibitions, dummy show pieces, and mirrors for buffets. There are several methods for preparing chaud-froid for nonedible displays. Some chefs simply mix light cream with unflavored gelatin. Others use sour cream, cream cheese with water, and unflavored gelatin. These methods give excellent results as far as the whiteness of chaud-froid is concerned; however, it is better to keep the cost of this type of chaud-froid to the minimum by using the above recipe.

MAYONNAISE CHAUD-FROID OR MAYONNAISE COLLÉE

A mayonnaise chaud-froid is made by mixing one part of mayonnaise with one part of cold liquid aspic jelly. Do not whip, as bubbles may form. Mayonnaise chaud-froid is usually used to coat fish.

If the mayonnaise is freshly prepared, it is important to use the chaud-froid as soon as it has reached the right consistency. A mayonnaise chaud-froid containing fresh mayonnaise is apt to break if reheated. A mayonnaise chaud-froid containing commercially made mayonnaise can be reheated safely. Mayonnaise collée is used mostly for fish.

BROWN CHAUD-FROID

A brown chaud-froid is made by melting equal parts of glace de viande and aspic jelly and combining the mixture with an equal part of tomato sauce. Generally, brown chaud-froid is flavored with Madeira or sherry wine and is used to coat roast meats such as beef, pork, turkey, and chicken.

How do you use chaud-froid sauce?

The method of application of a chaud-froid sauce on cold foods plays an important role in the success of a finished food platter. The temperature of the chaud-froid will determine the consistency of the sauce. A hot chaud-froid is light in consistency but when cooled becomes thicker and will congeal if kept under refrigeration or on ice. The sauce should be placed in a double boiler to melt.

When applying a chaud-froid sauce, several steps must be followed in order to be successful:

1. The food to be coated should have a smooth surface and be held in the refrigerator.
2. The food to be coated should be placed on a wire rack with a sheetpan underneath it.
3. When chaud-froid is at the right consistency, ladle it over the food. The method of application may have to be adjusted depending on the food product. A flat smooth surface, such as turbot or sole, can easily be coated with a mayonnaise chaud-froid just by pouring the chaud-froid over the surface. Because of their shapes, a ham, turkey, or galantine cannot be coated as easily. To obtain the best results, coat the sides of the item first, then the top.
4. During the process, the chaud-froid will have to be reheated in a double boiler, then cooled on ice, to reach the right thickness.
5. The item covered with chaud-froid should be refrigerated for a few minutes to allow the coating to congeal. Then apply a second coating.
6. A chaud-froid coating should be smooth and not too thick. Generally, two coatings, sometimes three, are sufficient. If lumpy chaud-froid has been used, remove coating and start all over.
7. The excess sauce that accumulates on the sheetpan can be used again.

Note: In today's modern kitchens chaud-froid is used only to enhance the food product. Contrary to the old teachings foods should be only partially covered so that guests can identify the food displayed

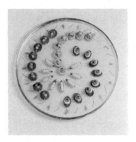

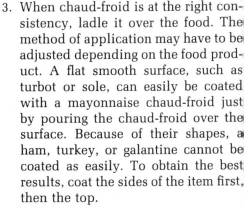

Arrangement of Finger Foods on a Chaud-Froid Mirror. Left: prosciutto on whole wheat croutons garnished with melon balls; top: marinated cucumber topped with seafood ceviche; center: barquettes filled with smoked salmon mousse garnished with keta caviar; right: stuffed quail eggs with beluga caviar on pumpernickel croutons.

5

Appetizers—Hors d'Oeuvre

Faire manger les sans appetit, faire briller l'esprit de ceux qui en ont et faire trouver à ceux qui en désirent, est le suprême rôle des hors d'oeuvre. ("To make hungry those without appetite, to give spirit to those with it, to reveal it to those who wish for it—these are the functions of the hors d'oeuvre.")

Hors d'oeuvre is a French expression and its true definition is, "a preparation served outside of the menu proper," at the beginning of a meal before the main course. Therefore, the hors d'oeuvre must be a small tidbit; it should be light, attractive, very delicate, and tasty. Hors d'oeuvre should not be spelled with a final s, since there is no plural form of the word in French.

There are four main types of hors d'oeuvre:

1. Cold hors d'oeuvre
2. Hot hors d'oeuvre
3. Zakuski/Scandinavian sandwiches
4. Canapés (hot and cold)

What are cold hors d'oeuvre?

The cold hors d'oeuvre can be divided into two categories:

1. The ready-to-serve variety, available in today's market in every conceivable type and form (such as antipasto, smoked or pickled fish, and sausages).
2. Those that require culinary preparation and that, when made properly,

have the advantage of being freshly prepared from fresh ingredients with maximum flavor and appeal. This is where fine cuisine can make a very important contribution to eating pleasure.

Cold hors d'oeuvre are also broken into further classifications:

1. Hors d'oeuvre frequently served at luncheons and generally known as *Hors d'Oeuvre à la Française*. This variety is served in small oval, oblong, or square dishes called *raviers*. The basic qualification of an Hors d'Oeuvre à la Française is that all of it be edible. Included in this group are small salads made from meat, fish, vegetables, and eggs, as well as various ham, sausage, or marinated fish dishes.
2. The hors d'oeuvre served before the meal.

The luncheon hors d'oeuvre is part of the meal and has its place in the proper se-

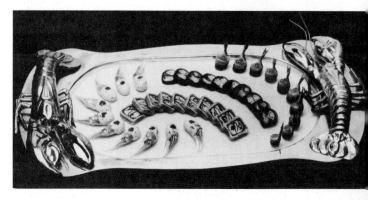

Left to right: Crab Mousse–Stuffed Claws; Pâté en Croûte; Scallop and Wild Mushroom Aspic; Steamed Smelts with Herbal Forcemeat.

quence of dishes served at the meal, while the dinner hors d'oeuvre is usually served with cocktails prior to the meal and is not a part of the menu. It is of vital importance that the chef be given enough time before service to prepare all hors d'oeuvre properly.

What are hot hors d'oeuvre?

Hot hors d'oeuvre are generally served at a cocktail party or before a dinner, but seldom if ever are served with a luncheon. Although some hot appetizers can be considered classical, many others are strictly prototypes that serve as a basis for many different preparations. As a matter of fact, every branch of cookery, when reduced to tidbit proportions, is or could be used in the preparation of hot hors d'oeuvre.

For example, from the pastry department we can secure the paillettes or allumettes, the beignets or frites, bouchées, croustades, petits pâtes, the rissoles, the ramequins, or the ever classic quiche Lorraine.

From the saucier and the entremetier, we can get the attereaux, one of the first hot hors d'oeuvre belonging to the old school of cookery. These are delicious when served in small morsels. The boreks, which are of Turkish origin; the blinis for caviar consumption; the oysters, Casino or Rockefeller; the soufflés; the cromesquis or croquettes, and many commercial preparations help to round out the endless list of hot hors d'oeuvre. While not essential to a meal, they are nevertheless the first contact the guest make with the culinary performance of the operation. The impression made by their preparation and presentation is the basis for the guests' expectations of the dinner.

What are Zakuski?

In the 1890s, Zakuski, or canapés à la Russe became very popular. These cold hors d'oeuvre of the canapé variety are classical made up of certain specified ingredients one of these is made of toast covered with smoked fish and scrambled eggs and finished with a thin gelée or aspic. Their presentation is left to the originality of the chef

How do you define the cold canapé?

These tiny open-faced sandwiches are cut into rectangular, round, or other shapes, the size and thickness depending on the nature of the ingredients used. Cold canapés are mostly made of toasted bread, crackers, or pumpernickel, covered with various butter spreads and topped with various accompaniments. As labor is the important factor in making cold canapés, this type of hors d'oeuvre should be ordered as early as possible. In costing the canapé, the price of labor should also be considered. In the past few years, canapés, hot or cold, have become very popular and are usually served at cocktail parties or other gatherings to foster the drinking of cocktails.

VEGETARIAN CANAPÉS

In the classical sense of the word, the vegetarian canapé does not exist. However, even Escoffier, the master, believed that new foods would be introduced and names would change. The lacto-vegetarian food influence is becoming stronger and therefore cooks must introduce new food concepts.

RED AND GREEN PEPPER CANAPÉ

Yield: 24 canapés
Ingredients

Red or green pepper, raw	3
Cream cheese	12 oz.
Yogurt	4 oz.
Chives, chopped	3 T
Mint, chopped	3 T
Lemon zest, grated	⅓ lemon
Salt and pepper, white	to taste
Cherry tomatoes, small, blanched and marinated in a vinaigrette	12
Black olives, pitted, small	24
Mint leaves, small	24

Method
Cut peppers into halves, then into squares. Mix cream cheese, yogurt, chopped chives,

Canapés. Assembled on the tray, from left to right: parma ham on croutons garnished with cantaloupe and honeydew melon and basil leaf, cucumber baskets filled with lobster ragout, barquettes filled with salmon mousse and salmon caviar, smoked mozzarella cheese on rye croutons garnished with basil leaf, roulade of smoked breast of duck on toasted croutons.

mint, and lemon zest. Season with salt and pepper. Pipe a rosette of the cheese mixture onto each pepper square, and decorate with half a blanched cherry tomato tossed in a vinaigrette, a black olive, and mint leaf.

SWEET AND SOUR MELON

Yield: 3 portions
Ingredients

Cantaloupe	1
Lemon	juice of 1
Red wine vinegar	½ cup
Sugar	3 oz.
Black pepper, ground	
Boiled or prosciutto ham, thinly sliced	3 oz.

Method
Cut melon into quarters and remove seeds and fruit meat from rind. Cube the fruit and toss it with lemon juice; chill. Combine vinegar and sugar and reduce over high heat to a syrupy consistency (about 5 minutes). Arrange the cubed cantaloupe on a serving dish, pour hot syrup over, season with pepper, and garnish with thinly sliced ham.

STUFFED MUSHROOMS CONTEMPORARY STYLE

Yield: 24 portions

Ingredients

String beans	24 oz.
Mushroom caps, large	24
Peanut oil	4 oz.
Salt, sugar, and pepper	to taste
Sherry vinegar	4 oz.
Cherry tomatoes, blanched and peeled	6
Water or chicken stock	6 oz.

Method

Cube string beans and cook them al dente. Sauté mushroom caps in oil till al dente. Season with salt, pepper, and sugar. Combine sherry vinegar, water or chicken stock, salt, pepper, sugar, and 4 tablespoons of peanut oil and marinate tomato wedges for 1 hour. Remove, add string beans, and marinate for 10 minutes. Fill mushrooms with tomato wedges and top with string beans.

GOAT CHEESE BALLS

Yield: 8 portions

Ingredients

New York goat cheese	1 lb.
Butter, softened	8 oz.
Nuts (pistachios, almonds), chopped fine	as needed
Seasonings (herbs, sweet paprika, coarsely ground black pepper)	as needed
Flavorings (ham, green olives, pumpernickel crumbs), chopped fine	as needed

Method

Combine goat cheese and butter and mix well. Mold into balls and chill. Roll in chopped nuts, herbs, and other seasonings and flavorings. Arrange on Boston lettuce leaves in grape clusters.

CARPACCIO OF STERLING ATLANTIC SALMON BALSAMIC VINAIGRETTE

Yield: 10 portions

Ingredients

Sterling atlantic salmon fillet	1 (2 to 2½ lb.)
Olive oil	1 cup
Red pepper, brunoise	½ cup
Green pepper, brunoise	½ cup
Yellow pepper, brunoise	½ cup
Shallots, diced fine	½ cup
Mustard seeds	1 tsp.
White wine	½ cup
Ketchup	½ cup
Chicken stock	½ cup
Balsamic vinegar	½ cup
Salt	½ tsp. or to taste
Pepper	to taste
Sugar	1 tsp.
Basil, fresh, chopped	1 T
Cantaloupe, peeled, seeded, and halved	1
Rice, boiled	20 oz.
Walnuts, coarsely diced, toasted	8 oz.

Method

Remove skin from salmon fillet and freeze to firmness for easy slicing. Slice paper-thin, place on a sheet pan, and keep cold. Heat one-third of the oil, and sauté the peppers, shallots, and mustard seeds. Deglaze the pan with wine; add ketchup and reduce by half. Add the chicken stock, balsamic vinegar, salt, pepper, sugar, and basil. Add rest of oil and chill.

Cut the cantaloupe into ten half-rings. Brush salmon slices with chilled vinaigrette and let rest for two minutes. Combine rice, walnuts, and remaining vinaigrette. Place a melon half on each plate, spoon rice salad onto cantaloupe, and surround with thin slices of salmon. Decorate with basil leaves.

LIVER MOUSSE AND ORANGE

Yield: 8 portions
Ingredients

Poultry livers	8 oz.
Salt	¼ tsp.
Pepper, allspice, grated orange zest	pinch of each
Butter	3 T
Shallots, diced	2
Whipped cream	4 oz.
Bread, toasted, cut into rounds	8 slices
Boston lettuce	8 small leaves
Oranges, medium	2
Grapes, green, seedless	8
Truffles, julienned	1 to 2 bunches

Method

Season livers with salt, pepper, allspice, and orange zest. Heat 1 tablespoon of butter in a pan, add shallots and sauté until transparent. Add liver and sauté for 4 minutes. Remove and cool. Purée liver and shallots in a blender. Press through a fine sieve. Carefully fold in whipped cream. Adjust seasoning. Brush white bread with butter and bake in oven until golden brown. Peel oranges and cut into eight slices. Spread toast with some liver mousse. Top with lettuce and orange slice. Pipe a rosette of liver mousse on top of orange. Decorate with grape and julienne of truffle.

SMOKED FISH ON RYE BREAD

Yield: 1 portion
Ingredients

Rye bread	1 slice
Butter	1 tsp.
Boston lettuce	1 leaf
Cottage cheese	2 oz.
Salt, sugar, and white pepper	to taste
Apple, small	½
Banana, small	½
Lemon juice	a few drops
Smoked trout fillet	3 oz.
Black pepper, coarse, crushed	to taste
Dill sprig	1

Method

Spread bread with butter and top with a lettuce leaf. Mix cottage cheese with salt, sugar, and pepper. Shred unpeeled apple coarsely. Peel banana, dice small, and sprinkle with lemon juice. Fold apples and banana into cottage cheese and spoon into lettuce leaf. Slice trout fillet and arrange on top of cottage cheese. Sprinkle with coarse crushed black pepper and decorate with dill.

GLACÉED CHICKEN LIVER WITH APPLES AND RED CABBAGE

Yield: 8 portions
Ingredients

Chicken livers, firm	2 lb.
Red cabbage, shredded	1½ lb.
Orange juice	¾ cup
Red wine vinegar (or as needed)	6 T
Salt, sugar, pepper	to taste
Olive oil	4 T
Apples (Granny Smith), peeled and quartered	4 ea.
Butter	2 oz.
Chicken broth	½ pt.
Walnuts, deep-fried	3 oz.

Method

Remove fat and sinews from the livers and cut into nut-sized pieces. Combine red cabbage, orange juice, vinegar, salt, sugar, and pepper, and add 2 tablespoons of oil. Set aside.

Heat remaining 2 tablespoons of oil and add 2 to 3 tablespoons of sugar. When the sugar is melted and golden brown, add apple wedges and toss until coated; keep warm.

Heat butter and sauté livers until light pink (2 to 5 minutes). Remove, add broth to pan, and reduce to a thin film. Add liver and toss to glacé.

Arrange marinated cabbage on plates. Garnish with liver, apples, and deep-fried walnuts.

OYSTERS WITH MUSTARD SAUCE

Yield: 12 portions
Ingredients

Oysters	12
White wine, dry	¼ cup
Water	¼ cup
Watercress	1 small bunch
Radicchio	¼ small head
Sour cream	2 T
Mayonnaise	1 T
Dijon mustard	1½ tsp.

Method

Shuck oysters and save bottom shells. Boil wine and water, add oysters and return to boiling for 1 minute. Drain, reserving liquid. Return liquid to a boil and reduce by two thirds. Add oysters and chill. Shred watercress and radicchio. Place in shells. In bowl, mix sour cream, mayonnaise, mustard, and cooking liquid. Arrange oysters on greens in shells. Top with sauce.

OYSTERS FLORIDA

Yield: 10 portions
Ingredients

Oysters	30
White wine	8 oz.
Cocktail Sauce (see recipe below)	10 T
Hot pepper sauce	dash
Grapefruit wedges	10
Pistachio nuts, chopped	to garnish
Cheese straws, small	10
Boston lettuce leaves	10

Method

Shuck oysters and poach in white wine and their own juice for 1 to 2 minutes. Chill.

Wash deeper part of shells and save. Prepare cocktail sauce flavored with hot pepper sauce. Set grapefruit wedges into shell. Add oysters, top with cocktail sauce, sprinkle with pistachio nuts and decorate with cheese straws. Arrange three oysters to a portion on Boston lettuce leaves.

OYSTERS CONTEMPORARY STYLE

Yield: 10 portions
Ingredients

Oysters, shucked	30
Tomato concassée	7 oz.
Pineapple, small, cubed	7 oz.
Titi shrimps	7 oz.
Lemon juice, ground black pepper	to taste
Boston lettuce leaves, small	10
Cocktail Sauce (see below)	10 T
Cheddar cheese, mild, grated	5 tsp.
Horseradish, freshly grated	5 tsp.
Pumpernickel	10 triangles

Method

Blanch oysters in their own juice. Chill. Combine tomato, pineapple, and titi shrimp and marinate with lemon juice and pepper. Line cocktail glasses with Boston lettuce. Add tomato, pineapple, and shrimp mixture. Top with oysters. Cover with cocktail sauce. Decorate with cheese, horseradish, and pumpernickel.

COCKTAIL SAUCES

A. 1 part tomato purée
   2 parts tomato ketchup
   1 part chili sauce
   Season with Worcestershire sauce, lemon juice, grated horseradish, salt and pepper to taste.

B. 1 part tomato purée or ketchup
   2 parts mayonnaise

Season with grated horseradish and bourbon whiskey to taste

C. 1 part sour cream
   1 part chili sauce
   Season with grated horseradish, salt, sugar, chopped dill, lemon juice, white pepper to taste.

OYSTERS GORDON'S GIN

Yield: 10 portions
Ingredients

Onions, diced	4 oz.
Oil	enough to sauté onions
Oysters, shucked	30
White wine, dry	1 cup
Red pepper, diced	2 oz.
Green pepper, diced	2 oz.
Chili sauce	3 oz.
Salt and pepper	to taste
Whipped cream	1 cup
Lemon juice	a few drops
Gin	1 T
American caviar	1 T
Boston lettuce leaves	10
Salmon caviar	10 tsp.
Dill sprigs	10

Method
Sauté onions in a little oil. Blanch oysters in their own juice. Remove them to a bowl and add white wine, sautéed onions, peppers, and chili sauce to poaching liquid. Reduce by two thirds. Chill and purée in a blender. Season with salt and pepper. Add to oysters and marinate for 1 to 2 hours. Whip the cream and carefully fold in the lemon juice, gin, and American caviar.

For each portion, outline a glass dish with Boston lettuce. Set in three oysters and some marinade. Top with rosette of whipped cream. Decorate with salmon caviar and dill sprig.

EGGPLANT TAHINI DIP

Yield: 4 portions
Ingredients

Eggplant	1 medium
Tahini paste	¼ cup
Lemon juice	¼ cup
Olive oil	⅓ cup
Garlic clove, crushed	1 clove
Tomato paste	1 T
Green pepper, chopped	1 small
Fresh mint, chopped	1 T
Fresh vegetables or crackers	as needed

Method
Cut eggplant in half lengthwise. Place on a sheet pan. Bake at 400°F for about 15 minutes or until soft. Remove skin from eggplant and blend or process with tahini paste, lemon juice, olive oil, garlic, and tomato paste until smooth. Stir in pepper. Arrange in a serving dish; cover, and refrigerate until service. Sprinkle with mint just before serving. Serve with fresh vegetables or crackers.

BEEF IN MUSTARD CRUST

Yield: 8 portions
Ingredients

Boiled beef or leftover pot roast	2 lb.
Boston lettuce	1 head
Watercress	1 bunch
Frisee	1 head
Cherry tomatoes	16
Salt, black pepper, sugar	to taste
Dijon mustard	6 T
All-purpose flour	3 oz.
Olive oil	as needed
Sauce Vinaigrette (see page 191)	½ cup

Method
Slice beef thinly. Clean lettuce, watercress, and frisee and cut into portion-sized pieces. Wash tomatoes and cut in half. Season beef slices with salt, pepper, and sugar. Brush on a thin layer of mustard, turn in flour, and

sauté slices on each side until golden brown. Toss lettuce, watercress, and frisee with vinaigrette, arrange on a plate, and place warm beef slices alongside. Serve immediately.

RABBIT HEADCHEESE

Yield: 6 portions
Ingredients

Beef tongue, cooked	3 oz.
Prosciutto ham	3 oz.
Mirepoix	1 cup
Peanut oil	2 T
Salt and white pepper	to taste
Rabbit	4 lb.
Sage, fresh	2 twigs
Thyme, fresh	1 twig
Bay leaf	½
Pâté spice	1 tsp.
Brandy	1½ oz.
White wine	1 oz.
Madeira aspic jelly	9 oz.
Sour cream	to garnish
Dill	to garnish
Croutons	to garnish

Method

Cube tongue. Cube ham a little smaller. Cut mirepoix small. Heat oil. Salt-and-pepper rabbit and sear. Add mirepoix, sage, thyme, bay leaf. Season with pâté spice, add brandy and flame, add white wine, cover and cook for 40 minutes. Remove fond. Remove meat from bones and cut in cubes. Reduce fond. Fold in Madeira aspic jelly and add rabbit, tongue, ham, and herbs. Spoon into terrine and chill. Slice and serve with sour cream, dill, and croutons.

CORNED BEEF AND SALAD WITH TOMATO-AVOCADO VINAIGRETTE

Yield: 10 portions
Ingredients

Corned beef	20 oz.
Bouquet garni	1
Peppercorns	10
Bay leaf	1

Salad Dressing for Mâche

Potatoes, cooked, riced while warm	6 oz.
Broth from corned beef	1 to 1½ cups
Vinegar	1 cup
Salt, pepper, and sugar	to taste
Shallots, diced	6 oz.
Peanut oil	1 cup
Mâche	10 oz.
Sauce Vinaigrette (see below)	18 oz.
Radishes, julienned	5 oz.

Method

Cook corned beef with bouquet garni, peppercorns, and bay leaf. Cool, chill, and slice the meat

Mix riced potatoes with broth, vinegar, salt, pepper, sugar, shallots, and oil. Dip mâche salad into dressing. Fan slices of corned beef and top with sauce vinaigrette. Garnish with mâche salad and julienned radishes.

SAUCE VINAIGRETTE

Yield: 18 oz.

Ingredients

Lemon juice	3 tsp.
Sherry vinegar	3 T
Salt, pepper, and sugar	to taste
Vegetable oil	6 T
Tomatoes, diced, blanched, peeled, seeded	6 oz.
Avocado, peeled and diced	6 oz.

Method

Mix lemon juice, vinegar, salt, pepper, sugar, and oil. Fold tomatoes and avocados into mixture.

MARINATED SCALLOPS, GARDEN STYLE

Yield: 12 portions

Ingredients

Shrimps	12
Court bouillon	2 qt.
Scallops, large	24
Marinade (see below)	4 oz.
Broccoli	16 oz.
Salt	to taste
Herb Dressing (see below)	4 oz.

Method

Cook shrimp in court bouillon. Chill, peel, and split lengthwise. Slice scallops thin and marinate 5 to 10 minutes (see below). Cook broccoli in salt water until tender-crisp (5 to 7 minutes), then shock under cold water. Marinate with herb dressing for 5 minutes (see below). Arrange on a plate.

MARINADE

Coriander seeds, crushed	2 tsp.
Parsley, chopped	2 T
Lemon or lime	juice of 1 large
Olive oil	2½ oz.
Salt and pepper	to taste

Method

Combine all ingredients.

HERB DRESSING

Green peppercorns, fresh	30
Egg yolks	4
Dijon mustard	1 oz.
Oil	14 oz.
Vinegar	2½ oz.
Sherry wine	1 oz.
White wine	2½ oz.
Salt	to taste
Shallots, diced	2 oz.
Parsley and chives, chopped	2 T
Water	as needed

Method

Crush green peppercorns. Combine with egg yolks and mustard. Add oil slowly to make mayonnaise. Gradually add vinegar, sherry, and white wine. Season with salt. Fold in diced, blanched shallots and herbs. If sauce is too thick, add a little water.

MARINATED SALMON JAPANESE STYLE

Yield: 10 portions

Ingredients

Salmon fillet	2 lb.
Green Peppercorn Marinade (see recipe below)	11 oz.
Limes	juice of 2
Shallots, finely diced	6
Olives, chopped	3 to 4 T
Toast	10 slices

Method

Set salmon fillet skin side down into a stainless steel or porcelain dish. Cover with pepper marinade and marinate for 2 to 3 hours. Remove from marinade and slice thinly. Arrange slices on a plate. Sprinkle with lime juice, top with some of the marinade, and sprinkle with shallots and olives. Serve with fresh toast.

GREEN PEPPERCORN MARINADE

Yield: 11 oz.

Ingredients

Green peppercorns, fresh, finely chopped	5 T
Salt	1 tsp.
Oil	10 oz.

Method

Combine all ingredients.

CARPACCIO OF FALLOW DEER IN BUTTERMILK

Yield: 10 portions

Ingredients

Buttermilk	1 pt.
Juniper berries, crushed	12
White pepper	to taste

Trio of Smoked Fish. A combination of smoked trout, smoked scallops, and smoked salmon, garnished with chive oil, pink peppercorns, candied grapefruit zest, whipped horseradish cream, and sliced brioche.

Rosemary	1 small branch
Fallow deer loins	2 lb.
Black pepper, coarsely ground	to taste
Field Salad Tossed with Vinaigrette	6 oz.

Method

Combine buttermilk, juniper berries, white pepper, and rosemary and let stand for 30 minutes. Slice semi-frozen loin into paper-thin slices, and place in marinade for 10 minutes. Remove from marinade, sprinkle with coarse black pepper, and arrange on Field Salad. Serve with farmer's bread.

LAMB CURRY SALAD

Yield: 2 portions

Ingredients

Lamb, cooked, julienned	9 oz.
Mayonnaise	3 to 4 oz.
Apple, grated, or applesauce	1
Madras curry powder	1 to 2 tsp.

Salt	to taste
White pepper	to taste
Mango, julienned or	½
Mango chutney	1 T
Coconut, grated	1 tsp.
Almond slices, toasted	1 tsp.

Method

Combine all ingredients. Mix well. Decorate with grated coconut and toasted almond slices.

SEA BASS AND SCALLOP TARTARE

Yield: 1 lb. 8 oz.

Ingredients

Fresh bass	17 oz.
Scallops	4
Cornichons	2
Capers	1 T
Green peppercorns, canned	1 T
Anchovy fillets	3
Parsley, chopped	1 T
Oil	3 T
Brandy	1 tsp.
Cayenne	1 dash
Egg yolks	4
Salt	to taste
Pepper	to taste
Croutons	as needed
Butter	as needed

Method

Skin fish; remove all bones. Grind fish and scallops through a fine plate. Dice cornichons, capers, green peppercorns, and anchovy fillets fine. Add parsley. Combine oil, brandy, cayenne, and egg yolks and mix with fish. Season. Serve with croutons and fresh butter.

CURED CATFISH WITH APPLE CUCUMBER SALAD

Yield: 8 portions

Ingredients

Sugar	2 T

Salt	2 tsp.
White peppercorns, crushed coarsely	8
Juniper berries, crushed	4
Catfish cutlets	8
Dill, coarsely chopped	4 T
Apples	2
Cucumbers	2 medium sized
Sour cream	½ pt.
Boston lettuce leaves	8
Black pepper, ground	to taste

Method

Combine sugar, salt, peppercorns, and juniper berries; rub into catfish fillets and sprinkle with dill.

Stack fillets in a plastic or porcelain container, cover with plastic wrap, and weight down with a board. Cure for 12 hours in the refrigerator. Peel apples and cucumbers, remove seeds, and slice. Combine with sour cream and season to taste with salt and lemon juice.

Remove catfish fillets. Scrape off spices and dill, and slice thinly on the bias. Place on Boston lettuce leaves and decorate with apple-cucumber sauce. Sprinkle with ground black pepper. Serve with fresh toast.

SMOKED SALMON ON PAPAYA

Yield: 12 portions

Ingredients

Papaya	3
Salmon, smoked, julienned	12 oz.
Kosher pickles or cucumbers	4 oz.
Asparagus tips, blanched al dente	4 oz.
Celery or celeriac, julienned, blanched	4 oz.
Onions, preferably red, sliced, blanched	2 oz.
Tarragon vinegar	2 oz.
Walnut oil	4 oz.
Dijon mustard	1 tsp.
Salt and pepper	to taste
Mayonnaise	4 oz.

Smoked Salmon on Papaya.

Dill, chopped	2 T
Quail eggs	12

Method

Peel papaya, remove seeds and save. Cut into wedges. Combine salmon, pickles, celery, and onions. Mix vinegar, oil, mustard, salt, and pepper. Marinate salmon mixture for 2 to 3 hours. Add asparagus to marinade for last 5 minutes. Drain mixture well, add mayonnaise and dill. Spoon over papaya wedges and decorate with quail egg and papaya seeds.

LOBSTER WITH PEACHES AND ASPARAGUS

Yield: 2 portions

Ingredients

Lobsters, boiled	2 1½-lb.
Peaches, ripe	2
Asparagus	12 spears
Bourbon	1 T
Herbs (dill, parsley, basil), chopped	1 T
Tomato Ketchup (see recipe)	1 T
Lemon juice	1 tsp.
Salt, fresh ground pepper	to taste
Oil	1 tsp.

Mayonnaise	1 T
Whipped cream	1 T
Black olives	4
Boston lettuce leaves	4

Method

Remove lobster meat from shell, remove claw meat and reserve.

Blanch peaches; shock and peel. Halve and remove pits.

Slice peaches and lobster meat, and dice asparagus.

Combine bourbon, herbs, ketchup, lemon juice, salt, pepper, and oil, and add to lobster, peaches, and asparagus. Toss well and adjust seasonings.

To serve, place lettuce leaves on two plates and arrange lobster salad on top. Combine mayonnaise and whipped cream and top salad with it.

Garnish each plate with lobster claws and peach slices.

SMOKED SALMON BRUSCHETTA

Yield: 4 portions

Ingredients

Pine nuts	3 T
Tomatoes, seeded and diced	2 medium
Mozzarella cheese, finely diced	4 oz.
Smoked salmon, finely chopped	4 oz.
Olive oil	3 T
Salt and white pepper	to taste
French country bread slices	4 large
Garlic	1 clove
Basil leaves, cut into thin strips	8

Method

In a small skillet, toast the pine nuts over medium high heat until golden. Remove from heat and let cool.

Preheat the broiler. Combine the pine nuts, tomatoes, cheese, salmon, and olive oil. Season with salt and pepper. Place the bread slices under the broiler and toast until golden on both sides. Immediately rub the garlic on one side of each bread slice and top with equal portions of the tomato-salmon mixture. Garnish with the basil strips and serve.

ARTICHOKE-FISH COMBO

Yield: 4 portions

Ingredients

Artichoke bottoms	4
Pearl onions	12
Fish, raw and firm (turbot, monk fish, tuna, swordfish), cut into small pieces	8 oz.
Salt and pepper	to taste
Olive oil	4 T
Mushrooms, small	12
Lemon	juice of 1
Water	6 T
Garlic, crushed or mashed	1 clove
Parsley, bay leaf, thyme	1 herb bag
Chili sauce	6 T
Boston lettuce leaves	4
Parsley, chopped	1 T
Toast points, trimmed	8

Method

Cut each artichoke bottom into 6 wedges. If pearl onions are raw, peel and blanch. Season fish pieces with salt and pepper and sauté in oil over high heat (sear). Add artichokes, onions, and mushrooms. Add lemon juice, water, garlic, and herb bag. Cover and braise till soft; 10 to 15 minutes. Add chili sauce and chill. Remove herb bag. Arrange on Boston lettuce; sprinkle with parsley and decorate with toast points.

CHINESE CABBAGE WITH SMOKED OR MARINATED SALMON

Yield: 4 portions

Ingredients

Chinese cabbage	6 oz.
Tomatoes, ripe	4
Eggs, hard-cooked	2
Vinaigrette (see recipe, page 191)	4 oz.

Dijon mustard	to taste
Juniper berries	2
Shallots	½ tsp.
Gin	dash
Rice, cooked	4 T
Smoked or marinated salmon, cut into large sticks	4 oz.
Dill, chopped	1 tsp.
Tarragon, chopped	½ tsp.

Method

Cut Chinese cabbage into julienne. Blanch, peel, and seed tomatoes and dice them coarsely. Peel eggs and cut into slices. Prepare dressing by combining vinaigrette, Dijon mustard, finely chopped juniper berries, finely diced shallots, and gin. Fold rice into marinade and add tomatoes and Chinese cabbage. Marinate for one hour. Arrange on a plate and sprinkle with salmon. Decorate with sliced eggs and chopped herbs.

TURKEY WITH PINEAPPLE

Yield: 4 portions

Ingredients

Pineapple slices, fresh, peeled, pencil-thick	4
Framboise liqueur	2 T
Powdered sugar	2 T
Mayonnaise	2 T
Whipped cream	1 heaping T
Cayenne pepper	a pinch
Red apple, julienned fine	1
Celery, julienned fine	1 stalk
Orange juice	1 T
Turkey breast, julienned	8 oz.
Green grapes, seedless	8
Walnuts or pecans	8

Method

Remove centers from pineapple slices. Arrange slices on plates. Sprinkle with Framboise and some powdered sugar. Chill. Combine mayonnaise with whipped cream. Add cayenne. Combine apple and celery, and marinate in orange juice for 5 minutes. Fold in turkey and mayonnaise. Mount onto pineapple slices. Decorate with grapes and walnuts.

CHICKEN SALAD WITH AVOCADOS

Yield: 8 portions

Ingredients

Vinegar	6 T
Gin	dash
Olive oil	4 T
Salt, sugar, and pepper	to taste
Chicken legs, cooked, boned, and cubed	6
Ripe avocados	2
Lemon juice	to taste
Tomatoes, blanched and cut into 8 slices	2
Crème fraîche or sour cream	4 T
Watercress or danishcress	1 bunch

Method

Combine vinegar, gin, olive oil, salt, sugar, and pepper. Add cubed chicken and marinate for 10 to 15 minutes. Peel avocados and cut into 16 wedges; season to taste with salt, pepper, and lemon juice. Arrange 2 wedges on each plate; spoon marinated chicken beside them. Decorate with tomato slices, dollops of crème fraîche or sour cream, and cress.

EGGPLANT PAPETON

Yield: 4 portions

Ingredients

Eggplant	2 medium
Shallots, chopped	2 medium
Olive oil	2 oz.
Butter	1 oz.
Eggs, beaten	3
Light cream	½ cup
Cornstarch	1 T
Salt	½ tsp.

White Pepper, ground	¼ tsp.
Aromat (optional)	¼ tsp.
Tomato Sauce	1 cup

Method

Peel eggplants; remove seeds and cube flesh. Sauté shallots in butter and oil. Add eggplant. Cook for 10 minutes over medium heat, stirring occasionally to prevent sticking. Purée eggplant mixture in a food processor. Beat in eggs, cream, and cornstarch. Season well with salt, pepper, and aromat. Pour in buttered individual oven-proof timbales and bake in a bain marie at 350°F until mixture is medium firm. To serve, unmold on warm plates, and pour hot Tomato Sauce over timbales.

SAUSAGE SALAD

Yield: 10 portions

Ingredients

Knockwurst	16 oz.
Onion	6 oz.
Salt	to taste
Sugar	to taste
Vinegar	4 oz.
Water	5 oz.
Oil	1 to 2 oz.
Black pepper, coarsely ground	to taste
Lettuce	10 leaves
Rye or pumpernickel bread	10 slices

Method

Skin sausage and slice. Slice onion thinly. Dissolve salt and sugar in the vinegar and water, and add oil. Mix with sliced sausage and onion. Add marinade, season with pepper, and marinate for 1 hour. Arrange on lettuce leaf. Serve with rye or pumpernickel bread.

Variation I

Knockwurst	10 oz.
Kosher pickle; julienned	1
Carrots, shredded and blanched	3 oz.
Onion, thinly sliced	2 oz.
Apple, peeled, cored, and julienned	1
Italian dressing	6 oz.
Chives, chopped	for garnish

Variation II

Tomatoes, blanched, peeled, seeded, and cubed	16 oz.
Red onions, thinly sliced	3 oz.
Garlic, finely mashed	1 to 2 cloves
Green pepper, julienned	1
Kielbasa or garlic sausage, sliced	7 oz.
Lemon juice	1 oz.
Olive oil	2 oz.
Salt and pepper	to taste
Mustard	1 T

HAM SALAD

Yield: 12 portions

Ingredients

Mushrooms, blanched and sliced	10 oz.
Mixed pickles, cubed	16 oz.
Boiled ham (leftover), cubed	8 oz.
Mayonnaise	3 to 4 oz.
Lettuce leaves	12

Method

Combine all ingredients and marinate for 1 hour. Serve on lettuce leaf.

TURKEY SALAD WITH FRUIT

Yield: 4 portions

Ingredients

Cooked turkey, cut into large julienne	8 oz.
Pineapple rings, canned or fresh, cut into large julienne	2
Kosher pickle, cut into large julienne	1
Tomatoes, peeled, seeded, cut into large julienne	2
Olives, Spanish, stuffed, halved	10

Mandarin oranges, canned or fresh	6 oz.
Vinaigrette	5 oz.
Egg, hard-cooked, diced	1
Parsley, chopped	1 T
Salt and pepper	to taste

Method

Combine all ingredients except eggs, parsley, salt, and pepper and marinate for 30 minutes. Fold in remaining ingredients and adjust seasoning. Serve on a lettuce leaf.

SKEWERED TURKEY LIVER NEW ORLEANS

Yield: 4 portions

Ingredients

Turkey liver	12 oz.
Slab bacon, cut in squares	4 oz.
Curry powder	to taste
Butter	for sauté
Onion, sliced fine	8 oz.
Soy sauce	to taste
Salt	to taste
Hard rolls, sliced	4

Method

Soak turkey liver in milk for 8 hours. Rinse well, drain, and dry. Alternate liver and bacon on skewers and roll in curry powder, chill. Heat butter to a foam and sauté skewers for 4 minutes. Remove from pan and keep warm. Add more butter to pan, add onions, and sauté until golden. Add soy sauce. Return skewers to pan. Heat for 2 minutes. Season with salt and serve with sliced bread.

CRANBERRY HERRING SALAD

Yield: 24 servings

Ingredients

Herring tidbits in wine sauce, drained, onions removed	6 lb.
Cucumbers, peeled, thinly sliced	8
Green apples, peeled, cored, and diced	8
Radishes, sliced thin	1 qt.
Leeks, small, washed, thinly sliced	4
Red onions, small, diced	4
Scallions, trimmed, sliced	8
Heavy cream, whipped	3 cups
Dijon mustard	¼ cup
Cranberry-Orange Relish	14 oz.
Salt	to taste
Lettuce leaves	as needed
Eggs, hard-cooked, chopped fine	12

Method

Combine herring, cucumbers, apples, radishes, leeks, onions, and scallions. Refrigerate until ready to serve. Fold in whipped cream, mustard, and relish. Add salt to taste. Decorate with lettuce and chopped eggs.

VEGETARIAN ANTIPASTO

Yield: 12 portions

Ingredients

Zucchini	2
Eggplant	2
Salt	½ to 1 tsp.
Mushroom caps or cèpes pieces	12 oz.
Olive oil	2 cups
Lemon juice	2 T
Vinegar	2 T
Chicken stock	2 T
Garlic, crushed	1 to 2 cloves
Dried thyme, oregano, basil	½ tsp. each
White pepper	⅓ tsp.
Fresh parsley, chopped	1 T
Lettuce leaves	12
Red peppers, large, fried and marinated (see recipe p. 23)	3
Olives, black or green	24

Parsley, deep-fried	2 bunches
Italian Toast	12

Method

Cut zucchini on a bias into ½-inch-thick slices. Slice eggplants into ½-inch-thick slices and salt. Rest for 30 minutes, rinse, and dry. Clean mushrooms and trim stems. Heat ½ cup of olive oil and sear zucchini and eggplant slices and sauté mushrooms. Remove.

Prepare a marinade from lemon juice, vinegar, chicken stock, garlic dried herbs, salt, pepper, and rest of olive oil. Pour over cooked vegetables and then marinate for 4 hours or overnight. Drain well.

Sprinkle with chopped parsley. Arrange on lettuce leaves together with red peppers and olives. Garnish with deep-fried parsley. Serve with Italian toast.

SMOKED CATFISH ON LENTIL SALAD

Yield: 8 portions
Ingredients

Lentils	6 oz.
Catfish fillets	2 lb.
Butter	2 oz.
Bacon, lean, diced	1 oz.
Onions, peeled and diced fine	2 medium
Leeks (mostly white, some green), cleaned and diced fine	12
Carrots	16
Tomato paste	1 T
Fish broth	1 pt.
Garlic, crushed	2 cloves
Heavy cream	¾ oz.
Salt, pepper	to taste
Red wine vinegar	to taste
Pickle fans	8

Method

Rinse lentils with cold water. Cut catfish fillets into 1-ounce pieces and smoke for 5 minutes or dry smoke. Heat butter and sauté bacon and vegetables until transparent. Drain lentils and add to sautéed vegetables; add tomato paste and heat. Add fish broth and garlic, and cook, covered, for 35 to 40 minutes or until lentils are cooked. Remove half of the lentils, add heavy cream, and purée with stick blender until creamy. Fold in rest of lentils. Season with salt, pepper, and vinegar. Garnish each plate with four pieces of smoked catfish and a pickle fan.

MARINATED MOCK ARTICHOKES

Yield: 10 to 12 portions
Ingredients

Iceberg lettuce cores	80
Water	3 qt.
White vinegar	3 oz.
Coarse salt	½ oz.

Dressing	
Carrots	3 oz.
Garlic	1 clove
Italian dressing	1 qt.
Parsley	⅓ cup
Radicchio leaves	10 to 12

Method

Trim lettuce cores of excess leaves and trim to a cone shape. Combine water, vinegar, and salt. Bring to a boil. Add trimmed lettuce cores and simmer for 10 to 12 minutes. Drain liquid and rinse cores with cold water.

To make the dressing, dice carrots brunoise and mince garlic. Combine with Italian dressing.

Add lettuce cores and marinate for 12 hours. Chop the parsley and sprinkle over the lettuce cores. Serve on radicchio leaves.

SMOKED TROUT WITH VODKA

Yield: 8 portions
Ingredients

Smoked trout	4 fillets
Whipped cream	4 T
Lemon, cubed	1½ T

Smoked salmon, cubed	2 T
Horseradish, grated	1½ T
Vodka	to taste
Sugar	a touch of
White pepper	to taste
Tomatoes, cut into julienne	6 oz.
Mushrooms, cut into julienne	6 oz.
salt	to taste
Dill, chopped	2 T

Method

Remove skin from trout fillets. Fold lemon, smoked salmon, horseradish, vodka, sugar, and white pepper into the whipped cream. Divide mixture evenly among eight dishes. Top each with a halved smoked trout fillet. Surround with seasoned tomatoes and mushroom julienne. Sprinkle with dill.

POTATO PANCAKES

Yield: 20 2-inch pancakes
Ingredients

Potatoes, grated	1½ lb.
Onions, grated	3 oz.
Eggs, whole	4 ea.
salt	⅓ oz.
Lard or 1 part oil and 1 part butter	4 to 5 oz.

Method

Drain grated potatoes well. Add grated onions, eggs, and salt; mix well. Heat fat. Drop mixture by spoonfuls into pan and brown until crisp on both sides. Remove from heat and place on a glazing rack to remove fat. Serve immediately, with smoked salmon, sturgeon caviar, or steak and fish tartar.

SWISS GRUYÈRE IN A PAPER BAG

Yield: 1 portion
Ingredients

Gruyère cheese	2 to 4 oz.
Slice of bread	1
Sweet Hungarian paprika	to taste
Green pepper, roasted, peeled, and deseeded	¼ to ½
Salt	
Butter	½ oz.

Method

Cut bread into rectangles and toast. Cut cheese into rectangles and dust with combined salt and paprika. Set on top of toast and top with green pepper. Set on buttered parchment paper and bake in 400°F oven for 2 to 3 minutes.

CRABMEAT BALLS

Yield: 12 portions
Ingredients

Bacon	12 slices
Crabmeat, lump	16 oz.
Breadcrumbs, fresh	2 cups
Sherry wine, dry	3 oz.
Lemon juice	2 T
Onion salt	1 tsp.
White pepper	½ tsp.
Prepared mustard	3 tsp.
Lemon wedges	12

Method

Cut bacon slices in half. Flake the crabmeat and combine with the bread crumbs, wine, and seasonings. Mix well and shape into two dozen small balls. Wrap with bacon slices. Broil under medium heat until bacon is crisp, turning to brown evenly. Serve with lemon wedges.

DEEP-FRIED MUSHROOMS

Yield: 12 portions
Ingredients

Mushrooms, medium size, firm	24
Ham or Meat Stuffing (see page 64)	
Salt and pepper	
Lemon juice	to season mushroom caps

Flour, egg, bread-
crumbs   to bread
                              mushrooms
Oil   for deep fat fryer

Method

Clean mushrooms and remove the stems. Season with salt and pepper. Stuff twelve mushroom caps and top with twelve mushroom caps. Sprinkle with lemon juice and bread, dipping mushrooms into flour, beaten egg, and breadcrumbs. Fasten with a toothpick. Deep fry at 350°F until golden brown and serve.

HAM STUFFING

Shallot, chopped fine	1
Butter	1½ oz.
Mushroom stems, ground fine	3 oz.
Ham, ground fine	3 to 4 oz.
Parsley, chopped	2 tsp.
Glace de viande (optional)	1 tsp.
Egg yolk	1
Salt, pepper, lemon juice	to taste

Method

Sauté shallots in butter. Add mushroom stems. Add ham, parsley, glace de viande, and egg yolk and season the mixture. Chill.

MEAT STUFFING

Green pepper	1
Mushroom stems	1 oz.
Butter	1 oz.
Salt	
Chicken or turkey or beef, ground fine	11 to 12 oz.

Method

Dice green pepper and mushrooms finely. Sauté in butter. Season and chill. Mix with ground meat and adjust seasoning.

PARMESAN CROQUETTES

Yield: 10 portions
Ingredients

Butter	2 oz.
Flour	2½ oz.
Milk	1 pt.
Egg yolks	5
Parmesan cheese	3 to 3½ oz.
Hot pepper sauce	a few drops
Salt, nutmeg	
Flour, egg white, white bread-crumbs	to bread croquettes
Lemon	10 wedges
Parsley, deep fried	2 bunches

Method

Prepare a colorless roux from butter and flour. Add milk and bring to a boil. Simmer 10 minutes. Fold in tempered egg yolks, bring to a boil, and remove from heat. Add Parmesan and seasoning and salt lightly. Pour onto greased sheet pan, approximately ½ inch deep. Cover with greased parchment paper. Chill well, cut into 2½-inch-long sticks. Dip in flour, egg white and bread crumbs. Deep fry 1 minute. Serve with lemon and deep fried parsley. This recipe makes approximately thirty croquettes.

WILD MUSHROOM MILLE FEUILLE WITH HONEY-ROASTED SHALLOTS AND RUBY PORT SAUCE

Yield: 10 portions
Ingredients

Filo dough	15 sheets
Olive oil (for sautéing)	6 T
Assorted wild mushrooms: shiitakes (trimmed and quartered), cremini mushrooms (small diced), cèpes (diced), chanterelles (trimmed and quartered)	8 to 10 cups
Garlic, whole, crushed	8 cloves
Salt, freshly ground black pepper	to taste
Ruby port	4 oz.
Fresh parsley, chopped	2 oz.
Mirepoix (onions, carrots, celery), diced	6 oz.

Smoked Fish Variation.

1. Small tartlet filled with a salad of diced cooked beets, grated horseradish, and apples, topped with a smoked sturgeon roll.
2. Poached slice of apple, topped with smoked fillet of mackerel and crushed black pepper.
3. Smoked trout in a cucumber circle with julienne of egg whites.
4. Fresh fig hollowed out and filled with a mixture of fig meat, cottage cheese, finely diced smoked herring, finely diced blanched celery cubes, salt, and pepper.
5. Scrambled eggs and chives, pressed and cut out in circles, topped with smoked eel.
6. White break crouton topped with rosette of lemon-flavored caviar whipped cream, a rose of smoked salmon, and dill garnish.

Mushroom trimmings (from above)	4 oz.
Tomato paste	2 oz.
Honey-roasted Shallots (see below)	
fresh herbs to garnish	as needed

Method

To prepare *filo squares*, cut filo sheets into 3-inch squares and arrange in stacks of three on a nonstick baking sheet. Lightly brush top square with olive oil. Bake in a 400°F oven until crisp and golden (about 5 to 7 minutes); remove from oven and reserve.

Prepare Honey-roasted Shallots (see below). Heat a little olive oil until smoking and sauté each type of mushroom separately with garlic cloves. Season with salt and pepper; deglaze with Ruby port. Drain mushrooms, reserving jus. Combine sautéed mushrooms and divide into two batches. Chop one batch coarsely in a food processor; reserve remaining mushrooms for garnish. Fold chopped parsley into chopped mushroom mixture.

Sweat mirepoix and mushroom trimmings in olive oil until soft. Add tomato paste and cook briefly, being careful not to brown. Deglaze with reserved mushroom jus and Ruby port; simmer until aromatic and slightly viscous. Adjust seasoning as needed. Purée in a blender, strain, and keep warm.

To assemble, place one 3-layer stack of baked filo in center of plate. Spread with a thin layer of chopped mushroom mixture and top with herb garnish. Repeat this procedure, ending with a third layer of filo. Arrange four roasted shallots around perimeter of plate; drizzle with sauce and serve.

HONEY-ROASTED SHALLOTS

Ingredients

Balsamic vinegar	16 oz.
Fresh rosemary sprigs	3
Salt and freshly ground black pepper	to taste
Whole shallots, small, peeled, trimmed	40
Olive oil	⅛ cup
Honey	¼ cup

Method

In a stainless bowl, combine vinegar, rosemary, and seasonings. Add shallots, cover, and marinate for at least 12 hours. Drain shallots, reserving marinade.

Preheat oven to 400°F. In a small saucepan, heat marinade over medium flame and reduce by half; reserve. In a separate pan, heat olive oil and slowly sauté shallots. Deglaze with reduced marinade; add honey.

Transfer to oven and continue cooking until liquid has evaporated and shallots are tender. Adjust seasoning as necessary.

SQUID AND CLAM APPETIZER

Yield: 6 portions
Ingredients

Squid tubes, cleaned	16 oz.
Clams, shucked	18
Lemon juice	¼ cup
Salad oil	⅓ cup
Parsley, chopped	1 T
Pimento, chopped	1 T
Salt	½ tsp.
Pepper	to taste
Lettuce, shredded	as needed

Method
A few hours before serving, cut squid lengthwise into ½-inch strips, then cut strips in half. Simmer in boiling water for 1 hour. Drain, reserving liquid.

Blanch the clams for 1 to 2 minutes in the squid stock.

In a bowl, combine lemon juice, oil, parsley, pimento, salt, and pepper. Add squid and clams. Marinate in refrigerator at least 1 hour. Allow to stand at room temperature 15 minutes before serving. Drain, reserving marinade. Toss shredded lettuce with marinade. To serve, arrange squid and clams on shredded lettuce.

SALMON RILLETTES

Yield: 3 lb.
Ingredients

White wine	3 cups
Shallots	10 oz.
Fresh salmon	1½ lb.
Olive oil	to cover salmon
Smoked salmon	1 lb.
Butter	to sauté
Unsalted butter, softened	6 to 8 oz.

Lemon juice	of 1 lemon
Salt	to taste
White pepper	to taste
French bread, toasted, cut into rounds, or cucumber disks	to serve

Method
Bring wine to a simmer, add shallots, and return to a simmering temperature of 160 to 170°F. Place fresh salmon in the simmering wine and poach until the salmon is flaky. Remove the salmon from the poaching liquid, place in olive oil, and refrigerate until cool.

Place smoked salmon in sauté pan with butter and cook slowly. Refrigerate in butter until cool.

In a mixing bowl, place the fresh cooked salmon and the smoked salmon, and mix until the mixture becomes creamy. Add the softened unsalted butter in small pieces and the remaining ingredients, and mix until smooth.

Place the mixture in a plastic-lined mold and chill. Serve with toasted French bread rounds or cucumber disks.

Note: Leftover poaching liquid can be used to make fish aspic. Leftover cooking butter can be used for fish sauces.

TUNA BITES

Yield: 3 dozen
Ingredients

White tuna, solid	14 oz.
Cream cheese, softened	4 oz.
Blue cheese	2 oz.
Chives, chopped	1 T
Lemon juice	½ tsp.
Salt	to taste
Parsley, chopped	½ cup

Method
In a food processor, combine tuna, cream cheese, blue cheese, and chives. Add lemon juice and season to taste with salt. Form into

small balls and roll in parsley. Chill for an hour or more before serving.

MACADAMIA NUT CHICKEN

Yield: 20 strips
Ingredients

Chicken breast, boneless	2 large
Flour	2 cups
Salt	1 tsp.
Macadamia nuts, finely chopped	12 oz.
Breadcrumbs, dry	1 cup
Eggs	4
Butter, melted	½ cup
Sweet Ketchup Sauce (see below)	1¾ cups

Method

Cut chicken into 3-inch-long strips. Preheat oven to 350°F. Mix flour with salt; mix nuts with breadcrumbs. Beat eggs lightly in a shallow bowl.

Dip chicken strips in melted butter to coat, then coat with flour. Dip in egg and coat evenly with the nut mixture.

Place chicken strips on a parchment-covered sheet pan. Bake for 10 to 15 minutes in a 400°F oven. Serve with sweet ketchup sauce.

SWEET KETCHUP SAUCE

Yield: 1¾ cups
Ingredients

Ketchup	1 cup
Red currant jelly	½ cup
A1 sauce	3 T
Hot pepper sauce	½ tsp.

Method

Combine all ingredients and heat to a boil. Serve hot or cold.

CRAB PUFFS

Yield: 3 dozen
Ingredients

Scallions, chopped	2 T
Celery, minced	2 T
Peanut oil	enough to sauté vegetables
Cream cheese, softened	8 oz.
Crabmeat, cleaned	8 oz.
Breadcrumbs, fresh	2 T
Hot pepper sauce	2 drops
Egg roll wrappers	9
Oil	for deep drying

Method

Cook the scallions and celery in a small amount of oil until tender. Cream the cheese and stir in crabmeat, scallions, celery, breadcrumbs, and hot pepper sauce. Cut each egg roll wrapper into four squares. Place equal amounts of the mixture in the centers of each square. Moisten edges, fold over the filling, and seal by pressing down moistened edges. Deep-fry at 350°F for 2 to 3 minutes.

MUFFIN FONDUE

Yield: 6 portions
Ingredients

Butter	2 T
Swiss cheese, grated	6 T
Kirschwasser	2 T
Salt	¼ tsp.
English muffins, split	3

Method

Combine the butter, cheese, Kirschwasser, and salt into a paste. Broil the muffin halves until golden brown. Spread the cheese mixture over muffins. Bake at 400°F until cheese is melted. Allow to cool, then cut into bite-size pieces.

CANAPÉS

Anchovy Canapé. Butter a canapé with anchovy butter; lay strips of anchovies on top, leaving a space in the center to be filled with chopped egg yolks mixed with parsley.

Shrimp Canapé. Butter a canapé with shrimp butter, arrange shrimp tails on top, finish with a sprinkling of fines herbes.

Caviar Canapé. Butter a canapé with caviar butter; place a layer of caviar on top, border with chopped yolks and whites of eggs, and sprinkle chives on top.

Caviar Cigarettes. Spread caviar on a very thin slice of bread; roll to form a cigarette.

Canapé Rigoletto. Butter a canapé with cayenne butter; sprinkle with a mixture of finely chopped whites and yolks of eggs, ham, tongue, fines herbes, and truffles.

Canapé à la Danoise. Butter a rye canapé with horseradish butter; arrange slices of smoked salmon, caviar, and fillets of marinated herring on top of canapé.

Canapé of Langostinos. Butter a canapé with langostino butter; arrange slices of langostino tails on top; decorate with langostino butter.

Canapé of Tongue. Butter a canapé with mustard butter; arrange slices of tongue on top and decorate with mustard butter.

Canapé of Ham. Follow same procedure as for tongue (see above), replacing the tongue with ham.

Canapé of Lobster. Butter a canapé with lobster butter; arrange slices of lobster on top; border with chopped eggs.

Canapé of Eggs. Butter a canapé with mayonnaise; sprinkle top with chopped whites of eggs; border with chopped yolks.

Canapé of Eggs à la Grecque. Butter a canapé with mustard butter; place a hard-cooked egg half on top; cover with mayonnaise; border with chopped eggs and sprinkle fines herbes on top.

Canapé of Game. Butter a canapé with cayenne butter; arrange small mounds of chopped game meat on top; border with fines herbes and chopped capers.

Canapé of Fish. Butter a canapé with herring roe butter; arrange slices of cooked fish on top of butter; cover with mayonnaise and border with chopped capers and fines herbes.

Canapé Cancalaise. Butter a canapé with tuna butter; top with a poached mussel; border with ravigote butter.

Canapé of Smoked Salmon. Butter a canapé with horseradish butter; place a slice of smoked salmon on top; border with chopped chervil and chives.

Canapé of Sardine. Butter a canapé with sardine butter; arrange a sardine fillet on top; decorate with anchovy butter.

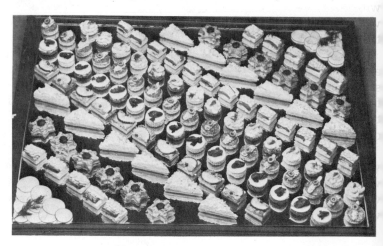

Arrangement of canapés.

Canapé of Lobster Eggs. Butter a canapé with lobster cheese, top with a sprinkling of lobster coral; decorate with lobster butter.

Domino Canapé. Butter domino-shaped canapés with truffle butter; cover with thin slices of gruyère cheese of the same shape. Cut holes in the cheese to simulate spots on dominoes and fill holes with pieces of truffle.

Canapé Rejane. Butter a canapé with lobster butter; top with a mound of chopped eggs and mayonnaise. Cover with a light mayonnaise and border with chopped lobster coral. (*Note:* When langostino or lobster coral cannot be obtained, substitute grated egg yolks that have been tinted during cooking.)

Canapé of Goujons à la Russe. Poach some cleaned goujons in a court bouillon of white wine; cool. Place on canapés, cover with gelatin mayonnaise and sprinkle lightly with chopped parsley.

Breast of Chicken Bombay. Place a slice of chicken breast in a tablespoon, fill cavity with mousse of chicken with curry added, then top with a second slice of chicken breast. Cover the combination with curried chaud-froid sauce and garnish with cutout radish and leek flowers.

Canapé of Sole à la Brasset. Butter round canapés with herring roe butter; place a small paupiette of sole on top and cover with a light mayonnaise. Decorate the sides with chopped coral and put a bit of chopped truffle on top.

Canapé à la Niçoise. Butter round canapés with anchovy butter; place three small stuffed green olives on the canapés; put a fourth olive on top of the three. Fill in between olives with anchovy butter and decorate as desired.

Canapé Paulette. Butter round canapés with anchovy butter; sprinkle half of canapé with chopped egg whites and the other half with chopped egg yolks; separate halves with a row of shrimp.

Small Brioche of Foie Gras. Place a small piece of truffle in the center of a ball of foie gras; wrap unsweetened brioche dough around foie gras, shaping it like a small loaf of bread. Bake and cool before serving.

Profiteroles. Bake a pâte à choux into tiny round shells. These may be garnished with any kind of purée of meat, fish, or cheese.

Canapé Vie Ville. Cover a canapé with tarragon butter, then top with a slice of ham; decorate with tarragon leaves.

Canapé à d'Arkangel. Cover one half of a small tartlet with caviar, the remaining half with purée of smoked salmon. Separate halves with a fillet of anchovy.

Note: Most canapés should be spread with either a butter- or cheese-flavored compound to complement the main ingredient to be placed on the canapé. A large variety of canapé ingredients is available on the market in cans or jars. These may be used either as hors d'oeuvre or as a garnish for canapés.

FISH AND SHELLFISH

Anchovies, Muscovite. On a large circle of cooked potato, arrange marinated anchovies to form a crown. Place caviar in the center of the crown. Garnish top of caviar with chopped egg white.

Boutargue (Mullet Eggs). These are available salted and smoked, to be served like caviar. They are very appetizing.

Salted Codfish à l'Indienne. Soak 2 pounds of codfish overnight; cut in scallop-sized pieces; roll in flour and fry quickly in hot oil. Saute 2 tablespoons of finely chopped onions in olive oil till golden; sprinkle with curry powder and simmer for one minute. Add 1 cup of dry white wine, juice of one lemon, three crushed garlic cloves and boil for 5 minutes. Place codfish pieces in this marinade, bring to a boil, cover and let cool. Serve cooled pieces with some of the marinade. Yield: 12 portions.

Langostine à l'Amiral. Defrost langostino carefully so the form of the shell remains intact. Bake small barquettes. Fill barquettes with a ragout made from langostino meat mixed with an anchovy mayonnaise.

Crayfish à la Moscovite. Remove the tail shell from cooked crayfish and serve tails with anchovy mayonnaise. Top with a sprinkling of chopped parsley.

Frog Legs à la Béarnaise. Sauté frog legs in olive oil; add diced tomatoes, white wine, lemon juice, and herbs; season with salt and pepper; simmer for 5 minutes. Serve with some of the liquor they were cooked in and sprinkle with fines herbes.

Goujons à la Russe. Poach some cleaned goujons in white wine and lemon juice. Remove goujons and reduce cooking liquor by one half. Arrange goujons on a small plate, top with mayonnaise thinned with some of the reduced cooking liquor. Use cucumber salad to complete the plate.

Lobster à la Boulognaise. Cut cooked lobster meat into small pieces; add an equal quantity of celery and finely chopped beets. Mix these ingredients with mayonnaise; season well with finely chopped chervil, tarragon, and cayenne. Arrange lobster mixture on lettuce leaves and sprinkle with finely chopped lobster coral.

Herring à la Dieppoise. Poach cleaned, fresh fillets of herring in a marinade of white wine, vinegar, carrots, onions à la russe, and herbs. Serve with some of the marinade.

Herring à la Livonienne. Remove fillets and reserve heads and tails of twelve salted or smoked herrings. Remove skin and dice fillets. Place in bowl with equal quantity of diced boiled potatoes and fresh apples. Season with the following dressing: ½ teaspoon salt; pinch of freshly ground white pepper; 1 teaspoon each, coarsely chopped parsley, chervil, fennel, and tarragon; 6 tablespoons olive oil and 3 tablespoons of red wine vinegar. Mix all ingredients well. On a service platter, mold this preparation into shapes resembling herring; place reserved heads and tails at each extremity, thus simulating the original fish; serve.

Herring à la Lucas. Salad of diced marinated herring in a Sauce gribiche. Season lightly.

Herring à la Russe. Arrange fillets of smoked herring on a ravier; border with sliced cold potatoes. Season with a fennel vinaigrette.

Trout à la Saint Menehould with Champagne. Place cleaned trout fillet in a pan. Sauté sliced carrots, onions, garlic in butter seasoned with freshly ground pepper, grated nutmeg, herb mixture, and salt. Add a bottle of Champagne and simmer for 30 minutes. Add trout fillets and cook for 6 to 8 minutes. Chill. Remove the trout from the fond. Strain and reserve fond. Serve trout with fond alongside. (Herring and salmon may be cooked in similar fashion.)

Mackerel In Marinade. Take twelve very fresh mackerel (about 1 pound each); remove the fillets and place them in a sauté pan; season with salt, freshly ground pepper. Sprinkle finely sliced onion, pinch of thyme, three parsley sprigs, one bay leaf, and the juice of two lemons over fish. Add sufficient dry white wine to cover and bring to a boil; cover and let simmer for 5 minutes. Remove from heat and allow to cool; place in refrigerator until jellied.

Marinated Mackerel à la Suedoise. Prepare small mackerel like Herring à la Dieppoise.

Mullets à l'Orientale. Prepare the same as Mullets au Saffron, eliminating the saffron.

Mullets au Saffron. Cook mullets in oil, chopped onions, diced tomatoes, white wine, fish stock, herb mixture, and saffron. Serve mullets in liquor with sprinkling of chopped parsley.

Mussels. Poach and clean some mussels; mix with mayonnaise flavored with lemon juice and thinned with poaching liquor reduced by two thirds. Sprinkle fines herbes on top.

Mussels à l'Antiboise. Garnish a mussel shell with a purée of sardines; place a

Far left and lower right: Pickled Herring and Glass Noodle Salad. Far right and lower left: Bitter Squash and Baby Squid on Seaweed Salad. Center: Shrimp and Saffron Rice.

poached mussel on the purée and a chervil leaf over the mussel; glaze all with aspic.

Mussels à l'Indienne. Prepare mussels in a curry sauce. Arrange within a turban of boiled rice.

Pickled Oysters. Steam forty-eight oysters in their own liquor; drain, and reserve liquor. Remove shells. Boil ½ pint vinegar with ⅓ teaspoon cloves, whole white pepper, whole allspice, a pinch of mace, and ½ teaspoon sugar for a few minutes, then add the oyster liquor, bring to a boil, strain, and pour over oysters. Let oysters marinate in refrigerator for 4 hours or overnight.

Slices of Pickerel à la Georgianne. Clean and completely bone a pickerel. Stuff with a highly seasoned forcemeat; wrap as a galantine and cook in a court bouillon made with white wine. When fish is done, cool and cut into slices. On each slice, place a small portion of Russian salad, then place a small slice of lobster on top of the salad. Glaze with aspic.

Salmon, Canadian Style. Cut 2 pounds fresh salmon in large dice, fry briskly in hot oil; season with salt and paprika. Place in a sauté pan; add 1 pound of small fresh okra, white wine, and the juice of two lemons; let simmer for a few minutes, season to taste, and cool covered. Sprinkle finely chopped green pepper over servings.

Horns of Salmon à l'Imperiale. Make horns of smoked salmon and garnish with caviar butter.

Barquettes of Fillet of Dover Sole Caprice. Fill small barquettes with cucumber salad, seasoned with cream and lemon juice. Arrange small paupiettes of sole stuffed with a purée of truffles over salad; glaze all with aspic.

Paupiettes of Fillet of Dover Sole. Stuff paupiettes (roulades) with forcemeat flavored with red pimentos; poach, cool, and cut into rings. Garnish dish with a salad of cucumbers; arrange rings on salad.

Tortillions of Dover Sole à la Diable. Tie slender bands of sole into a knot. Sauté in a little oil; then add white wine, lemon juice, a few grains of coriander seed, garlic, a little Worcestershire sauce, crushed thyme, and bay leaves. Bring to a boil. Cool sole; serve with liquor.

Smelts à la Caucasienne. Clean smelts; dry, flour, and brown in very hot oil. Place in vinaigrette.

Marinated Smelts (known in French cookery as *escabèche*). Fry forty-eight thoroughly dried and floured smelts in hot oil. When done, place in a deep dish and set aside. In the same hot oil, stir fry one large onion and one carrot (cut into very thin round slices) with eight unpeeled cloves of garlic. When slightly brown, drain the oil, then moisten with 1 tablespoon vinegar, the juice of one lemon, 1 quart dry white wine; add freshly ground white pepper, one bay leaf, a pinch of thyme, three parsley sprigs, three small pimentos, and salt to taste. Simmer for 15 minutes. When ready, cool. Remove garlic and pour over smelts. Marinate for 24 hours. Serve smelts with strained marinade.

Shrimp with Saffron à l'Orientale. Shrimp may be used with or without their shells in this dish. However, leaving the shell on is recommended. Heat 2 tablespoons olive oil. Add forty-eight medium shrimp and sauté over high heat for 2 to 3 minutes. Cover with dry white wine; add salt to taste, three parsley sprigs, two fennel leaves, pinch of thyme, one bay leaf, three cloves of garlic, a few peppercorns and coriander seed, and ⅓ teaspoon of saffron. Simmer for 6 to 8 minutes and allow shrimp to cool in this liquor. Remove shrimp, peel if desired, arrange on a platter, and strain liquor over them. Serve chilled with warm sesame bread alongside.

Sturgeon à la Russe. Cook fillet of sturgeon in a highly seasoned marinade; cool in this marinade. Make an aspic with some of the marinade. Cool the aspic over ice. Coat the bottom of a dish with this aspic. When aspic has set, arrange slices of sturgeon and smoked salmon over it.

Tuna à l'Antiboise. Make a salad of potatoes and tuna, garnish with slices of tomatoes, quartered eggs, and pitted olives; serve with mayonnaise dressing.

VEGETABLES

Artichoke à l'Egyptienne. Prepare small artichokes, leaving the stems attached. Cook in a combination of oil, white wine, lemon juice, coriander seed, salt, and pepper to which brunoise (carrots, celery, onions) has been added. Frozen artichoke hearts may be substituted for fresh artichokes.

Artichoke Bottoms. Cooked artichoke bottoms may be garnished in many ways (with, for example, purée of foie gras, or peas).

Cucumbers à la Danoise. Cut cucumber disks 1 inch thick, hollow, blanch, and drain. Put herring fillets and hard-cooked egg yolks through a fine sieve; add chopped chives, mustard, olive oil, and salt and pepper to taste. Fill cucumber disks with mixture; decorate with shredded horseradish.

Celeriac Ravigote. Julienne celeriac, parboil; chill and combine with a mixture of French dressing, mayonnaise, and French mustard.

Left to right, top: Smoked Breast of Duck with Pepper Salad; Salt-Dough Centerpiece; Cured Pork Fillet with Fruit Farce, Oriental Vegetable Salad. Left to right, bottom: Artichoke Bottom with Marinated Vegetables; Smoked Salmon with Horseradish–Cream Cheese Rose on a Marinated Turnip Slice; Stuffed Egg on Pumpernickel Bread; Chicken Roulade with Prosciutto and Cheddar Cheese; Rye Barquette with Smoked Shrimp and Spinach Mousse.

Marinated Carrots. Peel small carrots; cook in water, white wine, vinegar, herbs, garlic, olive oil, salt, and pepper. Serve chilled in cooking liquor.

Salsify à l'Italienne. Marinate salsify and beets separately in Italian dressing. Arrange slices of salsify with slices of beets in lettuce cups.

SALADS

The following salads can be used for hors d'oeuvre:

Tomato and Egg Salad
Tomato and Potato Salad
Potato and Chervil Salad
Potato and Fillet of Herring Salad
Potato and Shrimp Salad
Shrimp and Egg Salad
Shrimp and Tomato Salad
Celeriac Salad
Celeriac and Truffle Salad
Celeriac and Chervil Salad
Radish and Mint Vinegar Salad
Radish and Pickled Cherry Salad
Boiled Beef Salad
Cucumber Salad
Beet and Chopped Fennel Salad
Beet and Potato Salad
Mussels, Tomato, and Beef Salad
Oyster and Garlic Crouton Salad
Seafood Salad
Red Cabbage Salad
White Cabbage salad
Lentil, White Bean, Kidney Bean (all dried legumes) Salads
Eggplant Salad
Eggplant, Tomato, and Pimento salad

See also Chapter 16 for salad recipes.

BARQUETTES

Barquettes are small boats made of piecrust dough. They may be featured as follows:

Bagration. Chicken purée, chicken breast, truffles, and aspic.

Beauharnais. Chicken and truffles, covered with mayonnaise mixed with purée of tarragon and gelatin and decorated with truffles and aspic.

Cancalaise. Mousse of fish and oysters in aspic.

Marivaux. Small dice of shrimp and mushrooms with mayonnaise collée; decorate with hard-cooked egg and aspic.

Various other fillings can also be served in barquettes:

Anchovy salpicons
Smoked eel
Vegetables
Mussels
Compound butter
Caviar
Cucumber
Shrimp
Lobster
Foie gras
Herring
Olives
Eggs
Sausages
Tuna
Tomatoes
Truffles

The following may be used to decorate barquettes:

Capers
Gherkins
Fruit
Eggs

Parsley

Chervil

Tarragon

Lettuce

EGG DISHES FOR HORS D'OEUVRE

**Tips for Better Use of Eggs
in Garde Manger**

1. To prevent the yolk of a hard-cooked egg from becoming green-tinged:
   A. Use fresh eggs. The green substance, called ferrous sulfide, develops more readily in older eggs.
   B. Never boil the eggs longer than 15 minutes.
   C. Once cooked, quickly cool the eggs in cold water.
2. Eggs should be poached in vinegar-spiked water. The acid in the vinegar precipitates the setting of the egg white and thus gives the poached egg a more compact shape. The proper ratio is one tablespoon of vinegar per quart of water.
3. To hard-cook eggs, place the eggs in a proper-sized pot. Cover with cold tap water. Bring to a boil, then immediately lower the temperature. Simmer as follows: small eggs, 12 minutes; medium eggs, 13 minutes; large eggs, 14 to 15 minutes; extra-large eggs, 15 minutes. This method will always provide consistent results, with no overcooking or undercooking, as the water will not boil until the eggs reach a common temperature.
4. Hard-cooked eggs are easier to peel when hot. As the cooked eggs cool, the white starts to adhere to the shell's innermost membrane. To facilitate the peeling of a hard-cooked egg, start at the larger end and remove the shell under cold running water.
5. To prevent a boiled or soft-boiled egg from cracking, pierce the larger non-tapered end of the egg with a standard pushpin before placing in simmering water. This method is almost foolproof. It allows the air to escape from the pocket as it increases under heat. In garde manger, this method is often advisable if you must have a perfectly cooked, uncracked egg.
6. To tell if an unopened egg is raw or cooked, spin the egg on a flat surface. If the egg rotates effortlessly and smoothly, it is hard-boiled. The yolk of an uncooked egg changes position inside the egg, causing it to wobble as it turns.
7. When whipping egg whites, it is important that they do not come in contact with any fat. They reduce in volume if they contain any trace of yolk or grease. Make sure that all utensils used to mix or store egg whites are grease-free. Egg yolk or grease are the most common causes for low-volume beaten egg whites. In extreme cases, egg whites may not gain any volume and may have to be discarded.
8. To tell if a raw egg is fresh without breaking it, place it in a bowl or pot of cold water. If the egg sinks and lies on its side, it is fresh. If it stands partially on its tapered end, it is still edible but more than a week old. If it floats, it is not suitable for consumption.
9. A raw egg should be stored upright, with the larger end up. This helps retard spoilage because it keeps the egg yolk from coming in contact with the air pocket.

HARD-COOKED EGGS MIMOSA

Yield: 16 tarts
Ingredients

Green peas and diced carrots, mixed and cooked	1 cup
Celery, finely diced	½ cup
Ham, cooked, finely diced	¾ cup
Lobster, cooked, flaked	¾ cup
Mayonnaise	10 oz.
Heavy cream, whipped	2 oz.
Salt, ground pepper	to taste
Tart shells, 2-inch, baked	16
Whole eggs, hard-cooked	8
Egg yolks, hard-cooked	2
Parsley, chopped	

Method

Combine cooked peas and carrots, celery, ham, lobster, mayonnaise, heavy cream, salt, and pepper. Chill. Coat the bottom of the tart shells with this mixture and chill. Shortly before serving, fill the tart shells half full with the salad mixture. Cut hard-cooked eggs in half lengthwise and place one on each tart. Coat lightly with mayonnaise. Put the hard-cooked egg yolks through a sieve and sprinkle over eggs. Garnish with chopped parsley. Chill a few minutes for mayonnaise to set. Serve on a buffet table or on a meat, fish, or vegetable salad plate.

ASSORTED COLD STUFFED EGGS, RECIPE VARIATION NUMBER 1

Based on twenty hard-cooked or pickled eggs, each of the following recipes will top eight egg halves.

1. 4 oz. cream cheese
   2 T finely chopped herbs (chervil, parsley, dill)
   2 T heavy cream or yogurt
   Salt and white pepper

   For the garnish: small baby corn tip, green pepper triangle, and a pimento circle.

2. 4 oz. cottage cheese
   2 T grated carrots
   2 T grated pecan nuts
   Salt and white pepper to taste

   For the garnish: anchovy roll, tomato triangle, black olive.

3. 4 oz. cream cheese
   2 T Madras curry, slightly toasted
   2 T mashed avocado (optional)
   1 T lemon juice
   2 T heavy cream or yogurt

   For the garnish: sliced kiwi fruit halves and blue grape, dill sprig.

4. 4 oz. cream cheese
   1 T chopped dill
   Some grated lemon zest
   Salt and white pepper

   For the garnish: smoked salmon roll, red and black caviar, dill sprig.

5. 4 oz. cream cheese
   4 T tomato onion ketchup
   1 T Hungarian paprika (sweet)
   Salt and black pepper

   For the garnish: cherry tomato slice, gherkin fan, watercress leaf, Spanish stuffed olive half.

Note: For an à la carte appetizer, serve two different egg halves on a vegetable salad or plain Boston lettuce leaf with a crouton.

For a reception, arrange all eggs in rows on a food platter.

STUFFED EGGS STRASBOURG STYLE

(with *Foie Gras*)
Yield: 6 portions
Ingredients

Eggs, hard-cooked, peeled	6
Foi gras purée	3½ oz.
Truffles, chopped	2 tsp.
Aspic, aromatic	to serve

Method

Cut eggs in half lengthwise. Remove yolks and put them through a sieve. Add foie gras purée and mix well. Stuff the egg whites. Sprinkle with chopped truffles. Serve on a bed of chopped aspic.

STUFFED EGGS ROSCOFF

Yield: 6 portions
Ingredients

Eggs, hard-cooked, peeled	6
Lobster, finely diced, cooked	1 cup
Mayonnaise	½ cup
Salt and ground pepper	to taste
Coating mayonnaise	¼ cup
Mixed vegetables, cooked, cold	1 cup
Lettuce	to garnish

Method

Cut eggs in half lengthwise and remove yolks, leaving the whites intact. Reserve both yolks and whites. Combine lobster, ⅓ cup of the mayonnaise, and salt and pepper to taste. Spoon the mixture into the cavities of the whites, mounding it over the tops. Then coat the stuffed eggs thinly with coating mayonnaise. Chill until mayonnaise is set. Combine the cooked vegetables with the remaining mayonnaise and salt and pepper to taste. Arrange lettuce in the center of a plate and surround it with the stuffed eggs. Press the hard-cooked egg yolks through a sieve and sprinkle them over the eggs.

HERB-STUFFED EGGS

Yield: 6 portions
Ingredients

Eggs, hard-cooked, peeled	6
Butter, softened	4 T
Spinach, chopped, cooked, well drained	½ cup
Tarragon and chervil, dried	⅛ tsp. each
Watercress, finely chopped	2 T
Mayonnaise	¼ cup
Aspic, half-set	1 cup
Tarragon and chervil leaves	to garnish

Method

Cut eggs in half lengthwise. Remove yolks and put them through a sieve. Add softened butter and mix well. Heat spinach with herbs and watercress 1 minute, then cool. Drain, squeezing out as much of the liquid as possible. Purée spinach in a blender. Reserve 2 tablespoons of this purée for later use. Mix remaining purée with egg yolk mixture. Stuff the egg whites. Mix the reserved spinach purée with mayonnaise and coat eggs. Garnish with tarragon and chervil leaves. Coat with the half-set aspic.

Spread the remaining aspic over a serving platter and chill until set. Arrange the eggs on top.

PICKLED EGGS

Yield: 10 portions
Ingredients

Dry mustard	1½ tsp.
Cornstarch	1½ tsp.
White vinegar	1 pt.
Sugar	1½ to 2 tsp.
Turmeric	½ tsp.
Eggs, hard-cooked	10

Method

Dilute dry mustard and cornstarch in a little water. Add vinegar and spices. Boil 10 minutes. Add shelled eggs. Marinate for 2 hours or overnight. Good for stuffed eggs, salads, or snacks.

EGGS IN ASPIC COLINETTE

Yield: 6 portions
Ingredients

Eggs, poached, cold	6
Chaud-froid sauce	⅔ cup
Aspic	2 cups
Shrimp, peeled, deveined, cooked	18

Aspic croutons, cut ¼-inch thick	6
Truffle, thinly sliced	7 slices
Salmon, cooked	½ lb.
Heavy cream, whipped	3 to 4 T
Salt and pepper	to taste
Lemon juice	1 to 2 tsp.
Smoked salmon	to garnish
Parsley	to garnish
Truffle	to garnish

Method

Trim edges of the egg whites to shape eggs uniformly. Coat the eggs with chaud-froid sauce and chill until coating is set. Coat the inside of a 9-inch ring mold with aspic and chill until aspic is almost set. Decorate the bottom of mold with shrimp and truffle slices and place chaud-froid-coated eggs on top. Finish filling the mold with aspic. Chill until aspic is firm. Just before serving, unmold the ring onto a large serving plate and surround with aspic croutons. Flake the salmon and blend with cream, salt, pepper, and lemon juice. Chill until ready to serve, and then spoon into the center of the ring. Garnish with smoked salmon slices, a truffle slice, and sprigs of parsley. Serve at once, for a buffet or lunch or supper.

EGGS TARTARE

Yield: 6 portions

Ingredients

Tomatoes, medium size	4
Salt and ground black pepper	to taste
Vegetables, mixed, in ½-inch pieces, cooked	2 cups
Mayonnaise	1 cup
Eggs, poached, cold	6
Parsley, chopped	2 T
Gherkins, chopped	2 T
Lettuce	to garnish

Method

Blanch, peel, and halve the tomatoes. Scoop out the centers, and squeeze the pulp well to remove liquid. Dice the centers, and re-serve. Sprinkle the halves with salt and pepper. Combine the cold cooked vegetables and the tomato centers with ½ cup of the mayonnaise and salt and pepper to taste. Trim edges of the egg whites to shape uniformly. Coat the eggs with mayonnaise. Place one on each tomato half. Sprinkle with chopped parsley and gherkins. Line a serving plate with lettuce, over which arrange salad-filled tomatoes. Garnish the center of the plate with remaining half tomato.

EGGS FROU-FROU

Yield: 6 to 12 portions

Ingredients

Asparagus tips, cold, crisply cooked	24
Peas, cold, cooked	1 cup
Green beans, cold, cooked, cut into ½-inch pieces	1 cup
Mayonnaise, thick	1¼ cups
Salt and pepper	to taste
Eggs, poached, cold	12
Egg yolks, hard-cooked, sieved	2

Method

Combine all vegetables with ⅓ cup of the mayonnaise. Season with salt and pepper to taste. Pile in the center of a serving dish. Trim edges of the egg whites to shape eggs uniformly and coat each with mayonnaise. (If desired, use coating mayonnaise.) Sprinkle eggs with sieved hard-cooked egg yolks and arrange them around the salad. Serve for lunch or supper.

EGGS IN ASPIC

Yield: 6 to 12 portions

Ingredients

Water	to cover onions
Onions, sliced	1 cup
Butter	2 T
Flour	2 T

Milk	1 cup
Salt and ground pepper	to taste
Unflavored gelatin	1 T
Cold water	1 T
Heavy cream, whipped	¼ cup
Eggs, soft-cooked, cold, medium	12
Green and red sweet peppers	2 each
French dressing	to marinate

Method

Pour enough boiling water over onions to cover them, and let stand 5 minutes. Pour off water and drain onions well; cook them in the butter until they are soft. Remove from heat and blend in flour. Stir and cook 1 minute. Remove from heat and add milk. Stir and cook until the sauce is of medium thickness. Season the sauce with salt and pepper. While sauce is cooking, soften gelatin in cold water, add to the hot sauce, and mix well. Put sauce through a sieve, pushing as much of the onion through as possible, or blend a few seconds in an electric blender. Fold in cream.

Peel soft-cooked eggs and coat with the sauce. Chill until the coating is almost firm. Decorate top of each with three small green and three small red diamond-shaped pieces of sweet pepper. Arrange in a cold serving dish. Fill center of the dish with thin green pepper sticks marinated 30 minutes in French dressing. Serve for lunch or supper.

EGGS CASINO

Yield: 6 portions

Ingredients

Coating mayonnaise	⅓ cup
Tomato purée or ketchup	1 to 2 T
Eggs, soft-cooked in shells and cooled	6
Egg, hard-cooked	1
Chicken, cold, cooked, finely diced	¾ cup
Mayonnaise	3 T

Salt and ground black pepper	to taste
Pastry barquettes, baked	6
Asparagus tips, cooked	12
Ham, cold, cooked	12 slices

Method

Combine coating mayonnaise and tomato purée or ketchup. Peel the soft-cooked eggs. Coat six of them with the coating mayonnaise mixture. Using the white and the yolk of the hard-cooked egg, make a design on the top of each to simulate a daisy. Chill until set. Mix the chicken with mayonnaise and salt and pepper to taste. Spoon the mixture into the baked barquettes. Place two asparagus tips and a tomato mayonnaise-coated egg on each. Fold the ham slices in quarters and arrange six folded slices in a circle in the center of the platter; set three decorated barquettes on either side of the ham.

EGGS IN ASPIC WITH PARMA HAM

Yield: 6 portions

Ingredients

Soft-cooked eggs, medium, cold	6
Chicken aspic, very aromatic	3 cups
Truffle, thinly sliced	6 slices
Tarragon or parsley leaves	to garnish
Ham, cooked, thinly sliced	6 slices

Method

Peel eggs and set aside. Coat the insides of six small oval-shaped timbales with aspic and chill them until aspic is almost set. Decorate the bottoms of the timbales with truffles slices and tarragon or parsley leaves. Wrap each egg in a slice of ham and place one in each timbale. Finish filling the molds with half-set aspic. Chill until aspic is firm. There will be some aspic remaining; chill until set and reserve.

To serve, unmold eggs onto a cold serving plate, arrange them in a circle. Cube firm aspic and spoon it around the eggs. Serve for a buffet, lunch, or supper.

Penguin.

1. Mise en place: hard-cooked eggs, black olives, carrots, salami slice, toothpick, round cutter.

2. Slice off a little of the egg to make egg stand up straight.

3. Insert a small stick of carrot into the black olive and insert into egg with toothpick.

4. Peel off the olive skin, approximately ½ inch wide.

5. Cut out a small triangle from the peeled skin and place on either side of the egg.

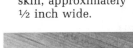

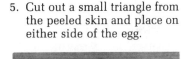

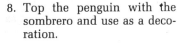

6. Cut out circles from olive skin and place on penguin for buttons.

7. Cut two slivers of black olive and place in front of penguin for shoes.

8. Top the penguin with the sombrero and use as a decoration.

EGGS IN ASPIC À LA JEANNETTE

Yield: 6 portions
Ingredients

Eggs, poached, cold	6
Aspic, half-set	1½ cups
Chaud-froid sauce	⅔ cup
Foi gras purée	⅔ cup
Butter, softened	¼ cup
Truffle	to garnish

Method
Trim edges of the egg whites to shape eggs uniformly. Coat with chaud-froid sauce. Place an egg in each of six custard cups and chill until coating is set. Finish filling cups with half-set aspic, but do not cover the top of the eggs. Combine foie gras and butter. Using a pastry bag and a fluted tube, garnish each dish with a flute ring of the mixture. Chill until ready to serve. Garnish the top of each egg with a bit of truffle. Serve for lunch, supper, or for a buffet.

Other Egg Hors d'Oeuvre

SLICED HARD-COOKED EGGS WITH MAYONNAISE

Allow one egg per serving. Split hard-cooked eggs in half lengthwise or cut in thick crosswise slices. Coat with mayonnaise. Arrange on a serving dish and garnish with chopped parsley. Serve as an hors d'oeuvre or on a meat, fish, or vegetable salad plate.

Hard-Cooked Eggs, Spanish Style (Oeufs à l'Espagnole). Make deviled stuffed eggs, place on marinated tomato slices. Refrigerate ½ hour before serving. Julienne celery and red peppers and marinate in salt, oil, and vinegar. Arrange tomato slices with

Salami Sombrero.

1. To make sombrero, cut the salami slice halfway to the center.

2. Roll into a cone.

3. Turn upside down.

4. Bend cone into a sombrero.

ggs in circle on platter; top with marinated celery and red pepper strips. Garnish with stuffed green olives. Julienne of truffles may also be added.

Boiled Eggs Moscow Style (Oeufs à la Moscovite). Prepare a light mousse of lobster. Cut into circles and top with half a hard-cooked egg decorated with a small slice of lobster and a small amount of caviar. Arrange these around a mountain of lemon-flavored whipped cream mixed with caviar.

Buttered toast is the perfect accompaniment.

Boiled Eggs Danish Style (Oeufs durs à la Danoise). Cut hard-cooked eggs lengthwise into halves. Remove egg yolks and stuff cavity with diced lobster salad blended with mayonnaise and egg yolks. Serve on lettuce leaf with danishcress and radish rose.

Hard-Cooked Eggs Stuffed with Seafood (Oeufs aux fruits de mer). Cut hard-cooked

Frog Egg.

1. Mise en place: Hard-cooked eggs, stuffed Spanish olives, pimentos, gherkins, toothpick, carrots, green peppers.

2. Cut off the bottom part of the egg at a 45-degree angle.

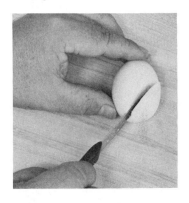

3. Remove a small wedge from top of egg.

4. Top egg with two ends of stuffed Spanish olives for eyes.

5. Cut pimento into long triangle for tongue.

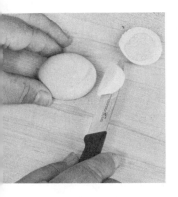

eggs in half. Stuff with combination of finely diced smoked eel, anchovies, and a few titi shrimp mixed with mayonnaise and lemon juice. Garnish with chopped lobster coral and coat lightly with aspic.

Russian Eggs (Oeufs à la Russe). Cut hard-cooked eggs in half lengthwise, top with tartar sauce, and decorate with a small amount of caviar.

Hard-Cooked Eggs, Norwegian Style (Oeufs à la Norvegienne). Cut hard-cooked eggs in half lengthwise. Pipe a small amount of creamed horseradish (blend of whipped cream, grated horseradish, sugar, salt) over egg. Garnish with tiny shrimp and salmon caviar. Serve on lettuce leaf with radish rose or parsley.

Eggs Piquantes (Oeufs Piquantes). Cut hard-cooked eggs lengthwise. Remove yolks and purée them with anchovies, then whip in a small amount of butter. Pipe yolk mixture into whites. Decorate with slice of radish or small sour gherkins or a bit of anchovy or smoked salmon.

Soft-Cooked Eggs Served in Tomatoes (Oeufs Mollets aux Tomates). Place a soft-cooked egg (4 to 5 minutes) in a marinated half tomato. Pipe on a flower made of mixture of egg yolk, tomato catsup, and butter. A few bits of caviar represent center of flower. Set tomato on blanched, marinated fine julienne of vegetable. Serve with Sauce Tyrolienne.

Soft-Cooked Eggs Farmer's Style (Oeufs Mollets à la Paysanne). Place soft-cooked eggs on an oval-shaped toasted crouton of white bread. Around eggs, arrange diced turkey or chicken, cauliflower rosettes

6. Insert pimento triangle into frog mouth. Cut gherkins into fans for feet.

7. Carve carrot with a paring knife into a hat and stick with toothpick into egg.

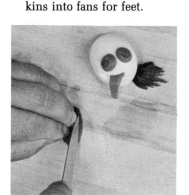

8. Cut green pepper into a flower and set frog next to it. It will be a highlight of your buffet.

sliced black olives, and fennel that has been marinated in lemon juice, oil, salt, and pepper. Sprinkle with chopped fresh parsley.

Soft-Cooked Eggs Niçoise (Oeufs à la Niçoise). Blanch tomatoes 15 seconds and peel. Cut in half, remove seeds. Marinate in combination of oil, vinegar, and salt; top tomato half with soft-cooked egg and arrange on platter with string bean salad. Just before serving, top with Sauce Green Goddess and garnish with a truffle slice.

Soft-Cooked Eggs on Croutons (Oeufs sur Crouton). Cut egg-size croutons from white bread and bake. Spread with herbal butter. Set soft-cooked egg on top of crouton and arrange croutons with eggs around a salad of mussels. Dredge mussels in flour, sauté in oil, then marinate for 24 hours in oil and vinegar. Add to marinated mussels tiny shrimp, small blanched cauliflower roses, chopped chives, parsley, dill, and mustard. Let stand for 1 hour.

Poached Eggs, Sicilian Style (Oeufs Pochés à la Sicilienne). Blanch medium-sized tomatoes, peel, halve, and remove seeds. Marinate in white wine, vinegar, salt, pepper, and oil. Shortly before serving, drain tomatoes and fill with a poached egg. Top egg with blanched marinated julienne of carrots, celeriac, mushrooms, and truffles (optional), and serve on a glass platter with watercress and garlic mayonnaise.

Poached Eggs, Gourmet Style (Oeufs Pochés à la Lucullus). Fill small tartlets with lobster mousse; top with poached eggs. Coat with Sauce Chantilly and garnish with truffle bits.

Eggs in Cocottes. With the hurried pace set for today's kitchen brigade and the shortage of labor, this method of preparing egg dishes is very welcome since it is not only fast but produces an item that is easy to serve. The appetizer can be made up ahead of time in any quantity. It is especially desirable for fast-turnover restaurants.

In most cases, we fill the cocotte (small china mold) with any one of several different mousses, then top the filled cocotte with either a cooked or a poached egg. It can be decorated with truffles, olives, tongue, tarragon leaves, or leeks; then the whole is coated with aspic. If salad is used as an underlining for cocotte, the eggs should be coated with mayonnaise. To serve, arrange on a doily or broken napkin covered platter.

Eggs Hungarian Style (Oeufs à la Hongroise). Mix cooked calves' brains, finely puréed, with a little sour cream, prepared mustard, chopped herbs (chervil, parsley, tarragon), salt, and sweet paprika to make a sauce. Put a hard-cooked egg in a cocotte and top with sauce.

Eggs Spatini. Mix French-cut string beans, cooked tender-crisp, with spicy mayonnaise. Place in china ramekins and top with a poached egg that has been coated with mayonnaise and pistachio nuts.

Eggs German Style. Purée smoked herring with butter; pipe into small ramekins. Top each with a poached egg and coat with lobster sauce.

Eggs Margaret. Make a tasty salad from raw, sliced button mushrooms and truffles, marinated in oil, lemon, and salt. Fill cocotte with salad and top with poached egg. Top with mayonnaise and a sprinkling of chopped herbs (dill and basil) and a slice of truffle.

Eggs with Asparagus Tips. Put poached egg in a cocotte; coat with Sauce Andalouse and garnish with tips of asparagus.

Tea Eggs. Boil eggs for 5 to 6 minutes, then cool and crush each shell lightly but do not remove shells. Immerse eggs in a strong tea solution, flavored with ginger anise, and vodka. Marinate for 1 to 2 hours or overnight, remove shells from eggs, and serve.

6

Foie Gras—Truffles—Caviar

FOIE GRAS

Nothing is new under the sun—Egyptian maps show slaves force-feeding geese. In 52 B.C., Metellus Pius Scipio, Pompey's father-in-law, used to cram geese with figs to obtain fat livers, which were used in various recipes. Romans also knew of foie gras, which they used to eat hot with raisins.

Nowadays, it is chiefly the French cities of Strasbourg Toulouse, as well as Israel, that are known for their foie gras. Geese from the region of Alsace (in the southwest of France) become plump, and their livers enlarge considerably, after intensive force-feeding that generally continues for about four weeks during the winter. A plain goose liver thus becomes a foie gras, or a fat liver. The livers, soft pink in color, weigh between 1 and 3 pounds. The birds are fed to the limit of their capacities, but their health is watched, and force-feeding is temporarily suspended if they exhibit signs of illness.

The first pâté de foie gras was made in France, in Périgueux, by a pastry chef whose name was Courtois. In 1780, a French chef by the name of Clause was the first to commercialize foie gras in Strasbourg. The pâtés of foie gras were prepared

in various ways—in terrines, en croûtes—and the taste varied considerably.

At the time, truffles, or "black diamonds" (described in detail on p. 88), were unknown in the region of Alsace. Francois Doyen, the chef for the Magistrate of Bordeaux, introduced truffles to Clause in 1789. As a result, the foie gras of Strasbourg reached the peak of perfection in gastronomy. All foie gras was then sold under the name "Pâté de Foie Gras de Strasbourg aux Truffes du Périgord."

Since that time the manufacturing of foie gras has grown to such an extent that several factories in Strasbourg, in the southwestern region of France, and in Israel are now exporting their delicacies all over the world.

How is foie gras prepared?
The fattened goose livers are sorted in the factories by color, size, and consistency. Ten years of experience are required before a sorter can predict the quality of the finished product. A cooked foie gras may turn into a fatty, tough piece of liver with no interest for connoisseurs. Therefore, profes-

Livers from carefully fattened geese are used in the preparation of foie gras. After liver is removed, it is cleaned and all sinews are removed before it is seasoned, stuffed with truffles, and poached or baked. Fresh foie gras is weighed and packed; it will keep from two to four weeks when refrigerated.

sionals are essential to ensure that the best livers are selected.

The livers are cleaned by removing all sinews. They are seasoned with a special spice mixture, stuffed with truffles, then poached in Madeira or Cognac. Some livers are baked in the oven. Every manufacturer has a particular method of preparation and cooking, although the results do not differ noticeably from one method to another.

Foie gras is sold fresh, in cans, and in terrines.

Fresh Foie Gras

Fresh foie gras, called *Foie Gras au Naturel*, has a noticeable flavor advantage over canned foie gras. It keeps well or can be refrigerated for two to four weeks, depending upon the product.

Manufacturers sell fresh foie gras under various names: Foie Gras Frais; Bloc de Foie Gras Truffé; Suprême de Foie Gras en Gelée; Melons de Foie Gras; Aspics de Foie Gras. Legally, all of these foie gras must contain a minimum of 75 percent goose liver unmixed with other ingredients, and a minimum of 5 percent truffles.

It should be clearly understood that the product described as a "pâté de foie" should not be confused with foie gras. Indeed, any French pâté de foie contains 80 percent to 90 percent of pork liver with less than 1 percent truffles and a small amount of goose fat.

Foie Gras in Cans or in Terrines

Cans or terrines of foie gras may be preserved for a much longer period than fresh foie gras, up to three months. Terrines of foie gras truffé come in various sizes, holding from 2 ounces to over 1 pound of foie gras with truffles. The earthenware jars are elaborately decorated. When freshly opened, a good foie gras should be covered with a thin layer of yellowish fat. This is rendered from the liver during cooking and should have an appetizing odor.

Canned foie gras is known by several names, determined by the size and shape of the can: Parfait Bloc de Foie Gras Truffé; Baby Bloc de Foie Gras Truffé; Bloc de Foie Gras Truffé; Terrine de Foie Gras Truffé. Canned foie gras should meet the same standards as fresh foie gras.

Canned foie gras products are also manufactured using trimmings and cut pieces of goose livers mixed with goose fat and pork meat. These are called purée, mousse, or crème de foie gras and should contain a minimum of 50 percent foie gras mixed with the other ingredients.

Use of Foie Gras

As an hors d'oeuvre to begin a meal, foie gras is served in chilled slices, decorated with a Madeira aspic, and accompanied by toast. It may also be served after the main course, before the cheeses or desserts; in this case, a red Bordeaux, a Burgundy, or a Champagne brut would be the most appropriate wines to serve with it. If foie gras is to be served as an hors d'oeuvre, a dry white wine such as an Alsace is acceptable.

Foie gras also finds its uses in hot cuisine, especially in sauces, and in various culinary preparations, such as Tournedos Rossini and Beef Wellington.

Perhaps it has best been described by C. Gerard who said, "The goose is a kind of living hothouse in which grows the supreme fruit of gastronomy."

For many years, this expensive culinary morsel, revered by gourmets, was available for our American guests only in cans. But now, finally, we have a small but excellent American production of duck foie gras, and it has become possible for professional chefs and amateurs alike to indulge in this delicate food. Our American duck foie gras is of the best quality and if well prepared, can be equal to any European counterpart.

Grade A prime duck foie gras is excellent for terrines and mousses; Grade B select duck foie gras is excellent for the hot kitchen. Duck foie gras for processing is good for pâté terrines, mousses, and parfaits. All duck foie gras is sold vacuum-packed.

Preparation of Duck Foie Gras

1. Soak the liver for 2 hours in icy, slightly salted milk or water. Keep the liver completely submerged.
2. Place the liver in lukewarm (110°F) water for 15 minutes.
3. Rinse well, drain, and dry with absorbent paper.
4. Remove any sinew or nerve strings carefully with tweezers.
5. Per pound of liver, marinate in ½ ounce brandy, ½ ounce port wine, ½ teaspoon salt, a knife tip of curing salt, and some white pepper (sugar may be added).

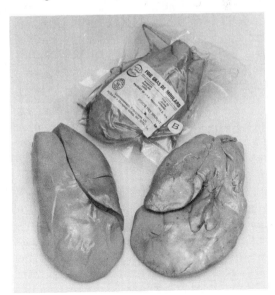

American duck foie gras (foie gras de moulard), from left to right: Grade A, Grade B, for processing.

6. Press nerve strings and sinew through a fine sieve.

7. Line a terrine with plastic wrap or thinly sliced fatback. Press liver into terrine. Add fine-pressed nerve string and sinew. Cover with plastic wrap or fatback. Cover with aluminum foil.

8. Place weight on top, cover, and rest for 12 hours in refrigerator.

9. Bake/poach in a water bath in a 200°F oven for 40 minutes or to internal temperature of 130°F. *Note:* Water bath should maintain 140°F at all times.

10. Remove from water bath and chill. Unmold terrine and clean. Reset into terrine. Decorate and cover with aspic jelly.

Note: Liver may be larded with truffles. It can be spooned out for service or cut into medallions. The trimmings can be made into a mousse.

Black truffles, native to Périgord, France, are dark brown or black. Here they are being inspected before processing.

Cooking Duck Foie Gras

Fat liver or foie gras is an extremely delicate food that can be destroyed if overcooked. American duck foie gras is more vulnerable to meltdown than its counterpart, goose foie gras, as three-quarters of the liver is pure fat. Therefore, it is *essential that utmost care is taken* to cook this specialty with low heat.

TRUFFLES

The black bits found in various food preparations, although called "Black Diamonds" or "Children of the Gods" by some knowledgeable professionals, are generally known as truffles. The truffle is a fungus fruit that matures underground; however, not all underground fungi are truffles. The value of the truffle has always been in its ineffable odor and flavor.

In the days of the Roman Empire, truffles were gathered with much effort and eaten with much pleasure in western Europe, southern portions of the British Isles, all around the Mediterranean, and throughout the Middle East. Pythagoras, Theophrastus, Pliny, and Orelius recorded their appreciation of truffles, which they considered vegetables. Large quantities were brought to Rome from Libya and Spain. This historical fact illustrates the limitation of the scientific knowledge of that age, for the far superior black truffles, now known to be abundant in Italy and France, seem not to have been much used.

After providing hundreds of years of good eating, classical cooking disappeared with the rest of Greek and Roman civilization; truffles also disappeared, at least from literature, and were reintroduced in Spain in the fourteenth century. Since then, they have rarely been neglected.

From 1729 to 1851, the Tulasne brothers of Paris, and two Italians, Pietro Micheli and Vittorio Pico, produced magnificent studies that have been the foundation of all later scientific work on truffles. Before 1729 the nature of truffles was unknown; they were considered to be products of the earth, since they were found under decayed leaves, branches of trees, and bushes. Even through the nineteenth century, truffles remained an enigma.

The real story of the growth of truffles is a strange one. The truffle is the fruit of a widely spreading system of colorless, microscopic branching threads that penetrate the soil for distances measurable in yards. These threads, known as hyphae, touch the furthest tips of the roots of trees or shrubs. The interaction of root and hyphae forms a compound structure, part plant and part fungus. However, this fungus cannot further develop without nutrient or vitamins. When the hyphae have absorbed enough raw material from the soil and the plant to which they are attached, they proceed to develop fruit, just as an apple tree or a grape vine does. The fruit that develops from a knot of hyphae is the truffle.

Before men gathered truffles, foxes, pigs, squirrels, and deer were very fond of the fungi. Nowadays, two animals are trained to assist in the gathering of truffles. In France, hogs locate the truffle by scent; Italians use trained dogs.

What do truffles look like?

Truffles vary in color from a smooth white surface to a dark chestnut brown or black. The rind is usually a compact, resistant layer composed of thick-walled tissue. They are usually round, although some species resemble fresh ginger in shape. The interior of the truffle has elaborate folds or chambers.

The flavor of truffles also varies considerably. One highly prized variety has a touch of garlic in its flavor; those best known to cooks and generally available seem to combine in one rich particle the savor of a filbert and a properly matured cheese. The odor of this is indescribable.

Many kinds of truffles are known: over thirty species are found on the European continent. Although fifty-eight species of truffles are found in North America, the consumption of truffles in the United States is negligible. Many of these specimens are so rare that they are preserved in museums.

In France, the region of Périgord, situated less than 50 miles from the Bordeaux region, is well known for its crop of truffles. Périgueux is the capital of the Périgord. In culinary art, Sauce Périgueux naturally contains truffles. The heart of Italy, especially the region of Umbria, produces practically the entire output of Italian black and white truffles. Geographically, the truffle regions are relatively close to wine regions. A good year for wines will probably result in a poor year for truffles and vice versa. The years 1983 and 1985 are perfect examples. Both were very good wine years, but truffle production fell markedly, resulting in a cost increase.

From a diet point of view, truffles are comparable to oysters. The composition of a truffle is 72 percent water, 8 to 10 percent protein, 4 percent fat, 13 to 15 percent carbohydrate, and 2 to 5 percent mineral substances.

How to Work with Truffles

Whether fresh or canned, truffles should be thoroughly washed and stored in lightly salted water. Before using, peel and slice, dice or cut into julienne, then marinate in sherry or port wine. Truffles are used to decorate a large variety of cold dishes.

The Elusive White Truffle

In the United States the first white truffles arrive in markets and specialty shops in early fall. These expensive Italian tubers have an intense perfume. A major supplier of white truffles from New York once remarked: "We do not have to try to sell them very much. They cost a lot of money, but nobody questions the price. Usually the people who buy them know about them."

The majority of white truffles are produced in Italy during the fall and early winter months. While they are also available in Yugoslavia, the quality is no match for the white Italian truffles, especially those from the little Piedmontese town of Alba, also a producer of wines. The quintessential Italian way to eat white truffles is shaved or thinly sliced over Parmesan-flavored risotto or homemade noodles. They are also used in green salads and to flavor chaud-froid sauces.

Contrary to popular belief, white truffles, unlike their black cousins, should not be cooked. They lose some of their fragrance when they are cooked. Their subtle rich scent is unique and incomparable. Fresh white truffles should be firm to the touch; they should not be spongy. They always impart a profound and distinctive aroma when fresh.

Store white truffles in a sealed container filled with raw Italian Arborio rice, and keep refrigerated. Before using, just brush them with a dry cloth to rid them of soil.

Because of the small supply and high cost of white truffles, their usage in the garde manger department is rather limited.

Mock Truffles

As truffles have become increasingly expensive and rare, various substitutes have been developed. To make mock truffles, use recipes given below.

Cook fatless pork skin until soft; purée while hot to a fine paste. Combine with equal amount of beef blood. Season with salt and pepper. Line a loaf mold with plastic wrap. Fill with mixture and bake in a water bath at 180°F for 2 hours. Remove and chill. Unmold and dice or slice or cut into fine strings. This recipe is good for truffle overlays or as truffle substitute in pâtés, terrines, or galantines.

If you are using truffles for decoration only, the following nonedible simulation can be used. Combine ½ pound used coffee grounds with ⅓ cup Kitchen Bouquet liquid. Heat in a water bath. Add 1 to 2 ounces powdered unflavored gelatin and mix well. Chill mixture slightly and roll into round balls. Set balls on parchment paper and chill.

CAVIAR

Though the word *caviar* brings the Cossack, and therefore Russia, to mind, it does not appear in the Russian language; there it is known as *ikra*. The word *caviar* is derived from the Turkish word *khavyah*. The precious roe was brought to Italy by the knights of the Holy Army. In Italy it was named *caviala* and became quite famous in the court of Pope Julius II, in A.D. 1300.

From Italy, caviar was introduced to all European countries. Shakespeare mentioned it in *Hamlet*, saying "T'was Caviare to the General!" Savarin's *Dictionaire de Commerce*, written around 1711, makes clear that it was not despised at the highest tables of France.

What is caviar?

What is this novelty that has such irresistible appeal to gourmets all over the world? The classic definition is "the salted roe of a species of fish called sturgeon," although the roe of salmon or other species is also called caviar.

Until industry and pollution came along, the sturgeon was found in rivers running into the Atlantic and Baltic, in the Rhine, and in North American lakes. Today, most sturgeon caviar comes from the Caspian Sea, caught by both Russia and Iran.

Of the varieties of sturgeon producing

The luxury of caviar and champagne cannot be matched. Caviar should be served simply but elegantly. (Photo courtesy of Romanoff Caviar)

caviar, the beluga is the largest, sometimes reaching 2,500 pounds and producing up to 130 pounds of roe. The next size is the ocictrova or osetra, weighing around 400 pounds, producing 40 pounds of roe. The smallest of the sturgeon family is the sevruga, which weighs 60 pounds and from which only 8 pounds of roe can be harvested.

Although larger-grain caviar usually commands a higher price, the size of the roe does not influence its flavor; however, its preparation is extremely important. The roe is taken from the fish, carefully sieved, and all tissues and membranes are removed. Then it is washed in clean fresh water. Following this, the caviar master determines exactly how much salt to add and, by hand, blends salt with the roe. Better eggs are always processed with the least amount of salt possible.

The amount of salt used depends on the grade of the sturgeon roe to be prepared, the weather, the condition of the roe, and the market for which it is destined. Only after the salt has been added to the sturgeon roe does it become caviar; therefore, there is no such thing as unsalted caviar. For the U.S. market, only salt is used as a preservative; in European countries, salt and borax may be used. Caviar prepared with salt and borax tastes sweeter.

Top-quality caviar is known as *Mallosol.* This word does not denote a type of caviar; it means "little salt," and it is used in conjunction with the words beluga, osetra, or sevruga.

Most fish containing roe are caught at breeding time. When they leave the deep sea waters, they seek shallow riverbeds in order to spawn. The best caviar is prepared from sturgeon caught between March and April, when the water is cool, and the fish roe firm and fresh. The other important catch season, in the fall, provides most of the caviar sold during the holidays.

Caviar prepared in Russia or Iran and qualifying for the Mallosol grade is packed in original tins weighing 2 kilos (4.2 pounds) and refrigerated throughout its trip to its destination. These tins are most often repacked in the United States into smaller units: 1-, 2-, and 4-ounce crystal jars, or 7- or 14-ounce tins.

Nonrefrigerated caviar, that is, pasteurized caviar, has a shelf life of twelve months or more. (Still, it is wise to buy caviar frequently, enough to meet current needs.) Pasteurized caviar is available vacuum-packed. After six months, white specks may appear; the spots are fat and crystallized salt, and are absolutely harmless, although not always appealing to the eye.

Caviar made by one special process is known as Paiusnaya, or "pressed" caviar. After eggs (roe) have been cleaned in the usual way, caviar is packed in linen bags and hung to drain like cottage cheese. This destroys the natural shape of the eggs, as they are pressed together. The caviar is then packed in 2-kilo tins. It has a much saltier taste than Mallosol caviar, and it looks very much like a solid mass. It is a great favorite in Russia and is greatly prized among connoisseurs.

There are two salmon caviars with a natural reddish hue: chum is a pale orange pink, and the roe from silver salmon (sometimes called *keta*) is closer to red. Golden whitefish is another naturally hued caviar. In addition, when cost is a consideration, there are black whitefish caviar and lumpfish caviars available in black, red, or golden. The last four caviars may be lightly rinsed and drained in a strainer to reduce running.

Mallosol caviar should always be served with toast and unsalted butter. A lesser quality can be served with lemon, toast, and butter. Salty caviar should be served with a garnish of finely chopped white onion, chopped hard-cooked egg white and yolk, lemon, toast, and butter. Sometimes, caviar is served with blinis (little pancakes made of fermented batter of buckwheat) and topped with sour cream (see recipe, p. 93). A mixture of whipped cream and caviar can also be made to be served in conjunction with blinis. Caviar should always be served on ice, as room temperature can alter its taste very rapidly.

(The above information was supplied through the courtesy of the Romanoff Caviar Company.)

The Revival of American Caviar

The American caviar industry is growing and its future looks good. It comes as something of a surprise to learn that this is not a new industry. At one point, caviar production in the United States exceeded that of Russia, and at the turn of the century 100,000 pounds a year were gathered from Atlantic sturgeons spawning in the Hudson and Delaware rivers and Pacific sturgeons in the Sacramento and Columbia. Most of the caviar was enjoyed in Europe, however, for the American palate had not yet developed a taste for such sophisticated treats (in New York, saloonkeepers put out bowls of free caviar for the same reason that they now give peanuts away—to make their customers thirsty). Eventually, however, dam building, pollution, and overfishing took their toll, and the sturgeon went the way of so many other fish, practically becoming extinct in American waters. By the end of World War I, the Caspian Sea was the center of worldwide caviar production.

Fresh Domestic Caviar

Sturgeon. The resurgence of interest in American products has stimulated the growth of a caviar industry in the United States. Both supply and quantity is uneven at this writing, but improvement is steady. Sturgeon of various species are present along all our coastlines and in the rivers leading into America's interior. However, only the sturgeon of the Tennessee River, also known as paddlefish, are numerous enough to justify commercial packing operations. Roe from sturgeon caught in the United States is generally about the size of sevruga roe. After processing, it is sold for about half the price of imported sevruga caviar.

Although some of the best American caviar is prepared using a process identical to the one used in Iran and Russia, the flavor is not always as good as that of Caspian Sea caviar. There are several reasons for this, including differences in species; geographical and climatic differences, which affect the diet of the fish; and the type of salt used (the Russians use a well-aged natural salt).

Probably the most significant difference, however, is the experience passed on from the caviar master to the beginner and from parent to child. Preparing caviar perfectly is as much an art as a science.

Golden Whitefish. The whitefish is native to the Northern Great Lakes. The natural golden color and small crisp grain of whitefish caviar is favored for all recipes, garnishings, and salads calling for caviar. The original technique for processing this caviar came from Sweden.

Black Lumpfish Caviar. The primary world source for lumpfish caviar is the cold clear waters surrounding Iceland in the North Atlantic. The roe of the lumpfish is processed into caviar in much the same manner as salmon and whitefish caviar. Lumpfish caviar is the largest selling type of caviar in the world, due to its availability and affordable price.

The roe is treated with natural food color, black, red, or golden.

Salmon Caviar. Salmon caviar has a very large grain (egg) and superior taste and quality. It is prepared in the Pacific Northwest in the same way that sturgeon caviar is prepared in Russia. There are two varieties: what is labeled "natural salmon" from the roe of chum salmon, and red or "keta" salmon, processed from silver salmon. Neither caviar contains any food color.

How is caviar purchased?

For all its mystery, caviar is not very difficult to buy and use. There are a number of good suppliers offering caviar from a wide variety of fish in a multitude of sizes, as small as 1 ounce and as large as the just-over-4-pound tin. Reliable caviar suppliers generally recommend that you buy in quantities reflecting only your current needs. Your orders should be frequent, not large.

Caution is the watchword, for there are many charlatans in the business, often trying to sell caviar of inferior quality. But there are a number of excellent suppliers who stand behind their products 100 percent. Get acquainted with one of them, then exercise your own quality control, insisting on tasting each order you purchase. With such a costly item, vigilance should be routine.

Blini with caviar. (Photo courtesy of Romanoff Caviar)

BLINI WITH CAVIAR

Yield: 36 blini

Ingredients

Milk	2½ cups
Butter or margarine	¼ cup
Buckwheat flour, sifted	3 cups
Sugar	3 T
Salt	1 tsp.
Egg yolks	3
Active dry yeast	1 pkg.
Water, warm (105 to 110°F)	¼ cup
Egg whites	3
Butter or margarine, melted	½ cup
Caviar, imported sturgeon, American sturgeon, black lumpfish, or golden whitefish caviar	3½ to 4 oz.
Sour cream	1½ cups

Method

Bring milk and butter to just below boil. Cool. Sift together flour, sugar, and salt. In large bowl, beat egg yolks until foamy. Alternately stir in milk and flour mixtures. Mix yeast and warm water; stir into batter. Cover; let rise 1 hour. Beat egg whites until stiff, not dry. Fold in. Cover; let rise until it reaches previous volume. Preheat lightly greased griddle. For each blini, drop a scant ¼ cup batter onto griddle. Lightly brown on both sides; keep warm. Each guest adds butter, caviar, and sour cream to taste.

Do-ahead note: Blini may be prepared up to a week before the party, then stacked with plastic film or foil between layers, overwrapped and frozen. Frozen blini may be unwrapped and reheated for 8 to 10 minutes in oven or toaster oven set at 350°F.

Forcemeat

A basic element in the preparation of many specialties, farce, or forcemeat, made of various seasoned ground foods, is widely used in garde manger preparation. Forcemeat, or farce, is the base for the preparation of pâtés, terrines, galantines, and ballotines. Farces are also used to stuff or garnish meat, eggs, fish, poultry, game, and vegetables, and in the preparation of French specialties such as quenelles and mousses.

Fish farces used in cooking are usually combined with panadas (see below). The amount of panada added to a farce should not exceed 20 percent of the weight of the farce. Most farces prepared with meat, poultry, or game are bound together with eggs or egg whites. Farces used for pâtés and galantines are seasoned with a special spice mixture described below.

PREPARING FORCEMEAT, OR FARCE, FOR PÂTÉS AND TERRINES

Forcemeat, or farce, is a ground meat mixture that can be seasoned either highly or subtly. Generally forcemeat is composed of the following combination:

2 parts, or 40 percent, dominant meat

1 part, or 20 percent, lean pork

2 parts, or 40 percent, pork fat

Seasonings and garnishes vary according to the recipe. To prepare forcemeat, grind each ingredient separately through the fine-to-medium plate of a meat grinder, then chill. Season meat with salt and run through food chopper or food processor. When it is smooth, add fat and combine, then add spices and mix well. All ingredients must be kept cold at all times (50 to 53°F).

How to Blend the Seasonings

Before adding the seasonings to the forcemeat, pulverize the herbs and spices in a blender, put through a wire sieve, and keep in a tightly covered container to preserve the aroma. Use only dried spices and herbs.

Here are four spice and herb combinations that can be blended into a forcemeat:

1. Recommended by master chef August Escoffier:

Bay leaf	½ oz.
Thyme	¾ oz.
Coriander	¾ oz.
Cinnamon	1 oz.
Nutmeg	1½ oz.
Cloves	1 oz.
Ginger	¾ oz.
Mace	¾ oz.
Black pepper	1¼ oz.

Cayenne pepper   ¼ oz.
White pepper   1¼ oz.
2. Recommended by the authors:
Cloves   ½ oz.
Ginger   ½ oz.
Nutmeg   ½ oz.
Paprika   ½ oz.
Basil   ⅓ oz.
Black pepper   ⅓ oz.
White pepper   ⅓ oz.
Bay leaf   ⅙ oz.
Thyme   ½ oz.
Marjoram   ⅙ oz.
3. Spice blend for fine forcemeat:
White pepper   1½ oz.
Coriander   ¾ oz.
Thyme   1¾ oz.
Basil   1¾ oz.
Cloves   ¾ oz.
Nutmeg   1½ oz.
Bay leaf   ½ oz.
Piment   ¾ oz.
Mace   ¾ oz.
Dried cèpes   1 oz.
4. Spice blend for special or game pâtés:
White pepper   ¾ oz.
Black pepper   ¾ oz.
Hungarian paprika   ¾ oz.
Marjoram   ⅓ oz.
Thyme   ¾ oz.
Basil   ¾ oz.
Nutmeg   ¾ oz.
Mace   ¾ oz.
Bay leaf   ¾ oz.
Cloves   ¾ oz.
Juniper berries   1¾ oz.
Dried wild mushrooms   3½ oz.

Note: For seasoning pâté forcemeats, mix 1 ounce or desired amount of pâté spice mixture with 16 ounces of salt and keep well covered. To season forcemeats, we recommend using ⅓ ounce per pound, or to taste.

PANADAS

A panada is a binding agent made of flour, bread, or other starch products. Fish quenelle forcemeats contain panadas, and other fine forcemeats, especially chicken or veal, contain a panada as a substitute for eggs. In some cases, both a panada and eggs may be called for. Several versions of panadas are used.

FLOUR PANADA

Yield: 2 lb.
Ingredients

Butter   8 oz.
Flour   8 oz.
Milk   1 pt.
Egg yolks   7
Salt and white pepper   to taste

Method

Heat butter and add flour to make a roux. Combine milk and eggs, add to roux, and slowly bring to a boil stirring constantly. Simmer 5 minutes. Season with salt and pepper. Place in a dish, cover with plastic wrap, and chill.

BREAD PANADA

Yield: 1 lb.
Ingredients

White bread, cubed, no crust   7 oz.
Milk   ½ pt.

Method

Combine cubed white bread and milk. Stirring, constantly, bring to boil. Cook until thick. Place in a dish, cover with greased parchment paper, and chill.

PÂTE À CHOUX

Yield: 3½ to 4 lb.
Ingredients

Water   1 lb.

Butter	½ lb.
Flour	1 lb.
Eggs	12 to 16

Method

Bring water and butter to a boil. When butter has melted, add flour. Stir until it forms a ball. Cook 2 to 3 minutes, stirring constantly. Remove from heat, cool 2 to 3 minutes. Stir in eggs one at a time. Refrigerate, covering with parchment paper to prevent forming of skin.

FORCEMEATS AND FARCES

Low-cholesterol Forcemeat: A New Concept of Healthy Eating

In response to recent consumer demand for healthier, more easily digestible, and higher-quality foods, the types of forcemeats traditionally used for pâtés, terrines, and mousses and the understanding of their preparation has evolved, incorporating new ingredients with classical culinary techniques. Although the established list of ingredients for traditional forcemeats (pork fat, or any type of animal fat; excessive amounts of eggs and cream; fatty meats; commercially blended spice mixtures; and alcoholic beverages, such as brandy and Kirschwasser) must be revised in order to address this concern, it by no means implies a loss of quality. In fact, the "new" ingredients must be of the highest quality to ensure the desired flavor, and no longer require manipulation through the addition of spice mixtures or alcoholic aromas.

A New Method for Preparing Forcemeats

The successful preparation of forcemeats does not depend solely on the basic ingredients of fish, meat, game, or vegetables, but on the compatibility of all of the components involved. For a successful emulsion, all ingredients must be measured to their proper proportion, particularly the fat. In the new method, fat must be easily digest-

ible; that is, a high-quality vegetable fat (oil) that is either mono- or polyunsaturated, such as olive oil, canola oil, sunflower oil, soy oil, corn oil, and so forth.

A meat emulsion works best when all ingredients bind together. To achieve this, one needs the high speed of a food processor. This enables the chef to prepare forcemeat à la minute, reducing preparation time and eliminating the need for overnight storage.

By substituting ingredients and changing old methods of preparation, the contemporary cook can create new recipes within the dictates of classical cuisine. The following basic recipe serves a variety of meats, poultry, and fish well; the suggestions on preparation that accompany it are not incompatible with the classical foundations of the profession and are based on sound culinary principles.

NEW-STYLE BASIC FORCEMEAT

Yield: 1½ lb.

Ingredients

Meat or fish, ground twice	16 oz.
Eggs or egg whites	2 whole or 3 whites
Fresh milk or half-and-half	3 oz.
Olive oil	3 oz.
Spices and salt	as needed
Glace	2 oz.

Method

Combine all ingredients in a food processor or blender and emulsify at high speed. The emulsion occurs at a temperature of 58°F.

Note: Bread and rice panadas are also useful in reducing fat and adding complex carbohydrates. For each 16 ounces of meat add 1 to 2 ounces of panada.

A Note on the Basic Preparation: The marination of basic ingredients is optional; however, the trend is toward a short marination, to enhance rather than dominate

Preparing Low-cholesterol Forcemeat.

1. Mise en place: white wine, milk, olive oil, salt, pepper, spices, ground meat (chicken), eggs, glace de volaille, and white bread.
2. Place ground meat, eggs, and panada into food processor and emulsify.
3. Slowly add milk.
4. Slowly add olive oil.
5. Add glace and seasoning and emulsify.
6. Make a test dumpling and simmer for 3 to 4 minutes or until done. Taste to check texture and adjust seasoning as needed. This forcemeat may be used as a soup garnish or in a terrine or timbale, hot or cold.

the flavor of the meat. For example, a turkey or chicken forcemeat needs only a 1-hour marination in salt, white pepper, some cayenne pepper, and a little dry white wine before grinding. Marination ingredients could be adjusted for different types of forcemeats, and other flavorings, such as fonds or vegetable purées, could be added or substituted.

If a lighter texture is desired, additional whipped cream, heavily reduced gelatinized fond whipped to a foam, or a higher percentage of vegetable oil may be added.

If the forcemeat is to be prepared from cooked ingredients, cut the cooked meat into small cubes and freeze. Grind through a cold grinder, place into a cold processor bowl, and emulsify with egg whites, vegetable oil, glace, and milk or cream.

BASIC FORCEMEAT FOR QUENELLES, MOUSSELINES, AND TERRINES

Yield: 26 to 30 oz.
Ingredients

Chicken, turkey, or fish, boneless	16 oz.
Salt, white pepper	to taste
White bread	2 oz. (optional)
Egg white	1
Heavy cream	1 to 1½ cups

Method
Cube meat or fish. Cube white bread and moisten with egg white and some cream. Chill. Season meat or fish and grind coarsely. Place in a food processor, add panada, and purée slowly. Add heavy cream until absorbed. Make dumpling test. Adjust seasoning.

FORCEMEAT FOR GALANTINES

Yield: 5½ to 6 lb.
Ingredients

Veal, fresh turkey, or pheasant	2 lb.
Pork butt	1 lb.
Salt	2 oz.
Fatback	2 lb.
Shaved ice	¾ to 1 lb.
Herb Purée (see below)	2 oz.
White pepper	½ tsp. or to taste
Cardamom	⅓ tsp. or to taste
Nutmeg	touch

Method
Cube meat, season with salt, grind coarsely, and chill. Cube fat and grind coarsely. Place meat in food processor or food chopper. Emulsify with ice. Add fat and blend well. Add herb purée and spices and blend. Fold in appropriate garnish.

Follow directions for how to make a galantine.

HERB PURÉE
Ingredients

Celery sticks, diced	2
Carrot, diced	2 med.
Onion, diced	1
Leek, white part, diced	1
Parsnip, diced	1
Milk	14 oz.

Method
Braise vegetables in milk, purée in blender, press through a sieve, and chill. Excellent for forcemeats.

GRATIN FORCEMEAT

Yield: 16 oz.
Ingredients

Fatback (pork), cubed	4 oz.
Lard	½ oz.
Turkey, cubed	4 oz.
Poultry livers, sliced	4 oz.
Shallots	1 oz.
Mushrooms, sliced	1 oz.
Bay leaf	¼ small
Thyme	⅓ tsp.
Salt	⅓ oz.

Pepper	⅓ oz.
Madeira	2½ oz.
Butter	2 oz.
Egg yolks	2
Glace de viande	1 T

Method

Sauté cubed fat in lard and remove. Brown cubed turkey and remove. Stiffen sliced livers in the hot fat. Add fat and turkey, shallots, mushrooms, bay leaf, and thyme. Season with salt and pepper and mix well. Add Madeira. Cover and braise for 6 to 7 minutes. Pour through a sieve to remove fat. Reserve fat. Remove bay leaf, and puree in a food processor. Add butter, egg yolks, glace de viande, and the reserved fat. Mix well. Adjust seasoning. Store in a clean dish covered with buttered parchment paper.

Note: To get a very fine product, force through a sieve. For different flavors, use pheasant or duck instead of turkey and livers.

CHICKEN LIVER PASTE FOR TERRINES, CANAPÉS, AND BARQUETTES

Yield: 2½ lb.

Ingredients

Marinade

Port wine	8 oz.
Bay leaves	2 small
Thyme	½ tsp.
Salt, black pepper	to taste
Chicken livers	38 oz.
Fatback or pork jowls, diced	10 oz.
Oil	to sauté livers
Heavy cream, whipped	4 T
Aspic	to line mold

Method

Combine wine, bay leaves, thyme, salt, and pepper. Add cleaned and washed chicken livers and diced fatback or pork jowls and marinate for 12 hours. Remove livers and fatback or pork jowls and dry. Heat some oil and sauté fat and livers. Do not overcook livers; they should be pink. Remove from sauté pan and chill.

Deglaze pan with marinade and reduce by two-thirds. Cool and blend in a food processor with all of the chilled livers and fat. Fold in heavy cream and season with salt and pepper. Use for timbales, fillings, piping, canapés, or barquettes.

8

Pâtés—Terrines

To many devotees of fine food, the pâté sets the standard for foods to come. Because pâtés take so many different forms and are so convenient to prepare and serve, they should become an important part of your daily menus.

Pâtés are made in many shapes and forms, including pâté en croûte, Pâté à la Maison, terrines, galantines, and mousses. Among the large variety of ingredients and garnishes used in pâtés, the most common are liver, truffles, various forcemeats, and seasonings. Fat goose or duck liver brings a particular flavor to pâtés. Chicken livers may be substituted.

Europeans have the advantage of having not only fresh goose liver, but also fresh, aromatic truffles, which play a major part in the preparation of pâtés and terrines. However, canned truffles can be used when fresh truffles are not available, and fresh Americans duck foi gras can be used instead of goose foie gras. (For more details on the use of truffles, goose liver, or duck liver, see chapter 6).

Pâtés can be prepared in advance, kept refrigerated, and served as appetizers or on buffets. A description of the major types of pâtés follows.

Pâté en Croûte is a meat, poultry, or fish

Clockwise from left: Pâté en Croûte; Pâté Maison; Vegetable Mousse; Terrine of Lobster (coarse forcemeat); Terrine of Salmon (fine forcemeat).

101

mixture encased in dough and baked in the oven, then filled with aspic jelly. The term *Pâté à la Maison* encompasses a meat, poultry, fish, or fruit mixture either in crust or without.

Terrines are meat, poultry, fish, or vegetable mixtures cooked in a mold (terrine) that is covered and baked/poached in a water bath. It can be served in the mold or unmolded.

Pâté en Croûte.   Terrine.

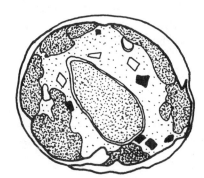

Galantine.

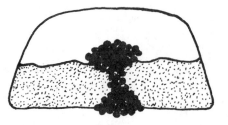

Mousse.

Galantines (see chapter 9) are meat, poultry, or fish mixtures enclosed in a natural casing, then poached and chilled in a strong flavored broth.

Mousses (see chapter 10) are mixtures of cooked foods, gelatin, mayonnaise, and whipped heavy cream chilled in special molds.

How to Work with Poultry Livers

As noted above, chicken livers can be substituted for goose or duck liver. It is essential to handle livers with care. Remove gall bladder, all veins, blood clots if any, and surrounding skin. Wash livers in cold water and soak in milk for 24 hours. Drain the livers thoroughly, season them, and keep refrigerated.

Pâté Dough

In most kitchens the chef seasons doughs for pâté en croûte with salt. However, you can add seasonings such as herbs and spices to the dough mixture to reach new heights of flavor. For example, for a rustic pâté, the dough could be seasoned with pepper and nutmeg, or for fish or poultry, ginger or lemon zest could be added. In addition, various types of flours (rye, whole wheat, or corn) could be used to enhance the diner's pleasure. If your menu should call for hot pâtés, a puff dough may be just what you need to make it better.

PÂTÉ DOUGH NUMBER 1

Yield: 4 lb.
Ingredients

Bread flour	2½ lb.
Baking powder	½ oz.
Salt	1 oz.
Dry milk powder (optional)	2½ oz.
Shortening	7 oz.
Butter	5 oz.
Eggs	3

| Water | 9 to 10 oz. |
| Lemon juice or vinegar | 1 oz. |

Method

Place dry ingredients, shortening, and butter in a food processor or food chopper and mix well. Remove; place in a mixing bowl. Combine eggs, water, and lemon juice and fold into flour mixture, using a dough hook. Rest for 1 hour.

PÂTÉ DOUGH NUMBER 2

Yield: 1½ lb.

Ingredients

Flour, all purpose	3½ cups
Salt	1½ tsp.
Vegetable shortening *or* butter	1 cup
Egg, whole	1
Vinegar (any flavor)	1 tsp.
Water	10 T

Method

Combine flour and salt; add shortening and mix thoroughly. Combine egg, vinegar, and water and add to flour mixture. Knead into a dough (do not overwork). Chill and rest dough in refrigerator for 1 hour. Temper before using.

Note: Herbs and spices can be added to vary flavor.

Preparation of Pâté en Croûte

1. Select a hinged mold, either round, oval, or rectangular (the type of mold will depend on the nature of the pâté); oil or butter the mold carefully.
2. Take three-fourths of the dough and roll it out with a rolling pin to about ⅛-inch thickness.
3. Cut dough into four pieces. Use 1½ pounds of dough per mold.
4. Press dough all around the walls and into the bottom of the mold. The dough should overlap the edge of the mold about ½ inch, and this overlapping dough will later be used to seal the lid.
5. Line the bottom and walls of the mold with thin slices of fatback or slices of ham (optional), then cover evenly with a thin layer of an appropriate forcemeat.
6. Place the ingredients in the mold as indicated in the recipe. The ingredients put in the center are usually an

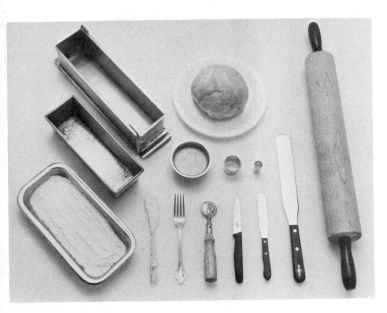

Mise en place for Pâté en Croûte: hinged pâté mold or loaf mold; pâté dough; rolling pin; large and small palette knife; paring knife; dough cutter; table fork; feather brush; flour for dusting; egg wash; round cutters.

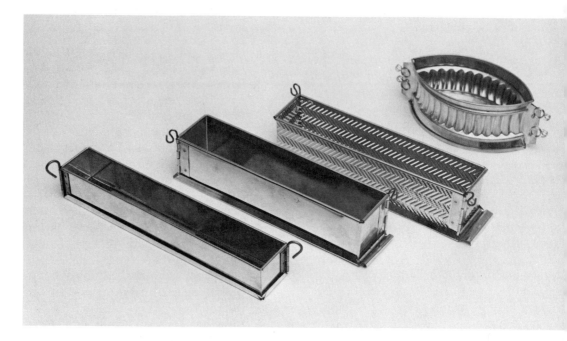

Hinged pâté en croûte molds. From left to right: hors d'oeuvre–size mold; smooth pâté mold; rectangular ridged pâté mold; oval pâté mold.

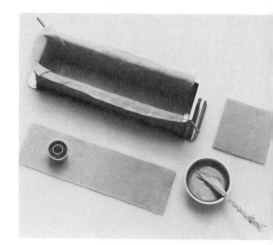

To Make Pâté en Croûte.

1. Roll pâté dough approximately ⅛ inch thick. Cut into four pieces as shown.

2. If loaf mold is used, outline bottom of mold with well-buttered parchment. Fold large piece of dough into the mold, letting it overlap by ½ inch. Brush corners with egg wash and fold smaller pieces over the end of the mold. Press overlapping corners or layers together to seal.

3. Layer the dough-lined mold with thinly sliced fatback or turkey, ham, or another thinly sliced cold meat (optional).

4. Fill the mold with forcemeat and garnish. Forcemeat must be pressed in firmly to avoid air pockets. Fold lining and dough over and brush with egg wash.

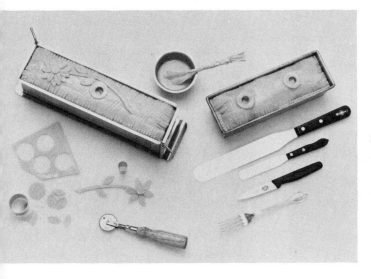

5. Top pâté with remaining dough. Crimp all sides with a dinner fork to seal. Cut holes (chimneys) into the dough cover to permit steam to escape. For garnish, cut out dough as shown. Brush dough well with egg wash and decorate. Bake per recipe instructions.

arrangement of various meats (veal, pork, poultry, ham, or tongue) and truffles that have been marinated in brandy, and will provide a decorative center for the finished pâté. The decorative center or garnish should be placed in the center of the mold and sealed with a small quantity of forcemeat. Fill the mold with the remaining forcemeat and cover with a thin slice of fresh pork fat or ham (optional).

7. Roll out remaining dough and cut into the same shape as the top of the mold. Moisten the edge of the dough with an egg wash and seal onto the top of the mold. Trim neatly with a knife.

8. Decorate the top of the mold with fancy shapes cut from the dough trimmings. Brush with egg wash. In the center of the mold, make a circular hole called a chimney, to allow steam to escape while the pâté is baking. A piece of parchment paper rolled into a tube may be placed in the chimney.

To Slice Pâté en Croûte.

1. Arrange a mise en place, using a pan of water and a carving knife.

2. To start slicing, slide knife forward as shown.

3. Continue slicing, bringing the end of the knife nearest you down slightly.

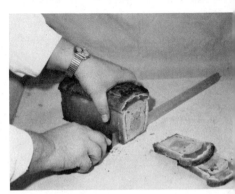

4. Cut straight down the rest of the way through the loaf, sawing back and forth to complete slices.

5. Place slices on a rack and brush with aspic jelly.

How to Bake a Pâté

The baking method, unless otherwise indicated in a specific recipe, is the same for all pâtés. To bake a pâté:

1. Preheat oven to 400 to 425°F. Bake pâté for 10 to 15 minutes, or until dough starts to brown.
2. Reduce temperature to 325 to 350°F, then bake pâté until well done.
3. To test the doneness of the pâté, insert a tester through the chimney all the way into the pâté; leave it there briefly. If the tester comes out dry and evenly warm, the pâté is ready. Or use a thermometer, which should read 160°F, internal temperature.
4. Take pâté out of the oven and allow to cool for 1 hour; fill the cavity of the pâté with aspic jelly; then place in refrigerator and chill.

Pâté en croûte. Note thickness of dough.

PÂTÉ OF CHICKEN AND LIVERS

Yield: 14 portions

Ingredients

Chicken (whole)	2½ lb.
Poultry livers, soaked in milk	9 oz.
Truffles, cubed	2 oz.
Port wine	1 oz.
Chicken leg meat, raw	12 oz.
Fatbakck, cubed	8 oz.
Shaved ice	1 to 2 oz.
Salt	1 oz.
White pepper, mace	to taste
Pâté dough with thyme and parsley	2 lb.
Madeira aspic jelly	1½ pt.

Method

Bone and skin the chicken. Save chicken breast; remove all meat from bones. Cut chicken breast in ½-inch strips. Clean, wash, and dry livers. Cut truffles into small cubes. Marinate chicken breast, liver, and truffles for 2 hours or overnight in port wine. Remove and blanch the liver for 1 minute in boiling water; then shock in ice water, drain, and dry.

Cube remaining chicken meat and chill. Cube fatback and chill. Grind and emulsify in food processor, adding 1 ounce of the marinated chicken liver and 1 to 2 ounces shaved ice. Season with salt, pepper, mace, and port wine. Remove from machine.

Fold truffles into forcemeat. Line pâté mold with dough and line with thinly sliced fatback. Line with forcemeat. Fill, alternate chicken breast strips, blanched livers, and forcemeat. Top with forcemeat.

Close with pâté dough; cut chimneys in the dough. Brush with egg wash and bake for 60 minutes in a preheated 350°F oven, or to 160°F internal temperature. Let rest for 1 hour and fill cavity with Madeira aspic. Chill for 12 hours.

PÂTÉ OF TURKEY EN CROÛTE

Yield: 2 4-lb pâté molds
Ingredients

Beef blood	8 oz.
Salt and pepper	to taste
Large turkey breast, cubed	16 oz.
Turkey liver	8 oz.
Turkey legs	12 oz.
Pork butt	6 oz.
Fatback	12 oz.
Salt with Spice Blend (No. 3)	½ oz. or to taste
Pistachio nuts, peeled	3 oz.
Pâté dough with powdered cépes, black pepper	4 lb. (approx.)

Method

Season beef blood with salt and pepper and marinate large cubed turkey breast overnight. Drain and dry 2 to 3 hours or overnight in refrigerator. Cut turkey liver into large cubes, blanch, and chill.

Grind turkey legs, pork butt, and fatback. Add salt with spice blend and chill. Place in food processor and emulsify (if machine labors, add up to 2 ounces ice). Fold dry turkey breast, pistachios, and blanched liver into forcemeat. Line pâté mold with dough and fill, following standard procedure.

Bake in preheated 350°F oven to 160°F internal temperature. Fill with clear aspic jelly. Chill and serve.

PÂTÉ OF LAMB, SHEEPHERDER STYLE

Yield: 12 to 14 portions
Ingredients

Lean lamb, diced	10½ oz.
Lean pork, diced	9 oz.
Pork fat, diced	10½ oz.
Pâté spice	2 tsp.
Basil	1 tsp.
Oregano	½ tsp.
Juniper berries, crushed	5
Garlic, crushed	1 clove
Orange zest, grated	from ½ orange
Salt	to taste

Garnish

Lamb fillets	2 to 3
Salt and pepper	to taste
Butter	1 oz.
Green peppercorns	1 T
Ham, diced	3 oz.
Pâté dough	2 lb.
Egg	1
Aspic jelly	2 pt.

Method

Grind lamb and pork. Season with salt; chill. Grind pork fat but do not season; chill. Emulsify pork and lamb in a food processor. Remove two-thirds of the meat from machine, add pork fat and purée fine.

Return the ground meat to processor and add all spices. Mix well. Make a test dumpling, simmer, and taste. Adjust seasoning.

Trim fillet and season with salt and pepper. Sear in butter; chill.

Fold peppercorns and ham into forcemeat. Roll out dough and line pâté mold. Fill half the mold with forcemeat, set lamb fillet in center and fill with forcemeat.

Close with dough cover and wash with egg wash. Bake in a preheated 350° F oven for 1½ hours or until it reaches 160°F internal temperature. Remove, let rest for 1 hour, and fill with aspic jelly; chill.

Note: You may want to line the pâté dough with prosciutto.

PHEASANT PÂTÉ

Yield: 1 pâté, 16 portions
Ingredients

Pheasant legs	10 oz.
Pork butt	5 oz.
Pork fat	10 oz.
Salt	½ oz. or to taste
Shallots, sautéed	½ oz.

Orange zest, grated	from ½ orange
White pepper	⅓ tsp.
Pâté spice #2	⅓ tsp.
Garlic, crushed	1 clove
Juniper berries	6
Pheasant breasts	4
Salt and pepper	to taste
Oil	to sear pheasant
Pheasant and chicken livers marinated in port wine and blanched	6 oz.
Pistachio nuts	2 oz.
Truffle, diced	1 oz.
Pickled tongue, boiled, diced	2 oz.
Pâté dough	2 lb.
Aspic jelly	to fill chimneys
Cantaloupe, sliced	to garnish
Cumberland Sauce	to garnish

Method

Cube pheasant legs, pork, and pork fat. Mix with all the seasonings and grind coarse. Grind again through fine plate. Place in a bowl and mix well, over ice if possible. Make test dumpling and adjust seasoning.

Season pheasant breasts and sear in oil. Chill.

Drain chicken livers, blanch, drain again, and dry. Combine with pistachio nuts, truffle, and tongue and fold into forcemeat.

Line pâté mold following standard procedure. Fill one-third with forcemeat, top with two pheasant breasts. Press well. Top with forcemeat, then with two pheasant breasts. Finish with forcemeat, pressing well to avoid air pockets. Finish pâté following standard procedure. Bake in a 350°F oven for 2 hours or to an internal temperature of 160°F. Cool, and fill with aspic jelly.

Serve with sliced cantaloupe and Cumberland Sauce.

PHEASANT PÂTÉ WITH DUCK FOIE GRAS

Yield: 2 pâtés, 32 portions

Ingredients

Pheasants, 2½ lb.	2
Pork butt	14 oz.
Turkey breast	14 oz.
Marinade	
Curing salt (saltpeter)	1/16 oz.
Salt	⅓ oz.
Garlic, crushed	2 cloves
Thyme	
Brandy	1 oz.
White wine	2 oz.
Duck foie gras	2 lb.
Curing salt, salt	pinch
Port wine	3 oz.
Fresh shiitake and chanterelle mushrooms	16 oz.
Butter	2 oz.
Madeira	5 oz.
Glace de viande	3 to 4 oz.
Heavy cream	4 oz.
Salt and pepper	to taste
Beef blood	2 oz.
Fatback	16 oz.
Poultry and pheasant livers	8 oz.
Egg yolks	3
Juniper berries, finely chopped	5 to 6
Pistachio nuts, coarsely chopped	¼ cup
Pâté dough	2 lb.
Pig caul	1
Egg wash	to coat pâté
Madeira aspic jelly	to fill chimneys

Method

Bone and skin pheasant. Trim breast for garnish. Cube legs, pork, and turkey, marinate overnight, and drain well. Clean duck foie gras and season with salt and some curing salt. Marinate in port wine overnight, drain well, and mold with plastic wrap into a roll. Refrigerate.

Wash mushrooms well, drain, and sauté in butter over high heat. Remove mushrooms and deglaze pan with Madeira. Reduce, add glace de viande and heavy cream. Reduce to a creamy consistency. Season with salt and pepper. Chill.

Sear seasoned pheasant breast, place in blood, and chill overnight. Drain blood and reserve, and dry breast in refrigerator for 2 to 3 hours.

Grind meat and fat coarse. Purée poultry livers with egg yolks and 1 ounce of the beef blood.

Combine ground meat, fat, liver mixture, any trimmings from foie gras, and mushroom sauce, and emulsify in a food processor. Season with salt, pepper, and juniper berries. Fold mushrooms and pistachios into mixture.

Line a pâté mold with dough. Line the dough with pig's caul and then with forcemeat. Place the foie gras roll into the middle. Top with forcemeat. Arrange pheasant breast outside of liver roll, and fill pâté with forcemeat, pressing well to avoid air pockets.

Enclose pâté following standard procedure. Cut chimney. Brush with egg wash.

Bake in a 350°F oven to internal temperature of 150°F. Rest for 2 hours and fill with Madeira aspic jelly.

DUCK PARFAIT

Yield: 4 lb.

Ingredients

Duck, 4 lb.	2
Red onions	3 oz.
Bay leaves, small	2
Juniper berries	10
White bread, cubed	10 oz.
Heavy cream	up to ½ pt.
Bacon	8 oz.

Salt, nutmeg, paprika	to taste (approx ⅓ oz. of salt per lb.)
Currants	1½ oz.
Livers	4 oz.
Pig's caul	1 to 2
Port wine aspic jelly	1 pt.
Cumberland Sauce	to garnish
Toast croutons	to garnish

Method

Bone duck, saving breast and leg meat and livers, and chill. Prepare an aromatic stock from bones, skin, heart, giblets, onions, bay leaves, and juniper berries. Strain and reduce to ¼ pint. Chill.

Moisten cubed white bread with some of the cream to make a panada. Dice bacon and render, strain, and chill. Grind duck meat and chill. Place in food processor and emulsify. Add panada, chilled bacon fat and reduced stock and remaining cream slowly. Season with salt, paprika, and nutmeg. Fold in currants.

Chop liver coarse. Season with salt and pepper and fold into forcemeat. Line a mold with pig's caul and fill with parfait mixture. Cover with pig's caul, then with parchment paper. Weight down with board and bake poach in a 250 to 300°F oven for 45 to 50 minutes or to internal temperature of 150°F. Cool and unmold, chill, and coat with port wine aspic jelly.

Serve with Cumberland Sauce and toast croutons.

LIVER PÂTÉ A L'ANCIENNE

Yield: 2 lb.

Ingredients

Fresh pork fat	1 lb.
Calf's liver	¾ lb.
Garlic, crushed	2 cloves
Brandy	2 T
Salt	½ tsp.
Black pepper, ground	¼ tsp.
Nutmeg, ground	⅛ tsp.

Lobster Armoricaine

Fallow Deer Variations. From left to right: Poached Sweet-
bread Disks with Marinated Leek and Pearl Onions; Loin of
Fallow Deer in Forcemeat Crust Rolled in Crushed Black
Pepper; Corn Salad; Turnip Barquettes with Marinated
Plum Tomatoes and String Beans; Game Pie; Game Head-
cheese.

Veal Combination Buffet Platter. From left to right: Marinated Vegetables in Dough Basket; Roast Loin of Veal; Galantine of Veal; Herbed Pâté en Croûte; Artichokes with Lentil Salad; Veal Headcheese; Broccoli Barquettes.

Terrine of Morels and Chanterelles; Quail Egg; and Chantilly Mayonnaise.

Fish and Seafood Variations. From left to right: Stuffed
Squid; Galantine of Red Shrimp; Poached Mahi-Mahi;
Shrimp and Pasta Salad; Lobster Medallions on Avocado
Mousse.

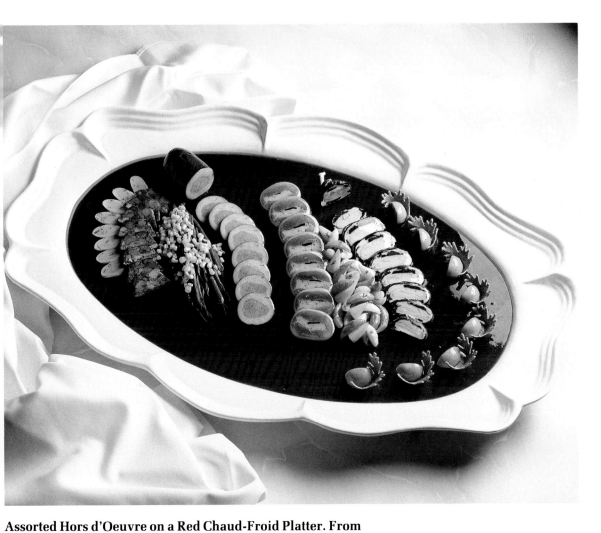

Assorted Hors d'Oeuvre on a Red Chaud-Froid Platter. From left to right: Marinated Leeks; Pheasant and Partridge Head Cheese; Corn and Haricot Vert Salad; Hot Smoked Pheasant Breast Stuffed with Herbed Farce; Cured Wild Duck with Truffle and Partridge Forcemeat Coated with Garlic Mustard Sauce; Root Vegetable Salad; Partridge Breast Coated with Wild Mushroom and Pickled Kale; Spiced Dough Antlers with Pumpkin–Apple Mousse.

Mille Feuille Filled with Marinated Morels, Asparagus, Ramps, and Fiddleheads served with Whipped Cream Vinaigrette, Chopped Chives, and Chervil.

Hors d'Oeuvre Platter with a Salt Dough and Saltiage Centerpiece. Counterclockwise from left to right: Glazed Shrimps in Rice Salad; Pheasant Galantine with Wild Mushroom Salad; Seafood Chaud-Froid with Cucumber Sticks; Duck Galantine with Orange Salad; Vegetable Chorizo Head Cheese; Salmon Mousse with Mango Salad.

Terrine of Salmon. From left to right: Marinated Cucumber Baskets with Marinated Vegetables; Fish Forcemeat in Crust; Sliced Terrine of Salmon; Red Pepper Barquettes with Asparagus; Sliced Poached Salmon; Marinated Snow Peas.

Turkey Medley. From left to right: Dough Leaves with Fruit and Nuts; Round Turkey Headcheese; Galantine of Turkey (using legs); Maryland Corn Salad; Pâté of Turkey (using breast meat); Marinated Spaghetti Squash with Tomatoes, Mushrooms, and Snow Peas; Dough-Leaf Centerpiece Filled with Chestnuts and Grapes.

Assorted Hors d'Oeuvre Platter on a White Chaud-Froid Platter with Green Leaf Pattern. From right foreground, ending at center, counterclockwise: Fruit Relish Terrine; Pressed Vegetable Terrine; Duck Breast with Pistachio Forcemeat and Mustard Chaud-Froid; Baby Onions stuffed with Caponata Salad on Polenta Croutons; Italian Sushi topped with Pork Sausage; Stuffed Apricots on Chicken Mousse; Cured Pork Slices wrapped in Purple Kimchi on a Marinated Dykon Base; Duck Prosciutto filled with Vegetable Mousse on Whole Wheat Crackers.

Sliced Roasted Chicken Breast, Stuffed Roasted Chicken Leg, Sweet Potato Topped with Chestnut, Sweet Potato Flower with String Bean Salad and Marinated Roasted Vegetable.

**Wild Mushroom Napoleon with Honey-roasted Shallots and
Ruby Port Wine Vinaigrette.**

Frisée Salad with Fennel and Beet Chips dressed with Orange Pistachio Vinaigrette.

The Ultimate Salad: Simple, Colorful, and Tasty. Fresh Boston Lettuce, Radicchio, Red Leaf and Mâche or Field Lettuce tossed in Olive Oil Vinaigrette with Fine Herbs.

**Composite salad: marinated cucumbers, pickled vegetables,
bean sprouts, snow peas, and palm hearts on radicchio with
a vinaigrette.**

Terrine of Scallop Mousseline with Tomato Basil Coulis.

Luncheon Suggestions. Clockwise from left: Grilled Lobster
in Marinated Sugar Pumpkins, Sweet Potato and Pumpkin
pudding, and Vanilla-flavored Velouté; Selection of Wild
Salad Greens, Stuffed Duxelles Morels, Pancetta Bacon
Rose, and Soft-boiled Quail Eggs with Red Wine Vinaigrette;
Jellied Consommé with Wild Mushrooms, Savoy Cabbage,
Pheasant Dumplings, and Truffle Royal.

More Luncheon Suggestions. Clockwise from lower left: Seared Foie Gras on a bed of Caramelized Onion and Apple; Braised Shank of Lamb on Stewed Lentils with gaufrette potato; Grilled Salmon Medallions with Mesclun Greens and Balsamic Vinaigrette.

Rosemary, dry	⅛ tsp.
Fatback, sliced	8 oz.
Bay leaves	2

Method

In a cold mixing bowl, grind the fresh pork fat with the calf's liver. Blend in garlic, brandy, salt, pepper, nutmeg, and rosemary. Line the bottom and sides of a suitable pâté or terrine mold with slices of fatback, reserving a few slices for the top. Spoon the liver mixture into mold. Cover with remaining fatback, top with bay leaves, then cover mold with aluminum foil and bake at 350°F in a bain marie for 2½ hours. Cool, then chill.

Serve cold as a spread with French toast or croutons.

PÂTÉ OF FALLOW DEER

Yield: 2 pâtés, 2 lb. each

Ingredients

Forcemeat

Fallow deer meat	2 lb.
Pork butt, 75% meat, 25% fat	2 lb.
Curing salt	a pinch
Salt	½ oz. or to taste
Pâté spice #2	½ oz.
Crushed juniper berries	8

Seasonings

Mushrooms, fresh, sliced	½ lb.
Golden Delicious apples, sliced	½ lb.
Shallots, sliced	¼ lb.
Orange zest, grated	from ½ orange
Lemon zest, grated	from ½ lemon
Butter	1 oz.
Eggs	3
Brandy	½ oz.
Orange liqueur	½ oz.
Port wine	½ oz.
Heavy cream	½ pt.

Garnish

Roland truffle	4 oz.

Pistachio nuts, coarsely chopped	4 oz.
Ham, cubed	8 oz.
Smoked beef tongue, cubed	8 oz.
Port aspic jelly	to fill pâté
Cranberry relish	to garnish

Method

To make forcemeat, cut fallow deer and pork into cubes, season with salt and spices, and chill. From bones and sinews, prepare a stock and reduce to a glace de gibier (extract). Chill.

Prepare seasonings: sauté mushrooms, apple, shallots, and orange and lemon zest lightly in butter, and cool.

Combine fallow deer and mushroom mixtures and grind through a ½-inch plate and again through a ⅛-inch plate. Place in a mixing bowl.

Gradually mix in the eggs, brandy, liqueur, wine, cream, and 2 ounces of the glace de gibier. Adjust the seasoning. Fold in the garnish ingredients.

Line a pâté mold with dough, following standard procedure. Fill with forcemeat, pressing down well to avoid air pockets. Enclose the pâté, cut chimney holes, and decorate (optional). Bake in a 350°F oven to an internal temperature of 150°F. Cool and fill chimneys with port aspic jelly. Chill and unmold. Serve with cranberry relish.

PÂTÉ OF RABBIT

Yield: approximately 3 lb.

Ingredients

Rabbit	5 to 6 lb.
Pork butt, lean	7 oz.
Salt	2 tsp.
Pork fat	14 oz.
Glace de Viande (see page 112)	2 T
Eggs	2

Green peppercorns, dried or fresh	½ tsp.
Mace	½ tsp.
Thyme	1 tsp.
Rosemary	⅓ tsp.
Mushrooms, cubed, cooked	4 oz.
Ham, diced	5 oz.
Pâté dough	2 lb.
Prosciutto or ham, thinly sliced	16 oz.
Egg wash	to coat pâté
Port wine aspic jelly	to fill chimneys

Method

Bone rabbit. Sear the loins and reserve for garnish. Trim the remaining meat (21 ounces) and cube. Cube pork, and combine with rabbit cubes; add salt and chill. Cube pork fat and chill.

Make the glace de viande (see below).

Grind rabbit, pork and fat through large plate (coarse). Combine eggs and glace and grind with rabbit meat and fat through fine plate. Place in a mixing bowl and mix with green peppercorns, mace, thyme, and rosemary. Mix well. Fold mushrooms and ham into the forcemeat.

Line a pâté mold with dough and thinly sliced prosciutto or ham. Fill half with forcemeat and place rabbit loin in center. Finish with forcemeat and press down well. Enclose with prosciutto or ham and dough. Brush with egg wash. Bake in a 350°F oven until internal temperature reaches 160° F. Let rest for 1 hour, then fill chimneys with port wine aspic jelly.

GLACE DE VIANDE

Yield: 2 to 3 T

Ingredients

Rabbit bones	2 lb. (approx.)
Veal or pork bones	16 oz.
Oil	3 T
Onion	1
Carrots	4
Celery ribs	4
Bay leaf	1
White peppercorns	5
Garlic	1 clove, small
Shallots, diced	4
Cardamom	⅓ tsp.
Water	to cover

Method

Cut rabbit bones and trimmings and veal bones small; brown in oil. Add onions, carrots, and celery, and brown. Add bay leaf, five peppercorns, garlic, shallots, cardamom, and water to cover bones by 2 inches. Simmer 2 to 3 hours, strain, and reduce to 2 to 3 tablespoons.

PÂTÉ OF SALMON MORNING GLOW

Yield: 14 portions

Ingredients

Milk	2 oz.
Flour	3 oz.
Egg yolks	3
Salt, pepper, nutmeg	to taste
Butter	1½ oz.
Striped bass or fresh sole or halibut, cubed	10 oz.
Egg white	1
White wine, cold	1 oz.
Brandy, cold	1 oz.
Fresh salmon, cubed	21 oz.
Pistachio nuts or peas	1½ oz.
Truffles	1 oz.
Aspic jelly	to coat pâté
Whipped cream flavored with ketchup	to garnish
Salmon caviar	to garnish
Dill sprig	to garnish

Method

Prepare panada by mixing cold milk with flour, egg yolks, salt, pepper, and nutmeg. Stirring constantly, bring to a boil. Stir until thick. Remove from heat and fold in butter. Return to heat and stir for 2 to 3 minutes. Chill for 30 minutes or until cold.

Cube fish (not salmon) and chill. Emulsify in a food processor. Add panada and lend well. Add egg white, white wine, and randy. Blend well. Cut salmon into ½-inch ubes. Season with salt and pepper, and hill.

Line a loaf mold with plastic wrap. Fill, lternating forcemeat, salmon cubes, pistachio nuts, and truffles. Cover with plastic vrap and aluminum foil that has been ierced. Preheat oven to 350°F. Set pâté in water bath, place in oven, and turn heat lown to 325°F. Bake for 1½ hours or until nternal temperature is 150°F. Press down ightly and cool. Let rest for 1 hour. Remove rom pâté mold and chill. Coat with aspic elly and decorate with a dollop of tomato etchup-flavored whipped cream, salmon aviar, and a sprig of dill.

VEAL AND HAM PÂTÉ

Yield: 12 portions

Ingredients

Pâté dough	1 lb.
Bundnerfleisch or ham, thinly sliced	10 oz.
Lean veal	21 oz.
Oil	2 T
Onions, finely diced	4 oz.
Parsley, chopped	4 T
Salt and pepper	to taste
Ham	21 oz.
Eggs, hard-cooked, sliced	2
Egg wash	to coat pâté
Veal aspic, strong	½ to 1 pt. (approx.)
Piccalilli	to garnish

Method

Line quiche mold or cake mold with dough, saving some for the top. Line with thinly sliced Bundnerfleisch or ham.

Sear the veal in the oil and slice it thinly. Cover bottom of the mold with veal. Sprinkle with some of the onions and parsley, salt, and pepper. Top with half of the sliced ham, sprinkle with more onions and pars-

ley, and top with one sliced egg. Repeat steps with the remaining ingredients.

Fold Bundnerfleisch over the eggs, cover with dough; seal, and brush with egg wash. Cut a chimney in the dough, and decorate. Brush decoration with egg wash and bake in a 450°F oven for 15 to 20 minutes. Remove and cool. Fill with aspic and chill. Serve with mustard vegetables (piccalilli).

CHICKEN A LA OMA PREITNER

(*The recipe of a country lady*)

Yield: 2 to 2½ lb.

Ingredients

Chicken, whole, 2½ lb.	1
Salt	to taste
Juniper berries, finely chopped	4
White wine	1 oz.
Chicken livers	4 oz.
Madeira	2 T
Small cépes or shiitaki mushrooms	6 oz.
Walnuts, chopped coarsely	2 oz.
Pistachio nuts	1 oz.
Salt and Spice Blend No. 3	⅓ to ¼ oz.
Pig's caul	1 to 2
Basic forcemeat (see recipe p. 99)	1 lb.
Black pepper, ground	2 T
Butter	to grease mold
Orange wedges in vinaigrette, poached apple, red currants, grapes	to garnish

Method

Bone and butterfly chicken. Remove breast and leg meat. Save skin. Butterfly chicken breast and pound lightly. Cube chicken legs. Season breast meat with salt and juniper berries and marinate in white wine for 2 hours. Drain and dry.

Season chicken livers with salt and marinate in Madeira for 2 hours. Drain and dry.

Combine cubed chicken leg, mushrooms, walnuts, and pistachios. Season with salt blend and fold into forcemeat.

Grease a triangular 1- to 2-quart mold, dust with black pepper, and line it with pig's caul. Line with chicken skin and chicken breast. Fill with forcemeat, pressing to avoid air pockets. Fold skin and pig's caul over forcemeat and sprinkle with ground pepper. Cover with aluminum foil and bake in water bath at 300°F for 1½ hours or to internal temperature of 160°F. Cool, unmold, and chill.

Garnish with orange wedges marinated in vinaigrette and poached apple filled with red currants or grapes.

FISH PÂTÉ EN BRIOCHE

Yield: 12 portions
Ingredients

Shallots, finely diced	3
Butter	1 tsp.
Fish fillet, cooked	8 oz.
Salt	½ tsp.
White pepper, nutmeg, mustard powder	pinch
Bread panada (optional)	1½ oz.
Egg white	1
Heavy cream	4 to 6 oz.
Dill, chopped	1 T
Tarragon, chopped	1 tsp.
Brioche dough	2 lb.
Salmon *and/or* other fish fillet	12 oz.
Egg wash	1 to glaze
Green Peppercorn Sauce (see recipe page 176)	1½ to 2 pt.

Method

Sauté shallots lightly in butter without browning. Chill. Cube the fish and season with salt and spices. Grind fish and shallots through medium plate. Place in food processor with panada and egg white and emulsify. Slowly add heavy cream. Make a test dumpling, and adjust consistency if necessary. Fold in chopped herbs.

Roll out brioche dough ⅛ inch thick. C[ut] into oval shape or use fish cutters (one lar[ge] for bottom, one small for top). Spread on[e] half of the forcemeat on dough. Allow [a] 1-inch border. Place seasoned salmon fill[et] on top and cover with remaining forcemea[t.] Brush border with egg wash and top wi[th] dough. Cover to seal well. Avoid air poc[k]ets.

Decorate with dough flowers if desire[d.] Cut chimney and brush top with egg was[h.]

Bake in a 450°F oven for 10 to 15 minute[s.] Reduce to 350°F and bake for 35 to 45 mi[n]utes or internal temperature of 145 to 150°[.] Let rest for 10 minutes before slicing. Ser[ve] with Herb Sauce.

Note: Leftover cooked fish can be use[d] in this recipe. If fish is in poor conditio[n] substitute cooked scallops for half the spe[c]ified amount. This dish can be served h[ot] or cold.

SEAFOOD TIMBALE GATE OF INDIA

Yield: 12 3-oz. portions
Ingredients

Red onion, finely diced	1 oz.
Butter	1 T
Sole	18 oz.
Salt	1 tsp. or to tas[te]
White pepper	⅓ tsp.
Mustard powder (optional)	½ tsp.
White bread without crust	1 cup
Egg whites	2 to 3
Heavy cream	up to 1 qt.
Flour	to dust
Curry powder	pinch

Shrimp Garnish

Raw shrimps, cubed	1½ lb.
Green onions, chopped	¾ cup
Butter	2 oz.
Madras curry powder	1½ tsp.
Sherry wine	5 T

Fish velouté	1½ cups
Chili sauce	2 to 4 tsp.
Mango chutney	4 tsp.
Salt	to taste
Bananas, firm, small	2
Cornstarch	to dust
Butter	1 oz.
Dill, chopped	to garnish

Method

Sauté red onion lightly in butter. Cool. Cube fish fillet and season with salt, pepper, and mustard powder, and chill. Soak cubed white bread in egg whites and some cream. Place fish in a food processor and run for 2 minutes to emulsify. Add bread panada and blend well. Slowly add heavy cream.

Make test dumpling. Adjust seasoning. Coat twelve oval timables with butter. Dust with flour seasoned with curry powder and fill with forcemeat, being careful to avoid air pockets. Enclose with plastic wrap and bake/poach in a water bath at 200° F for 20 minutes or to an internal temperature of 150°F.

Make the shrimp garnish while the timbales are cooking. Sauté shrimps and green onions in butter for 2 to 3 minutes and remove from pan. Add curry and sherry wine and heat. Add velouté, chili sauce, and mango chutney. Season with salt and simmer 3 to 4 minutes. Add shrimps and bring to a boil. Cube bananas, dust with cornstarch, and sear in butter over high heat (1 minute). Fold into shrimp mixture.

Surround seafood timbales with this mixture and sprinkle with chopped dill. Serve hot.

RIVER SALMON PÂTÉ

(hot or cold)
Yield: 12 portions
Ingredients
Panada (optional)

Milk	½ pt.
Salt, pepper	to taste
Butter	3 oz.
Flour	4 oz.
Egg yolks	4

Forcemeat

White mushrooms	7 oz.
Butter	3 T
Salmon	28 oz.
Shallots, finely diced	3 T
Parsley, chopped	1 T
White wine	3 oz.
Salt, pepper	to taste
Egg whites	4
Heavy cream	up to 1 pt.
Truffles, diced (optional)	2 oz.
White wine sauce or dill mayonnaise	to garnish

Method

Bring milk, salt, pepper, and butter to a boil. Add sifted flour and work like pâte à choux until mixture loosens from the pot. Add egg slowly, one by one. Chill. Julienne mushrooms and sauté in butter. Chill. Cube 8 ounces salmon and sear over high heat quickly. Chill. Sauté shallots and parsley in butter, and add white wine. Reduce by half and pour over salmon pieces. Chill.

Cube the remaining 20 ounces salmon; add salt and pepper. Chill. Blend in food processor into a fine paste. Add panada and blend well. Add egg whites and blend for 3 to 4 minutes. Add heavy cream slowly and blend well. Remove from machine and make the dumpling test (cook a dumpling in water). Fold marinated and drained salmon and mushrooms into the forcemeat.

Line a loaf mold with plastic wrap. Fill with forcemeat. Cover with plastic wrap and aluminum foil. Poach in water bath in a preheated 200 to 225°F oven 1½ hours or until internal temperature reaches 150°F.

Note: If served cold, add 2 ounces diced truffles to forcemeat. If hot, serve with white wine sauce; if cold, serve with an herb mayonnaise.

SHRIMP PÂTÉ, GULF OF MEXICO

Yield: 3½ lb.

Ingredients

Sole, boned and skinned	16 oz.
Veal suet, watered	16 oz.
Salt, pepper, ginger, pâté spice	to taste
White bread, diced	8 oz.
Egg whites	3 to 4
Heavy cream	½ pt.
Truffle, diced	2 oz.
Pistachio nuts, peeled	3 oz.
Shrimps, cubed and scalded	6 oz.
Dill mayonnaise	to garnish

Method

Grind sole and veal suet. Chill well and season with salt and spices. Blend in a food processor. Add white bread moistened with egg white; blend well. Add heavy cream slowly. Make test quenelle. Adjust seasoning.

Line a long loaf mold with plastic wrap. Fold diced truffle, peeled pistachio nuts, and shrimps into the forcemeat. Fill mold with forcemeat and enclose with plastic wrap. Top with a board and tie with string. Bake/poach in a water bath in a preheated 200°F oven for 2 hours or until internal temperature reaches 150°F.

Chill. Decorate. Serve with dill mayonnaise.

TERRINES

Terrines contain the same ingredients as pâtés. The only difference is that they are cooked in a fireproof earthenware or china dish also called a terrine and are always served cold.

Preparations of a Terrine

1. Select a terrine mold appropriate to the occasion.
2. Line it with plastic wrap.

For terrines, use the covered Le Creuset (left) or a cast-aluminum mold.

To make a two-part terrine, fill a terrine first with salmon forcemeat (dark side of the drawing). Chill. Then fill remainder of the terrine with sole forcemeat to complete the design.

3. Line terrine with appropriate food (ham, chicken, fish, fatback, pig's caul, or vegetables).
4. Fill cavity with forcemeat or create your individual design. For example, use two forcemeats, pink (salmon) and white (sole), or three forcemeats, green chicken (with herbs), yellow chicken (with saffron), and red chicken (with tomato).
5. Fold the plastic wrap and "food lining" over the forcemeat. Cover with a lid.
6. Place terrine into a deep container such as a roasting pan, fill with boiling water until terrine is three-quarters

To make a tricolor terrine, tilt the terrine and fill with herbal forcemeat. Fill the opposite side with saffron forcemeat; fill the center with tomato forcemaet.

submerged, and finish in a preheated 200°F oven or according to recipe.

7. Cook to an internal temperature of 150 to 160°F. Remove and chill.

8. Unmold, remove plastic wrap, and place upside down into terrine. Glaze

with aspic jelly or chaud-froid sauce and decorate. Terrines can be unmolded, sliced, and served on buffets.

RILLETTES

(This is a French regional specialty from Tours.)
Yield: 4 lb.
Ingredients

Pork shoulder	5 lb.
Pâté spice	1 tsp.
Salt	1 tsp.
Black pepper, ground	½ tsp.
Bay leaves	2

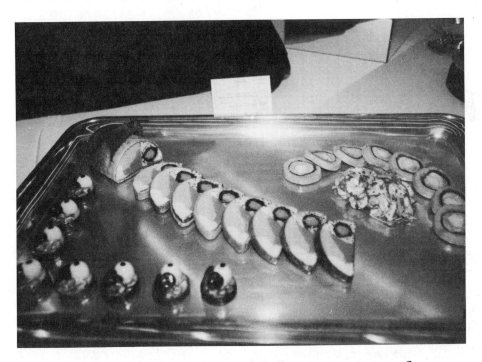

Terrine of Salmon, Sole, Monkfish, and Scallops. Various textures, flavors, and colors can be incorporated into your terrine, as shown here. This terrine is garnished with marinated cucumbers decorated with tomato, quail eggs, and shrimp; a shrimp salad; and a galantine of salmon and monkfish.

Method

Bone pork shoulder and separate fat from meat. Cut the fat and meat into large julienne. Season with spice blend, salt, pepper, and bay leaf.

Cook in a heavy pot over very low heat for 4 hours or until meat falls apart. Strain fat and reserve. Crush meat into coarse fibers with a fork. Press into an earthenware terrine and pour strained fat over the meat. Let cool.

When cold, cover with foil. This dish may be kept for several months.

TERRINE OF AMERICAN DUCK FOIE GRAS

Yield: 16 portions

Ingredients

Duck liver foie gras, prime or select	2 to 2½ lb.
Raisins	2 oz.
White wine	as needed
Salt, sugar, white pepper	to taste
Brandy	2 T
Brioche or toast	to garnish

Method

Prepare foie gras as directed on p. 87. Rinse raisins and soak in white wine. Season liver with salt, sugar, and pepper. Sprinkle with brandy and cover with white wine. Marinate overnight.

Drain raisins and liver and dry on absorbent paper. Line terrine with plastic wrap. Place half the liver in the terrine and press to cover bottom. Sprinkle with raisins, top with the other half of the liver, and press well to avoid air pockets. Smooth top with a palette knife and cover with plastic wrap. Close with lid. Place in a water bath and bake/poach at 200°F for 35 minutes. Chill and unmold. Slice or serve with a spoon. Serve with brioche or toast.

Terrine of Sole with Salmon Flower Inlay. Design and presentation of terrines is limited only by your imagination.

TERRINE OF SALMON GREEN GODDESS

Yield: 2 to 2½ lb.

Ingredients

Butter	2 oz.
Onion, finely diced	1 med.
Salmon, boned and skinned	2½ lb.
Powdered gelatin	to dust
White bread, without crust	4 oz.
Eggs	1
Heavy cream	up to 1 pt.
Salt	1 tsp. or to taste
White pepper	½ tsp.
Nutmeg	⅓ tsp.
Dill, finely chopped	½ bunch
Chervil, finely chopped	1 bunch
Parsley, finely chopped	½ bunch
Whipped cream, flavored with vodka and lemon	to garnish
Salmon caviar	to garnish

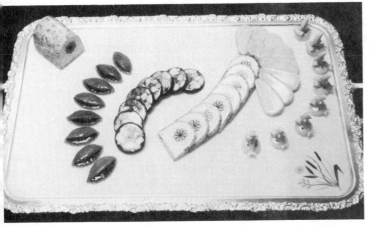

Fish Variations on a Chaud-Froid Mirror. From left to right: Terrine of Scallops with Saffron; Tomato Clams with Julienne of Vegetables; Seafood Headcheese; Sliced Terrine of Scallops; Poached Stuffed Salmon; Marinated Dolphins Carved from Squash.

Method

Sauté diced onions until transparent and cool. Trim the salmon fillet to fit the terrine. Dust with powdered gelatin and set aside. Cube the resulting salmon trimmings (approx. 20 ounces) and season with salt and pepper. Cube white bread and soak with eggs and some of the cream. Place salmon trimmings in food processor. Add onions, bread, salt, and seasoning and emulsify. Add heavy cream slowly. Line terrine with plastic wrap. Fill one-third full with forcemeat. Press salmon fillet in center. Top with forcemeat, pressing to avoid air pockets. Enclose with plastic wrap. Cover with lid. Bake/poach in a water bath at 170°F for 40 to 50 minutes or to an internal temperature of 140°F, and chill.

Unmold and roll in finely chopped herbs. Roll in plastic wrap and chill for 1 hour. Remove wrap, slice, and serve with vodka- and lemon-flavored whipped cream and salmon caviar.

TERRINE OF HONEYCOMB TRIPE

Yield: 2 lb.

Ingredients

Honeycomb tripe	2 lb.
Mirepoix (carrot, celery, onion)	4 oz.
Veal fond	1½ qt.
Bay leaf	1
Salt	to taste

Ham Mixture	
Boiled ham, cubed	1 lb.
Peanut oil	1 oz.
White pepper	⅓ tsp.
Egg, whole	1
Egg whites	2
Broth from tripe	1 to 2 oz.
Gelatin	½ oz.
Heavy cream	2 oz.
Aspic jelly	to coat terrine
Zucchini salad	to garnish

Method

Cook tripe, vegetables, and bay leaf in veal fond for 2 to 3 hours or until tender. Chill, cut tripe into julienne, and season with salt.

Place ham in a food processor. Add oil and pepper and purée fine. Add egg, egg white, tripe broth, and gelatin. Mix. Add cream and blend well.

Line terrine with plastic wrap. Fill, alternating tripe and ham mixture. Finish with ham mixture. Enclose with plastic wrap, weight down with a board, and bake in a water bath in a 350°F oven for 30 minutes. Chill. Coat with aspic jelly. Serve with zucchini salad.

Terrine of Salmon with Field Salad, Whipped Horseradish Cream, and Caviar.

Terrine and Wild Game Platter. From left to right: five-bean terrine, savoy cabbage salad, smoked stuffed breast of pheasant with wild rice, radicchio salad with balsamic vinaigrette, wild mushroom terrine, roasted loin of rabbit, herbed butternut raviolis, smoked breast of squab on rye crouton, roast loin of fallow deer, black bean and lentil salad, and hot smoked quail breast.

TERRINE OF CHICKEN LIVERS

Yield: 2½ lb.

Ingredients

Marinade

White wine	4 oz.
Madeira	2 oz.
Brandy	1 oz.
Salt, white pepper, tarragon	to taste
Curing salt	1 pinch
Garlic, mashed fine	2 cloves
Onion, sliced	2 oz.
Chicken breast	12 oz.
Pork butt	20 oz.
Chicken livers	20 oz.
Eggs	2
Flour	1 T
Salt, pepper, nutmeg	to taste
Green peppercorns	1 oz.
Aspic jelly	to coat terrine
Orange salad	to garnish

Method

Combine marinade ingredients. Cube chicken, pork butt, and 8 ounces of the chicken livers. Place in a plastic container and marinate overnight. Remove from marinade and grind coarse, then grind through fine plate. Place in a mixing bowl and add eggs, flour, 3 tablespoons of marinade, salt, pepper, and nutmeg and blend well.

Scald remaining chicken livers in boiling water. Shock in ice water and dry. Mix with green peppercorns and season with salt. Fold chicken livers into forcemeat.

Line terrine with plastic wrap and fill with forcemeat, pressing to avoid air pockets. Enclose with plastic wrap, cover with lid, and bake/poach in a water bath at 300°F for 2 hours or to an internal temperature of 150°F. Chill and unmold. Remove plastic wrap. Place upside down into terrine. Coat with aspic jelly and decorate.

Serve with an orange salad.

TERRINE WITH SWEETBREADS AND DUCK FOIE GRAS

Yield: 12 portions
Ingredients

Sweetbreads, soaked in cold water	22 oz.
Chicken or veal fond	1 qt.
Gelatin	1 to 2 oz.
Duck foie gras, select	1½ lb.
Mixed vegetables: carrots, celery, broccoli, lima beans	32 oz.
Leeks, blanched	2 to 3
Herb vinaigrette	to garnish

Method

Trim sweetbreads and cut into large cubes. Braise in 8 ounces of the chicken fond for 15 to 20 minutes, covered. Remove sweetbreads and chili; reserve sweetbread fond. Bloom the gelatin in the remaining chicken fond; then add sweetbread fond, and clarify, following standard procedure. Clean and trim duck foie gras (see p. 87). Roll in plastic wrap to 2 inches in diameter and poach, covered, at 160°F for 20 minutes. Chill in stock.

Prepare vegetables: peel carrots, cook soft, and chill. Peel celery, cook soft and chill. Cut broccoli into rosettes, cook al dente, and chill. Blanch lima beans and chill.

Line terrine with plastic wrap. Line with blanched leeks. Mix sweetbreads and vegetables. Fill halfway with mixture.

Place foie gras roll in center. Fill with rest of vegetable mixture. Fill mold with aspic jelly. Close with leeks and plastic wrap.

Chill well. Unmold and slice into portions. Serve with herb vinaigrette.

Note: Smoked salmon and smoked sturgeon could be used instead of sweetbreads and duck foie gras.

CREAM CHEESE–SWEETBREAD TERRINE WITH ZUCCHINI COULIS

Yield: 8 portions
Ingredients

Sweetbread	10 oz.
Dry white wine	1 pt.
Chicken stock	1 pt.
Cream cheese	8 oz.
Crème fraîche	3 oz.
Yogurt	3 oz.
Gelatine	1½ oz. (5 leaves)
Salt and pepper	to taste
Port wine	2 T
Chervil, fresh, coarsely chopped	1 twig

Method

Poach cleaned sweetbread in white wine and chicken stock. Chill and dry well. Combine cream cheese, crème fraîche, and yogurt and melt over medium heat. Dissolve soaked gelatine leaves in the mixture and add salt, pepper, port wine, and chervil. Line a terrine with plastic wrap. Pour some cheese mixture into mold; top with thinly sliced sweetbread. Alternate layers to fill terrine; chill. Serve with Zucchini Coulis (recipe follows).

Note: Sweetbreads may be substituted with an equal quantity of smoked salmon.

Serve terrine with a salad made from a shredded apple and pear marinated in 2 to 3 tablespoons of sour cream. Add 1 tablespoon each of nuts, sunflower seeds, and pumpkin seeds, and 2 to 3 tablespoons of oat flakes.

ZUCCHINI COULIS

Yield: approximately 1 pt.
Ingredients

Zucchini	1 medium
Garlic	1 clove
White port wine	1 oz.
Crème fraîche	½ cup
Salt and pepper	to taste

Method

Place zucchini, garlic, port wine, and crème fraîche into a blender, purée, and season with salt and pepper.

EGGPLANT–RED PEPPER TERRINE

Yield: 2½ lb.

Ingredients

Eggplants	4 large
Salt and pepper	to taste
Olive oil	as needed
Red peppers, roasted, peeled, and seeded	5
Basil–Oregano Pesto (recipe below)	2¼ cups

Method

Slice eggplants lengthwise in ⅛-inch slices. Salt and place slices in a colander to drain for 20 minutes. Rinse and dry slices between layers of paper toweling, and weight down with a heavy object. Lightly season eggplant with salt and pepper and sauté in a pan with barely any olive oil in it. Drain sautéed slices between layers of toweling and weight down with a heavy object. Line a terrine mold with eggplant slices; let the slices hang over the sides of the terrine. Alternate 2 or 3 layers of eggplant with a thin coating of pesto and a layer of red peppers. Continue layering until all the eggplant and peppers are used. Fold the eggplant slices over the top, and then cover terrine with plastic wrap. Weigh down with bricks and refrigerate for at least 2 days.

Note: At service, this terrine can be served with thin zucchini slices. Serve with Tomato–Basil Coulis (page 173).

BASIL–OREGANO PESTO

Ingredients

Pine nuts, lightly toasted	2 oz.
Garlic cloves, roasted	6
Basil leaves, fresh	15
Oregano leaves, fresh	15
Black pepper	1¼ tsp. or to taste
Parmesan cheese, grated	2 oz.
Pecorino Romano cheese, grated	1 oz.
Virgin olive oil	1 cup

Method

Place all ingredients except the olive oil in a blender and purée. Add the oil slowly, pulsing the blender on and off to incorporate, until all the oil has been added. Adjust seasoning with salt and pepper.

Note: For Creamy Pesto, fold in 2 cups of heavy cream.

9

Galantines

Galantines are always served cold, either as entrées or à la carte items, or attractively displayed on buffet tables. They consist of ground, boneless poultry meat or fish stuffed into a natural or synthetic casing, then shaped symmetrically, and cooked in a rich stock.

The word *galantine* comes from the old French word *galine*, meaning chicken. At one time galantines were made only of poultry; today, galantines are prepared using a variety of meats, fish, or seafood.

How does a ballotine differ from a galantine?

In a list of French culinary terms, the word *ballotine* could be confused with *galantine*. A ballotine is usually prepared from a boneless leg of poultry that is stuffed with forcemeat. In the case of fish, a fillet is stuffed, rolled, and shaped like a cone. Ballotines usually are baked or braised and served as hot entrées, while galantines are poached and served cold. What distinguishes the ballotine from the galantine is the shape and the method of cooking.

CHICKEN GALANTINE

Yield: 3 lb.

Ingredients

Roasting chicken	1 3-lb.
Pork, fresh lean	4 oz.
Veal, fresh lean	4 oz.
Pork fatback	3 oz.
Brandy	3 T
Eggs	2
Salt	⅓ oz. per lb. of forcemeat
Pâté spice	¼ tsp. per pound of forcemeat

Garnish

Ham, diced, cooked	4 oz.
Giblets, diced, cooked	4 oz.
Truffles, diced	1 oz.
Pistachio nuts, peeled	2 oz.

Method

Remove wingtips and make a cut along the back of the chicken from the neck to the tail. Remove the skin and flesh over the back, and on reaching the wing and thighs, find the joints and cut through the ligaments, detaching them from the carcass.

123

To Prepare a Chicken Galantine.

1. Mise en place: chicken breast for garnish; chicken skin; butcher twine; truffle, corn, and mushroom garnish; chicken forcemeat; chicken and vegetable trimmings for the poaching stock.

2. Place chicken skin on a sheet of plastic wrap. Spread with forcemeat.

3. Add a layer of truffle, corn, and mushroom garnish on top of the forcemeat. Fold the skin over the fillings, then use the plastic wrap to roll tightly into a cylinder shape.

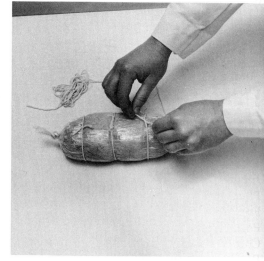

4. With twine, tie roll at both ends and around the middle to hold shape while cooking. Poach in a strong chicken stock made from trimmings.

Continue towards the breast, carefully cutting away the meat attached to the breastbone. The center bones can now be removed. Then bone the thighs, with the exception of a small portion of the knuckle, which should be left in position to retain the shape and hold the forcemeat in place. Debone the wings to the first joint.

Save the chicken tenderloins and combine with veal, pork, and fatback. Chill all meat and grind through the fine plate of a meat grinder. Chill again and repeat. Add brandy, eggs, salt, and pâté seasonings. Combine forcemeat with garnishes. Mix well and chill.

Prepare a rich chicken stock with the carcass bones. Strain. Place boned chicken skin side down on a moist linen cloth or cheesecloth. Spread the forcemeat over the chicken. Roll the chicken into the shape of a large sausage. Wrap the cheesecloth tightly around the chicken and tie both ends. Also tie roll loosely with string three times through the middle to hold in shape.

Simmer the galantine submerged in chicken stock for 1½ hours or to internal temperature of 160°F. When cooked, remove from heat and refrigerate in stock for 24 hours. Decorate as desired.

GALANTINE OF PHEASANT

Yield: 12 to 14 portions
Ingredients

Pheasant	1
Fresh pork fat, semifrozen	3 oz.
Pork, lean, chilled	7 oz.
Chicken meat, lean, chilled	6 oz.
Poultry and pheasant livers, chilled	6 oz.
Eggs	2
Heavy cream, chilled	7 oz.
Flour	1 oz.
Pâté spices	⅓ tsp.
Salt	½ to 1 oz.

Garnish

Veal tongue, diced	1
Small gherkins, diced	3
Truffles, diced	2 oz.
Mushrooms, whole, sautéed	3½ oz.
Cumberland Sauce with fresh grapes	to garnish

Method
Prepare pheasant as directed for chicken in preceding recipe for Chicken Galantine. Cube pork fat, pork, chicken, and livers; run through a food processor to make a smooth paste. Combine the paste with the eggs, heavy cream, flour, and seasonings; mix well. Fold garnish into the prepared forcemeat. Prepare galantine as described in preceding recipe. Serve galantine with a Cumberland Sauce containing fresh seedless grapes.

Clockwise from top left: Smoked Duck; Cranberry Relish on Lettuce Leaf; Galantine of Pheasant.

COMBINATION VEAL GALANTINE

Yield: 5 lb.
Ingredients

Veal breasts	3 lb.
Pork butt	7 oz.
Turkey breast	7 oz.
Pork fat	3 oz.
Salt	⅓ oz. per lb.
Shaved ice	2 to 3 oz.
Heavy cream	4 oz.
Veal fillets	2
Dry seaweed soaked in aspic	2 sheets
Pork tongue, pickled	16 oz.
Truffles	1 oz.
Aspic	8 oz.
Carrots	⅓ cup
Onions	⅓ cup
Celery	⅓ cup
Tomato paste	2 tsp.

Method

Bone veal breast and butterfly. Cube the pork, turkey, and pork fat and season with salt. Grind coarsely. Emulsify with ice in a food processor. Add heavy cream and blend well. Chill.

Salt veal fillet and sear on all sides. Chill well. Roll into seaweed. Cube the tips of tongue coarsely; trim the rest of the tongue. Dice the truffles. Fold diced tongue and truffles into forcemeat.

Set veal breast skin side down on oiled cheesecloth. Fill 1 inch high with forcemeat. Set pork fillet on one side and pork tongue on the other side. Cover with remaining forcemeat. Pull one side over pork fillet and the other side over the tongue. Seam veal breast. Roll into cheesecloth and tie with string.

Dice carrots, onions, and celery, and place in pan. Top with galantine and roast in a 350°F oven until 160°F internal temperature is reached. Remove. Set into a clean pan, press lightly, and chill. Add tomato paste to the vegetables and brown. Add two large ladles of aspic, purée in a blender, and strain through a fine mesh strainer. Brush cold galantine with this mixture and chill.

Note: Garnish with zucchini baskets filled with kernel corn or with tomato mousse medallions and asparagus.

GALANTINE OF SCALLOPS

Yield: 2 to 2½ lb.
Ingredients

Fresh scallops	20 oz.
Fillet of sole (fresh)	10 oz.
Salt, pepper	to taste
Bread panada	6 oz.
Egg whites	4
Heavy cream	up to 1 pt.
Gin	1 oz.
Dill, chopped	4 T
Fish fumet	1 gal.
Gelatin, powdered	2 oz.
Cantaloupe balls	to garnish
Pittsburgh Sauce (see below)	1½ pt.
Dill sprigs	to garnish

Method

Blend dry scallops and fish fillet in a food processor. Add salt, pepper, and panada and blend well. Add egg whites; blend well. Slowly add heavy cream. Season with gin and chill for one hour.

Mix half of the forcemeat with the chopped dill. Spread dill forcemeat on plastic wrap. Refrigerate 10 minutes. Top with plain forcemeat and roll. Tie, pierce with a needle, and poach in fish fumet strengthened with 2 oz. gelatin powder at 160°F for 30 minutes. Cool in stock.

Unmold and slice; brush with fish aspic. Decorate with cantaloupe balls and a sprig of dill. Serve with Pittsburgh Sauce.

PITTSBURGH SAUCE

Ingredients

Mayonnaise	16 oz.
Tomato ketchup	8 oz.
White wine	4 T
Chervil, chopped	2 T

Method

Combine all ingredients.

GALANTINE OF DUCK

Yield: 3 to 4 lb.

Ingredients

Duck, 4 lb.	1
Pork butt	16 oz.
Salt	⅓ oz. per lb.
Shaved ice	up to 12 oz.
Duck livers (poultry livers), soaked in milk	10 oz.
Eggs	2
Pâté spice	½ tsp.
Curry powder	½ tsp.
Cayenne pepper	to taste
Applejack	3 T
Pig's caul, large, soaked in cold salt water	1
Truffle	1 to 2 oz.
Strong stock	to poach
Apple baskets, cranberry relish	to garnish

Method

Butterfly duck, starting with the backbone. Remove all bones. Remove all meat from skin. Set skin on a tray in refrigerator and chill. Cube duck and pork butt; season with salt and chill. Cube duck fat and chill.

Emulsify duck, duck fat, and pork butt together with shaved ice in a food processor. Add 4 ounces poultry liver and blend well. Add eggs, pâté spice, curry, and a touch of cayenne; blend well. Chill. Marinate remaining 6 ounces of poultry liver in applejack for 20 minutes, remove, scald, shock, and dry.

Set duck skin on moist cheesecloth. Top skin with pig's caul and spread the forcemeat over it. Place marinated and blanched chicken livers in the center of forcemeat and line each side with truffle sticks. Cover garnish with the rest of the forcemeat.

Roll into a galantine. Make sure all meat is covered by caul and duck skin. Tie with string to keep shape. Poach in a strong stock at 180°F until 160°F internal temperature is reached. Press lightly and chill in stock.

Remove and slice for service. Serve with poached apple baskets filled with cranberry relish.

Note: Galantine may be coated with chaud-froid or glace de viande.

Apple Valley Duck. From left to right: Galantine of Duck; Apple Mousse and Cranberry Aspic Centerpiece; Pickled Carrots and Corn Mousse; Pâté of Duck; Poached Apples with Cranberry Relish.

Galantine of Duck Garnished with Hearty Greens and Poached Pears in a Red Wine Vinegar Reduction.

Galantine of Chicken with Sauce Andalouse Garnished with Vegetable Salad.

GALANTINE OF VEAL

Yield: 4 lb.

Ingredients

Veal breast, boned	3 lb.
Salt	to taste
White wine	1 oz.
Marjoram	½ tsp.
Lemon zest	⅓ tsp.
Butter	1 oz.
Onions, diced	2 oz.
Garlic, finely diced	1 clove
Cooked sweetbreads	8 oz.
Gelatin	½ tsp.
Veal tongue, smoked	3 oz.
Pistachio nuts	2 oz.
Veal forcemeat (see recipe, p. 99)	1 lb.
Aspic	to coat

Method

Butterfly veal breast. Sprinkle with salt white wine, marjoram, and lemon zest. Refrigerate for 1 hour.

Heat butter, and sauté onion and garlic until golden; chill.

Dust sweetbreads with gelatin and fold together with veal tongue and pistachio nuts, into forcemeat.

Spread forcemeat over veal breast. Roll into oiled cheesecloth and tie. Roast on a rack in a preheated 350°F oven to an internal temperature of 160°F. Press between 2 boards, cool. Remove cheesecloth and slice. Brush with aspic.

BALLOTINE OF SHRIMPS

Yield: 10 portions

Ingredients

Chicken or turkey breast, raw	7 oz.
Shrimps, raw	4 oz.
Salt and pepper	to taste
Egg whites	3
Brandy	½ oz.
Heavy cream	½ pt.
Truffle	1 small
Mushrooms	3 oz.
Pistachio nuts *or* frozen peas	1 oz.
Tomatoes, firm	10 large
Lemon aspic jelly	to coat ballotine
New Orleans Sauce (see below)	approx. 2 pt.

Method

Cube chicken meat and 3 ounces of the shrimps and chill. Purée in a food processor. Add salt and pepper. Add egg whites and brandy and mix well. Slowly add heavy cream.

Dice remaining shrimps, truffle, and mushrooms. Peel pistachio nuts and mix into forcemeat. Hollow tomatoes carefully, starting with stem, and fill with forcemeat. Cover tightly with plastic wrap and aluminum foil. Set on a wire rack over some water. Cover and steam at 175° to 180°F for 25 minutes.

Remove plastic wrap and aluminum foil; remove tomato skin. Chill. Glaze with lemon aspic jelly. Garnish with tournéed marinated cucumbers and New Orleans Sauce (see below).

NEW ORLEANS SAUCE

Ingredients

Mayonnaise	1½ pt.
Curry	1 T
Lemon	juice of 1
Tomato ketchup	7 oz.
Sour cream *or* yogurt	4 oz.

Method

Mix well.

GALANTINE OF SALMON

Yield: 5 to 5½ lb.

Ingredients

Salmon	5 to 6 lb.
White bread, crusts removed	10 slices
Egg whites	4
Salt	1 T or to taste
White pepper	1 T
Nutmeg	to taste
Heavy cream	2 cups
Pistachio nuts	1½ oz.
Red pepper, blanched, peeled, cut in large dice	10 oz.
White truffle paste	1 oz.
Gelatin powder	½ tsp.
Aspic	to coat
Cucumber pieces	16 oz.
Cantaloupe melon balls	16 oz.
Cherry tomatoes, peeled	16 oz.
Dill vinaigrette	4 oz.

Method

Remove head and tail of salmon. Bone salmon, starting with backbone, without damaging the skin. Remove salmon meat, keeping skin and meat intact. Chill meat and salmon skin.

Start a fish fond from salmon bones, head, and tail.

Cube 32 ounces of the salmon. Place into a food processor. Add white bread moistened with egg whites and emulsify. Add salt, white pepper, and nutmeg, and slowly blend in heavy cream. Remove and fold in pistachio nuts, red peppers, and white truffle paste. Poach a teaspoonful of forcemeat in boiling seasoned water. Taste and adjust seasoning.

Cube remaining salmon. Season with salt and dust with gelatin powder. Fold into forcemeat.

Spread moist cheesecloth on table and place salmon skin on top. Spread forcemeat over skin, leaving ½-inch border on both sides. Fold skin over and seam together. Roll in cheesecloth, tie both ends, and tie loosely 3 or 4 times between the ends. Strain fish fond. Add enough water to cover the galantine. Bring fond to a simmer, 170°F, and cook galantine to a 150°F internal temperature. Remove from fire. Weigh down and chill in the fond. Remove from fond. Remove cheesecloth carefully, without damaging the skin. Slide the galantine into ¼-inch-thick disks and brush with aspic. Toss cucumbers, melons, and cherry tomatoes with dill vinaigrette and serve with the galantine.

10

Mousse

The cold mousse is a delicacy that is sure to delight the eye and the palate of patrons. In the garde manger department, a mousse is defined as a mixture of cooked ingredients, puréed and held together with unflavored gelatin, velouté sauce, mayonnaise, or aspic jelly, then mixed with cream and flavored with wine. As a garde manger preparation, the mousse is always served cold, attractively molded.

Other preparations, called mousselines, are served hot. A fish quenelle forcemeat (see page 99), baked in a mold and served hot with a fish sauce, is called a mousseline. Some other hot fish mousses are Mousseline of Dover Sole Joinville and Mousseline of Salmon Americaine. Other delicacies such as Chocolate Mousse, Peach Mousse, and Strawberry Mousse, are served as cold desserts.

Whether served cold, hot, or as a dessert, the mousse is light and delicate. This chapter will explain the preparation of the cold mousse.

How is a cold mousse prepared?

A mousse is made with cooked meat, fish, poultry, or vegetables. The method of preparation is similar for all recipes: the ingredients are puréed and mixed with a binding agent containing gelatin. Then heavy cream and seasonings are blended in. A well-prepared mousse can be an impressive dish for service on a luncheon menu or on a cold buffet table.

The following recipes are for various mousse preparations, using either freshly cooked ingredients or leftovers.

BASIC MOUSSE

Yield: 2 lb.

Ingredients

Pheasant, duck, fallow deer, or rabbit, boneless, cooked	16 oz.
Strong aspic jelly	8 oz.
Thick béchamel or velouté	2 oz.
Salt, pepper	to taste
Whipped cream	6 oz.
Aspic	to coat molds

Method

Purée diced meat fine in a blender. Add cold liquid aspic jelly, béchamel, salt, and pepper. Fold in whipped cream. Spoon into aspic-coated molds. Chill.

ARTICHOKE MOUSSE

Yield: 2 lb.

Ingredients

Artichoke bottoms	16 oz.
Lemon	juice of ½
Chicken velouté	4 oz.
Aspic jelly	16 oz.
	(reduced to 8 oz.)
Salt and pepper	to taste
Whipped cream	6 oz.

Method

Purée artichoke bottoms. Add lemon juice, liquid velouté, and cold, reduced aspic jelly. Adjust seasoning. Fold in whipped cream.

Molds for mousse come in a variety of shapes. The most common are the rib mold and the oval timbale, shown here in different sizes.

LOBSTER MOUSSE

Yield: 2 lb.

Ingredients

Lobster meat, cooked	14 oz.
Coral, cooked	2 oz.
Béchamel	2 oz.
Aspic jelly	16 oz.
	(reduced to 8 oz.)
Whipped cream	6 oz.
Salt and pepper	to taste

Method

Grind cooked lobster and cooked coral through fine plate. Mix with béchamel and reduced aspic jelly. Fold in whipped cream. Adjust seasoning. Pour into mold and chill.

SALMON MOUSSE

Yield: 2 lb.

Ingredients

Salmon meat, cooked	16 oz.
Velouté	2 oz.
Aspic jelly	16 oz.
	(reduced to 8 oz.)
Whipped cream	6 oz.
Salt and pepper	to taste

Method

Purée salmon with velouté and reduced aspic jelly. Fold in whipped cream. Season with salt and pepper. Pour into mold and chill.

TOMATO MOUSSE

Yield: 12 portions

Ingredients

Aspic jelly	to line molds
Tomatoes, blanched, peeled, and seeded	6 oz.
Tomato ketchup	3½ oz.
Tomato paste	2½ oz.
Salt, sugar, cayenne pepper	to taste
Unflavored gelatin	⅓ to ½ oz.
Tomato juice	5 T
Tomato concassée (diced tomatoes)	8 oz.
Heavy cream, whipped	6 oz.

Method

Line timbales with aspic jelly and chill. Purée tomatoes, ketchup, tomato paste, and add seasonings. Dissolve gelatin in tomato

Mousse of Apple and Cranberry Aspic. To make this type of mousse, mold shortening into the shape desired (here, an apple). Prepare extra-strong gelatin aspic and place in mold. When aspic is almost set, submerge the shortening in the aspic, hold in place with wood dowel until set, and chill. Unmold and cut the aspic in half; carefully remove all the shortening. Put aspic back in the mold, cut a chimney into the aspic, and pipe mousse through the chimney until the cavity is full. Chill and unmold.

juice and fold, with diced tomato, into whipped cream. Fill timbales with mousse mixture. Chill. Unmold.

Serve with marinated tomatoes, asparagus, shrimps, and dill.

HAM MOUSSE, STRASBOURG STYLE

(Mousse de Jambon Strasbourgeoise)

Yield: 2½ lb.

Ingredients

Pullman ham or leftover baked ham	1 lb.
Goose liver pâté	4 oz.
Unflavored gelatin	1 oz.
Water	½ cup
Velouté sauce	1½ cup
Mayonnaise	½ cup
Heavy cream	½ cup
Beet juice (optional)	to color
Salt	1 tsp.
White pepper	¼ tsp.

Method

Grind ham and liver pâté through fine blade. Combine gelatin with warm water and add to ham mixture. Mix in velouté sauce and mayonnaise. Whip heavy cream and carefully fold into ham mixture. Add a touch of beet juice to intensify pink ham color. Season with salt and pepper and pour into a mold.

MOUSSE OF SMOKED SALMON AND TROUT WITH CAVIAR

Yield: 2 lb.

Ingredients

Salmon Mousse

Aspic jelly	to line mold
Salmon, lightly smoked or Gravlax (p. 153)	5 oz.
Fish velouté (no salt)	3½ oz.
Gelatin	⅓ oz.

(continued)

Mousse of Smoked Salmon and Trout with Caviar (continued)

Fish stock	5 T
Heavy cream, whipped	4 oz.
White pepper, salt	to taste
Beluga caviar	4 oz.

Trout Mousse

Smoked trout fillet	5 oz.
Fish velouté or mayonnaise	3½ oz.
Gelatin	⅓ oz.
Fish or chicken stock	5 T
Pepper, salt	to taste
Whipped cream	4 oz.
Molds, lined with aspic jelly and decorated with truffles, thinly sliced	2

Method

Line mold with aspic jelly and decorate with truffle circles. Cut smoked salmon into pieces and purée with warm velouté. Dissolve gelatin in stock, and add to mixture while machine is working. Fold in whipped cream, adjust seasoning, and put into mold. Mold should be half filled with smoked salmon mousse. Place a row of caviar down the middle.

Prepare trout mousse, following the same procedure. Place on top of salmon mousse and caviar, and chill. Unmold and serve.

Note: Golden whitefish caviar or salmon caviar can be substituted for beluga caviar.

MOUSSE OF CHICKEN ROTHSCHILD

Yield: 5 lb.

Ingredients

Base

Chicken breast meat, cooked	2 lb.
Chicken aspic jelly, very strong	2 pt.

Truffles, chopped	1 to 2 T
Applesauce, flavored with applejack	2 to 3 oz.
Green peppers, medium, blanched, peeled, and diced	2 to 3
Pecan nutmeats, whole, soaked in hot water	2 to 3 oz.

Layers

Lobster, cooked	2 oz.
Lobster coral, cooked	2 T
Tomato ketchup	1 to 2 T
Madeira and brandy	a touch of each
Heavy cream, whipped	2 to 3 cups
Light chaud-froid sauce	to coat mousse

Method

Purée meat and warm aspic jelly to a very fine consistency. Press through a sieve and separate into five equal portions. Fold the chopped truffle into one portion. Purée remaining meat mixture one portion at a time with remaining ingredients to make small amounts of apple, pepper, pecan, and lobster mousse base.

Fold equal amounts of whipped cream into each part and pour in layers into a glass bowl. Let each layer chill before topping with next layer. Pour apple mousse first, then pepper, truffle, pecan, and lobster, in that order. Chill and top with a layer of light chaud-froid sauce. Decorate with lobster claw, chicken breast, truffle, green pepper wedges, and whole pecan nutmeats.

CHICKEN LIVER MOUSSE

Yield: 2 lb.

Ingredients   Soak in milk overnight

Chicken livers	1½ lb.
Butter or rendered chicken fat	¼ lb.
Onion, chopped	½ lb.

Garlic, minced	2 cloves
Milk	1 pt.
Sherry	2 oz.
Curry	¼ tsp.
Thyme	1 tsp.
Bay leaves	6
Double strength aspic	1¼ cups
Salt, if needed	1 tsp.
Hot pepper sauce	½ tsp.
Heavy cream	1¼ cups

Method

Remove connective tissue from the liver. Melt butter or chicken fat in a sauté pan, add onions and garlic and sauté until soft and translucent. Add all other ingredients except heavy cream. Cook, covered for 10 minutes, stirring occasionally. Remove from heat and cool for 5 minutes.

Whip cream to medium stiffness. Remove bay leaves from liver mixture. Purée the liver mixture in food processor until smooth. Pour into a large stainless bowl and then fold in the whipped cream. Immediately pour into prepared molds and chill.

BROCCOLI MOUSSE

Yield: 10 portions

Ingredients

Sherry aspic jelly	to line molds
Beef loin, roasted pink (or leftover roast beef)	8 to 9 oz.
Carrots, cut into a large circle	2
Truffles, cut into a smaller circle	2
Gelatin	⅓ to ½ oz.
Beef stock	6 T
Broccoli, cleaned	12 oz.
Salt	½ tsp.
White pepper	to taste
Nutmeg	a touch
Thyme and basil	to taste
Heavy cream, whipped	8 oz.

Pâté dough	32 oz.
Egg yolk	1

Method

Line two round molds with sherry aspic jelly. Shingle chilled roast beef slices on top of a circle of carrots and truffles. Dissolve gelatin in beef stock. Cook broccoli in salt water until soft, drain, and chill. Purée in a blender with salt. Add prepared gelatin and herbs and spices; fold in whipped cream. Fill aspic molds and chill for 12 hours.

Roll out pâté dough to ⅓ inch thick and cut larger than mold in star shape, if possible. Let pâté dough rest for 15 minutes before baking. Brush with egg yolk, pierce, and bake for 10 to 12 minutes in 400°F oven.

To serve, unmold mousse onto baked pastry circle.

FISH MOUSSE

Yield: 2 lb.

Ingredients

Salmon, sole, halibut, pike, or similar fish, cooked	1 lb.
Unflavored gelatin	1½ T
Liquid fish aspic	½ cup
Salt	1 tsp.
Pepper	1 pinch
Worcestershire sauce	1 dash
Dill, chopped	2 tsp.
Mayonnaise	½ cup
White wine, dry	¼ cup
Heavy cream, whipped	½ cup

Method

Carefully remove all bones and skin from fish. Dissolve gelatin in aspic. Put fish into chopper, and gradually add the aspic. Add seasonings and blend the mixture to a paste consistency.

Transfer the fish mixture to a stainless steel bowl. Add mayonnaise and wine. Mix well with a wooden spoon, then cool on ice. When mixture has partially congealed, fold in whipped cream.

Fish mousse can be poured into aspic molds and served on buffets. The mousse can also be used as a filling for various items used to accompany the mousse, such as barquettes, vol au vent, cucumbers, tomatoes, mushroom caps, and artichoke bottoms.

An interesting variation can be prepared by mixing several kinds of fish mousse in combinations such as one-half trout mousse and one-half sole and golden caviar mousse, or one-third salmon mousse, one-third sole mousse, and one-third crabmeat mousse.

11

Marinades—Cures—Brines

MARINADES

A marinade—a seasoned liquid either cooked or uncooked—is used to season the food steeped in it and thus to improve its flavor. A marinade can also soften the fibers of certain meats, and make it possible to hold fish and meat longer.

How long can meat be kept in a marinade or brine?

The length of time foodstuffs should be left in a marinade or brine depends on their size and texture and on the temperature of the marinade or brine. In winter, large cuts of meat or game such as deer (venison) should be left in a marinade up to six days. In the summer, however, they should be marinated only 24 to 28 hours; only very large pieces can be left in the marinade for longer periods of time. It is important to watch the marinating product closely in hot weather to be sure it does not spoil.

Marinades may be cooked or uncooked. Use a brine if the ingredient placed in it is to last a longer period of time.

All marinated meat must be thoroughly dried before roasting or sautéing. Wet meat will not brown properly.

COOKED MARINADE

Yield: approximately 4 qt.

Ingredients

Carrots	3
Onions	2
Shallots	3
Black peppercorns	½ tsp.
Cloves	2 to 3
Parsley stalks	4
Thyme or rosemary	pinch
Bay leaf	1
Water	2 qt.
White wine	2 pt.
Vinegar	½ pt.
Salad oil	¼ cup

Method

Combine all ingredients except oil and simmer for 1 hour. Cool. Pour marinade over meat; add oil. If the meat (or game) is fresh, it will take less time for it to marinate. Large pieces will require 24 hours, smaller pieces, 4 to 5 hours. For game marinade, add juniper berries and coriander.

UNCOOKED MARINADE FOR BEEF, LAMB, OR VENISON

Yield: 2 qt.

Ingredients

Red wine	2 qt.
Thyme twigs, fresh	2
Bay leaf	1½
Peppercorn, freshly crushed	12
Juniper berries, crushed	10
Cloves	3
Rosemary	2 pinches
Garlic, crushed	1 clove
Oil	½ cup

Method

Combine all ingredients and pour over meat. Marinate 3 to 4 days, turning meat once every day.

BEER MARINADE FOR BEEF, LAMB, OR GAME

Yield: 2½ qt.

Ingredients

Ale or dark beer	4 pt.
Lemon juice	½ pt.
Sugar	5 oz.
Onion, medium, sliced, blanched	2
Bay leaf, small	2
Cloves	6
Black pepper, coarsely ground	1 tsp.
Juniper berries, crushed	1 oz.
Allspice, crushed	½ tsp.

Method

Mix ingredients in a crock. Put meat in it and hold it down with a weight. Meat should be well covered with liquid. Keep in a cool place. Marinate for up to one week.

MARINADE FOR GAME MEDALLIONS, NOISETTES, OR CUTLETS

Yield: ½ pt.

Ingredients

Vinegar or lemon juice	2 oz.
Red or white wine	6 oz.
Walnut oil	1 oz.
Juniper berries, crushed	½ tsp
Thyme	⅓ tsp
Dried, powdered wild mushrooms	1 T

Method

Place the small cuts of game in a chin dish. Mix ingredients and pour the liqui over the meat and marinate 8 to 24 hours Turn meat once or twice.

CURES

Curing is a process of surrounding fish poultry, or meat with salt only or sal sugar, nitrite-based curing salts, and spices The process dehydrates the meats and pre serves them.

Salt is by far the most important ingredient. It inhibits the growth of bacteria yeasts, and molds, it preserves food by re moving moisture from the tissue, and adds flavor.

Sugar or dextrose in a cure reduces th strong flavor of salt, lowers the pH (acid variance, and assists in reducing bacteria growth.

Nitrites, also known as saltpeter, help t control the growth of botulism. Nitrites als react with the pigment found in meat an give it a pink color. Nitrites are suspecte carcinogens, and there has been much pul licity against their use. However, until a effective alternative additive that can con trol the deadly botulism-causing bacteria found, nitrites must continue to be used They should always be added sparingly.

Spices such as cinnamon, black and white pepper, coriander, garlic, nutmeg, paprika, oregano, and others are added for aroma and flavor.

Dry Cure

Dry cure is a combination of salt and spices applied directly to food. Some recipes may call for sugar too, especially for fish cures. Dry cures are applied for a measured amount of time, determined by the thickness and weight of the food. When ready, the cure is rinsed off.

ALL-PURPOSE CURE

Yield: 1¾ lb.
Ingredients

Coarse salt	1¼ lb.
Sugar (dextrose)	7 oz.
Curing salt	2 oz.

Method

Combine all ingredients and rub firmly on all sides of the meat. Pack meat into a stainless steel or plastic container and cure in a cold place for 7 days, turning the meat daily. Remove, rinse, dry, and hot smoke at 190°F or roast until a 153°F internal temperature is reached.

CURE FOR PORK, DUCK, OR LAMB

Yield: To cure 3 to 4 lb. of meat
Ingredients

Salt	2 tsp.
Black peppercorns, ground	⅔ tsp.
Thyme or sage	⅓ T
Bay leaf	1
Allspice	⅓ T
Garlic, crushed	1 clove

Method

Mix all ingredients and rub mixture into the surface of the meat. Place in a covered plastic or stainless steel bowl. Marinate 12 to 24 hours. It is helpful to turn the meat once in a while. Before cooking, rinse and dry the meat well.

CURE FOR FISH

Yield: 2½ lb.
Ingredients

Coarse salt	1½ lb.
Curing salt	½ oz.
Ground mace	1½ tsp.
Ground Juniper berries	1½ tsp.
Garlic powder	1½ tsp.
Onion powder	1½ tsp.
Brown sugar	9 oz.

Method

Combine all ingredients and keep in a closed container until ready to use. This cure is excellent for smoked fish such as trout, bluefish, and salmon.

BRINE

Brine is a combination of salt, nitrites, sugar, spices, and water, which maintains a specified degree of salinity. Brines can be reused up to four times, providing the salinity is maintained. Meats can be covered with brine and marinated according to a recipe. Or a brine pump can be used to inject the brine liquid into the muscle at various points. This method cures meats faster than the steeping method.

BRINE FOR POULTRY

Yield: 1 gal.

Ingredients

Water	1 gal.
Coarse salt	½ lb.
Curing salt	½ oz.
Madeira	½ cup
Honey	1 cup

Method

Combine all ingredients and bring to a boil. Cool before using.

BRINE FOR PORK LOINS, BUTTS, AND HAMS

Yield: 3½ gal.

Ingredients

Water	3 gal.
Coarse salt	2¼ lb.
Curing salt	10 oz.
Sugar	10 oz.

Method

Combine all ingredients. This brine can be used for steeping or pumping.

SOFT BRINE FOR MEAT, POULTRY, AND FISH

Yield: 2 gal.

Ingredients

Water	2 gal.
Salt	1½ lb.
Curing salt	1 oz.
Sugar	1 cup
Herb bag of bay leaf, thyme, peppercorns, juniper berries, basil, ginger, marjoram, and sage	4 T

Method

Combine all ingredients. Boil for 3 minutes, stirring frequently to dissolve salt and sugar. Cool, remove herb bag, and chill before using.

FALLOW DEER HAM

Yield: 1 ham

Ingredients

Leg of fallow deer	3½ lb.

Brine

Water	3 qt.
Framboise	3 oz.
Juniper berries	1½ T
Fresh green peppercorns or black pepper	1½ tsp.
Coriander, whole	1 tsp.
Salt	9 oz.
Curing salt	½ oz.
Garlic	2 cloves
Bay leaf	1
Sugar	to dust

Method

Bone the leg of fallow deer, trim, and remove the sinews. Cut meat into two pieces and tie with string. Prepare the brine by combining all the brine ingredients, and submerge the fallow deer in it. Make sure the meat is completely covered. Top with a wooden board and refrigerate for 10 days.

Remove the meat from the brine, dry it, and dust with some dextrose sugar. Hang in cooler for 24 hours to dry. Smoke in cold smoke for 6 hours and chill well. Hang in a cool dry room for 2 months or roast in a 200°F oven to a 150°F internal temperature. Slice thin and serve with mushroom salad or wedges of melon sprinkled with coarsely ground black pepper.

PICKLED OR SMOKED DUCK, TURKEY, OR CHICKEN

Yield: 2 ducks or chickens, 1 turkey breast

Ingredients

Ducks or chickens, whole, or	2
Turkey breast	1
Poultry Brine (see recipe p. 139)	

Method

f desired, poultry can be boned, rolled, and
ied. Submerge poultry in brine for 2 to 3
lays in refrigerator. Remove and rinse well.

For pickling, prepare a court bouillon
water, carrots, celery, onions, peppercorns, parsley, bay leaf). Truss or tie the
poultry and simmer for 1 to 1½ hours, until
it reaches an internal temperature of 160°F.
Serve hot or cold.

For smoking. Use mock smoke method
on p. 154. Use 3 to 4 cups hickory sawdust.
Smoke roast for 35 to 45 minutes. Internal
temperature should be 160°F. Chill and
serve with Waldorf or tomato salad.

12

Essential Ingredients

Meat, poultry, game, fish, and shellfish are basic ingredients of the principal dishes prepared in the garde manger. The reputation of the garde manger department depends on proper selection and handling of these basic items. Many useful books present detailed information about the selection and preparation of these ingredients.

This chapter only briefly summarizes areas of importance in garde manger work. Techniques that assure proper preparation of these important ingredients are also illustrated and explained in this chapter.

MEAT

An average foodservice operation spends 25 percent of its food dollar on meat. This investment certainly makes meat an item of importance. Preparation of all meat items should be planned for maximum efficiency; this is where chefs can use their talents to create excellent dishes not only from expensive prime cuts but also from cheaper cuts. Chefs in the garde manger (or cold kitchen) department use their skills to transform these inexpensive cuts of meat into the full-flavored, attractive food items that are most appealing to the general public.

Beef

The quality of beef varies considerably and is revealed in the marbling, smoothness, and fineness of the grain of the meat, as well as by the color of the bones, which should be white. The finer the muscle fibers, the more tender the meat will be.

The prime beef cuts most suitable for buffet and à la carte presentation are tenderloin, shell strip, butt, strip loin, and rib. Beef cuts of lesser quality can also be used but are usually most satisfactory when cooked slowly and combined with sauces, marinated, or used in salads. (See chapter 205 for meat salads.)

Veal

Veal is the flesh of specially fed calves approximately sixteen weeks old. Veal has less fat and more moisture than beef and will dry out if cooked too long or at too high a temperature. Firm flesh is important; whereas white flesh is often touted as being superior, a pink tinge is common and perfectly acceptable.

Quality veal cuts, such as the saddle, rack, loin, and leg, are usually used in garde manger to make cold roasts and medallions. In forcemeats for pâtés and terrines, lower-quality cuts, such as the shank and breast, are used. Calves' feet and veal bones are essential to aspic and stocks. Calves' liver and spleen are excellent for mousses, pâtés, and terrines.

Pork

Pork is usually tender, as hogs are bred solely for their meat and are marketed at an early age. The best cuts of pork have a coating of fat, and the meat is white to pink.

Many different methods of cookery are used in the preparation of pork in the garde manger department, and many lesser-quality cuts are used. Fresh pork fat has many uses, especially in pâtés, galantines, and forcemeats. Pork caul is used in special recipes. The liver goes into pâtés and forcemeats. The shoulder, fresh ham, or loin can be smoked, cured, roasted, or boiled.

Smoked hams are specialties in many countries and in individual regions of the same country. A great variety of sausages is derived from pork, and there are countless other pork recipes, such as rillettes (see Chapter 20), headcheese, pâté de campagne, and blood sausage.

Game

The word game refers to many different types of animals, including venison, fallow deer, elk, bear, buffalo, pheasant, quail, partridge, and geese. These are all excellent food items for à la carte, hot or cold service, or on buffets.

Wild venison has not been as popular as it should be. For years we did not have enough quality venison to satisfy everybody, and many times elk or reindeer was substituted. As people have discovered the nutritional values of venison and chefs have become more interested in cooking game, farmers have developed ways of raising venison without a gamey taste. This animal, known as fallow deer, has very little fat or cholesterol, is moist, and has a fresh,

Saddle of Fallow Deer, farm-raised.

Loin and fillet removed from fallow deer carcass.

pleasing odor. Parts generally used in the cold kitchen are the leg, saddle, fillets, rack, tongue, and liver.

POULTRY

From the culinary standpoint, poultry is divided into two classifications: domestic birds (chicken, duck, turkey, goose, and

Saddle of Fallow Deer Stuffed with Figs, on Liver Mousse, Surrounded by Tartelets with Marinated Corn and Mushrooms.

Fallow Deer Combination. From left to right: Barquettes of Spinach on Carrots; Loin of Deer in Herbed Forcemeat Coating; Terrine of Wild Mushrooms; Field Corn Salad and Okra; Sliced Pâté Champagne; Tomato Pastry Shell with Kumquat Marinade.

Cornish hen) and game birds (pheasant, grouse, partridge, woodcock, mallard duck, wild goose, and wild turkey).

Domestic birds are sold fresh or frozen throughout the year. They are usually plucked and drawn; some fresh birds are sold New York–dressed, which means they are not eviscerated, and some are labeled "range-fed," which means the animals are not force-fed or given drugs and other additives in their diets. Frozen poultry is always sold plucked and eviscerated. The giblets (neck, liver, heart, and gizzard) are wrapped separately. Chickens are also cut into breast, legs, or wings, and these parts are sold separately.

The flesh of domestic birds should be firm but pliable, with a fine texture. There should not be too much fat, especially in the cavity area, and there should be no cuts or blood patches. The color of the skin does not indicate quality, as it depends on breed and feed.

Wild game birds are available mostly during the fall hunting season which extends through part of winter. Domestically raised game birds are available year-round, fresh or frozen. Although domestic fowl does not have the distinct flavor of wild, it is a very good substitute.

Freshly shot game birds should be aged or, as it is usually described, hung for a period of time to ensure tenderness. If water birds such as mallard ducks are used, only young birds should be used, as old birds have a strong, fishy odor.

Trussing Poultry, Method 1.

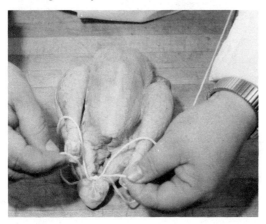

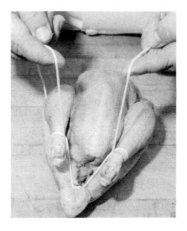

1. Positioning bird on its back, run butcher's twine twice around tail, leaving enough twine to complete trussing.

2. Wind twine around lower ends of thigh bones and pull tight against side of bird.

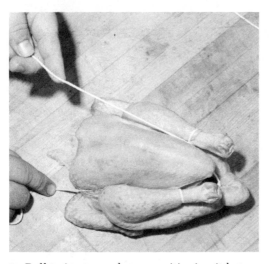

3. Pull twine toward you, positioning it between thighs and back of bird.

4. Tighten twine and wind it around bird's nec pull it tight and knot it.

Preparation of Poultry

Today, with modern facilities and processing systems, poultry preparation has been considerably simplified. In some cases, no further preparation of raw poultry is required after it arrives in the kitchen. Both fresh and frozen poultry can be obtained "oven ready" or cut into portions.

Before roasting, sautéing, or boiling, do mestic or game birds should be thoroughly washed or rinsed, dried, and then tied. Do mestic birds are often rubbed inside and outside with lemon juice so the meat be comes whiter and fresher in flavor.

Some lean birds, such as pheasant, are

Trussing Poultry, Method 2.

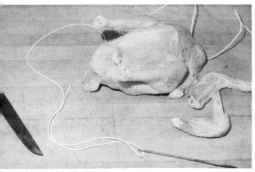

Remove wings and position bird on its back. Have trussing needle threaded with butcher's twine at hand.

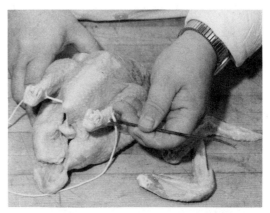

2. Bring thighs close to body and insert needle through both thighs to hold in place.

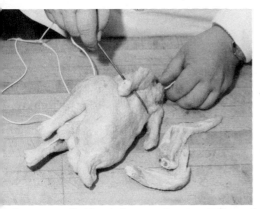

3. Insert needle through one wing, push through neck skin, which has been folded back, and then through other wing.

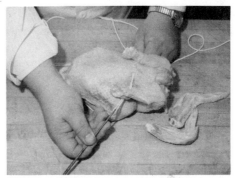

4. Pull needle all the way through, then pull twine tight to hold wings in position.

5. Tie twine tightly to keep bird neatly trussed.

barded with thin slices of bacon or pig caul. Another method of preparation requires trussing the bird, especially for poultry specialties produced in the garde manger or kitchen. Poultry requires boning and cutting if it is to be used to make pâtés or galantines. Frozen birds should be thawed be-

fore cooking, preferably in the refrigerator.

How to Cook Poultry

Poultry can be prepared in various ways. It can be roasted, grilled, sautéed, or boiled and served cold, decorated or coated with

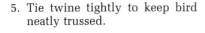

Carving a Roast Chicken for Display.

After whole roast chicken has been cut into sixteen portions to meet service needs, pieces can
be neatly arranged for display and easy service,
as shown here. A carrot flower with green pepper leaves make an attractive attention-getting
display.

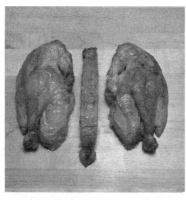

Depending on the type of service or portion desired, there are several ways to carve a roasted
chicken. Above is shown a chicken split in half,
with backbone removed, ready for luncheon or
dinner service.

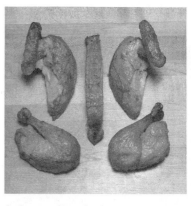

After halving the chicken and removing th
backbone, the breastbone is removed and th
chicken is portioned as shown above, good f
picnic or lunch basket.

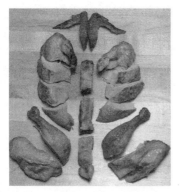

For party service, cut the breast and legs into
twelve pieces and cut the backbone and serve
with chicken wings.

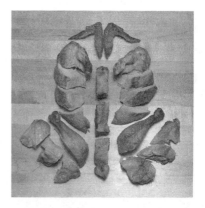

For maximum usage, cut into sixteen pieces, in
cluding the meaty backbone and chicken wing:

To carve a chicken for a cold buffet, slice breast into even slices. Stuff the cavity with chicken mousse or a vegetable salad and place breast slices back on the chicken in sequence as shown. Coat with clear aspic.

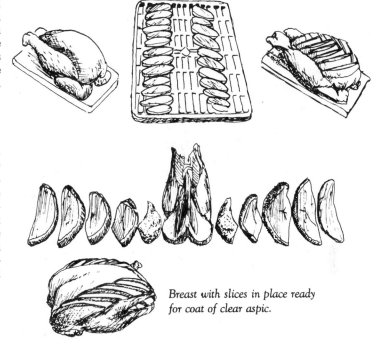

To carve a capon for a cold buffet, remove breast and fill cavity with a mousse of liver or a vegetable salad. Slice breast into thin slices; place slices in sequence on a tray so they can be replaced in order on the chicken. Put slices of capon back into the breast cavity, starting at the top of the capon and overlapping the slices.

Breast with slices in place ready for coat of clear aspic.

aspic or chaud-froid. It can also be made into forcemeats for use in pâtés, galantines, or timbales. Birds that are roasted, grilled, or sautéed must be young and of good quality. Older birds are usually boiled or used in forcemeats, although in today's kitchen, forcemeats are generally made with young, tender birds.

Domestic or game birds, whole or in pieces, are always decorative when coated with aspic. The aspic (see pp. 40–41) should be flavored with care, then brushed over the birds and decorated with truffles or other garnishes.

Jellied poultry molds (headcheese) are usually made from boiled chicken. This type of preparation is a good way to use leftovers, which can be enhanced with the use of tomatoes, cucumbers, or hard-cooked eggs.

Carving Poultry

The method of cutting or carving a bird de-

pends on its size and how it is to be served. Cut small birds in half or divide them into four parts. Large birds can be carved in various ways, depending on whether the slices are to be portioned on a dish or returned to the carcass.

When serving large birds with slices taken from breasts and rearranged on the carcass, it is advisable to cut off the under part of the carcass so that the bird will be flat on the dish, making the presentation neater and more decorative. Carving is usually done in the kitchen but can also be done on the buffet. When carving is to be done on the buffet, large birds are required.

FISH AND SHELLFISH

Many kinds of fish can be used in garde manger work. The fish may be purchased whole or cut into steaks or fillets. After it is cleaned, the fish is usually poached, unless the final preparation requires some other style of cooking. Fish for garde manger use can also be purchased frozen (in cans), marinated, or smoked.

How can you tell that fish is fresh?
When buying fresh fish, be sure to check for these important points:

1. Skin should be bright in color
2. Scales should adhere tightly
3. Eyes should be bright and transparent
4. Gills should be light in color
5. Flesh should be firm and stiff

Buying, Handling, and Storing Seafood

The following is an excerpt from *The Complete Cookbook of American Fish and Shellfish,* by John Nicolas, published by Van Nostrand Reinhold.

Handling and Storing Fish and Shellfish

Seafoods spoil more rapidly than any other food product and should be handled and stored with the utmost care. Freshly caught fish and shellfish that is brought to the pan quickly is in a class by itself. The flavor of seafood diminishes if processing, storing, or cooking are mishandled.

Fresh fish should be refrigerated on ice at 35 to 40°F (1.5 to 4.5°C) as soon as they are received. Seal the fish if necessary before placing on ice. Keep shellfish, especially clams and oysters, cold, but do not pack on ice. Use a separate refrigerator, if available, or at least a section of the refrigerator, avoiding contact with other foods. Fish should not be exposed to air unnecessarily as oxidation may alter the flavor. Fillets of fish lose their flavor more rapidly than whole fish and should be processed without delay. Purchase whole fresh fish if available. Eviscerate as soon as possible.

The source of supply is an important factor when purchasing fish and shellfish. It is therefore necessary to select a reliable fish dealer. There is no bargain in buying stale fish at any cost.

Different environmental conditions can cause a particular fish to have different flavors. Apart from the problems caused by water pollution, several species of fish found in northern waters are more palatable than the same species caught in southern waters. A bass or perch caught in muddy warm water is inferior to the same species caught in cold clear water. The same applies to hatchery trout, which seldom have the delicate flavor of wild brook trout.

Refrigerated smoked fish should not be placed in contact with ice. Smoked fish, especially trout, salmon, finnan haddie, and herring, should always be well sealed with wax paper and foil to contain their penetrating odors.

Thawing Fish Products

Schedule thawing so that fish or shellfish will be cooked soon after thawing. Thawed seafood should be held no longer than one day before cooking.

Place the package of frozen seafood in the refrigerator to thaw. Allow 3 to 6 hours per pound for thawing a package. If quicker thawing is necessary, place the package under cold running water.

Allow 1 to 2 hours per pound. Do not thaw fish at room temperature or in cold water, as it loses moisture and flavor. Thawed seafood should not be refrozen.

How Quality is Lost

The primary causes of quality breakdown in fish products are oxidation, dehydration, enzymatic action, and bacterial growth. When oxidation occurs, the oil or fat in the fish flesh can cause the fish to become rancid. Do not expose fish products to air unnecessarily, and wrap tightly before freezing. Dehydration is caused by improper packaging. Excessive drying out in frozen fish is known as freezer burn. Enzymatic action in the flesh of fish causes deterioration. Low temperatures slow enzymatic action and preserve the original quality. Bacterial growth increases mainly when the storage temperature is too high and when sanitation in handling fish is poor.

Scaling roundfish.

Boning roundfish.

Skinning roundfish.

Preparation of Roundfish

Scaling

Most fish cooked or served with the skin should be scaled. Scale the fish (using a fish scaler or back of a knife) starting at the tail and moving toward the head. Then remove the back, belly, and breast fins. After scaling, rinse the fish thoroughly.

Boning

To utilize most of the fish, cut off the head with two cuts along the gill bone and remove the head, leaving a V shape, then remove fins and rinse the fish.

To fillet, starting from the back, slide the knife along the backbone carefully, avoiding cutting into the flesh. Remove the bones, which can be used for fish fond.

Skinning

Place the fish fillet skin side down on a cutting board. Make a small cut at the tail end, between the skin and flesh. Take hold of the skin end and slide the knife, wiggling, pressing blade downward, over the skin until the flesh is separated.

Preparation of Flatfish

Skinning

Lay the fish dark side up on a cutting board. Cut through the skin across the base of the tail. Use a knife to pry a flap of skin away

Skinning flatfish

from the meat. Get a hold of the flap with one hand, hold down the tail with the other hand, and pull skin toward and then over the head. Turn the fish over and pull the skin toward and off the tail. To get a better grip, dip fingers into salt.

Boning

To fillet, cut the fish, starting near the head, along its center, following the seam, then follow the bone structure and remove fillets.

Sautéing and Poaching

To sauté fish fillets, start sautéing with bone side of the fillet down first, then turn (this is done because of shrinkage of the fillet). To poach, start with the bone side of

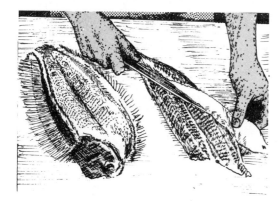

Boning flatfish.

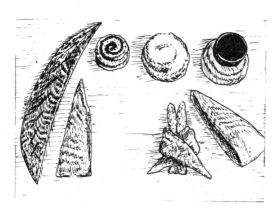

Sautéing and poaching techniques.

the fillet down. If the fish is stuffed, the bone side should be the outside, for better color. The drawing (lower left) shows several ways flatfish may be prepared for poaching or sautéing: lightly pounded and folded; fillet half folded over; folded over asparagus tips; fillet half filled with fish forcemeat and other half folded over; plain rolled; spread with farce and rolled; and molded around a greased timbale (to be filled after poaching).

To portion large flatfish first remove the fins and the head and belly, then remove the tail. Then, following the seam, slide the knife along the bone structure and remove fillets. Cut into portions or poach whole. To poach flatfish, use the poaching instructions for salmon (p. 153).

Fish for Use in the Cold Kitchen

Trout (rainbow or Golden). Available all year. Good for poaching, smoking.

Pike (walleye, yellow perch). Available all year. Good for forcemeats.

Atlantic cod. Available all year. Good for forcemeats.

Sole or Flounder (lemon, yellowtail, dabs, plaice). Available all year. Good for poaching, forcemeats.

Salmon (coho, sockeye, Atlantic, Norwegian, Scottish imports). Available all year. Good for pickling, smoking, poaching, forcemeats.

Monkfish. Available all year. Good for medallion, garnish, forcemeats.

Herring. Available all year. Good smoked, pickled, or marinated.

Halibut. Available all year. Good for forcemeat and medallions; good poached. Small halibut are called chicken halibut.

Working with Salmon

To poach for à la carte buffets:

1. Fillet salmon, remove soft bones, trim belly.

Stuffed Halibut with Lobster Medallions.

2. Sprinkle lightly with salt and brush with oil. Wrap whole fillet in plastic wrap. Pierce with needle.
3. Place in a poaching pan.
4. Cover with hot (160°F) court bouillon enforced with gelatin (3 ounces per gallon).
5. Poach at 140 to 150°F (10 to 12 minutes per inch of thickness).
6. Chill in court bouillon.
7. Remove all impurities from the fillet and cut into desired slices or portions.

GRAVLAX OR MARINATED SALMON

Yield: 4 to 5 lb.

Ingredients

Salmon	10 to 12 lb.
Lemons	juice of 2
Oil	¾ oz.
Brandy	¾ oz.
Sugar	8 oz.
Fine salt	7 oz.
White peppercorns, crushed	7 oz.
Fresh dill, chopped	2 bunches

Method

Fillet salmon; remove soft bones. Do not remove skin. Brush fish with mixture of lemon juice, oil, and brandy.

Mix sugar, salt, peppercorns, and dill, and pack around salmon fillets. Roll in plastic wrap. Set into stainless steel or plastic tray, skin side up. Weight down and marinate for 4 to 5 days in the refrigerator. Remove from marinade, scrape off peppercorns, and slice thin to serve.

Preparation of Cold Smoked Salmon

1. Fillet whole fish
2. Cure (dry salt)
3. Rinse (optional)
4. Dry in refrigerator
5. Cold smoke

CURED SMOKED SALMON

Yield: 5 lb.

Ingredients

Salmon fillets	6 lb.
Kosher salt	12 oz.
Sugar	¾ oz.
White peppercorns, crushed	¾ oz.
Curing salt (optional)	¾ oz.
Dill twigs	1 cup

(continued)

Cured Smoked Salmon (continued)

Lemon	6 slices
Orange	6 slices
White wine	1 qt.
Milk	1 qt.

Method

Lay salmon fillets in a 2-inch hotel pan skin side down.

Combine salt, sugar, pepper, and curing salt and distribute over salmon flesh (use more salts on the thicker part of the fillet), scatter dill, lemon, and orange over top. Cover and refrigerate for 12 hours.

Add wine to pan and turn fillets over so that the skin is up. Cover and refrigerate for 10 hours.

Pour off liquid from pan and replace with milk. Cover and refrigerate for 8 hours (minimum). As soon as possible the next morning, remove from milk (do not rinse), place skin side down on a rack, and dry in refrigerator.

Cold smoke for 8 hours at 85°F. To give a polish to the fish, bring temperature to 100°F for 15 minutes. (This will bring some of the oil to the surface.)

CURING TIME FOR SMOKED FISH

Thickness of Boned Fillet	Fat Fish	Lean Fish
¾ inch	8 hours	4 hours
1 inch	9 hours	5 hours
1½ inch	12 hours	7 hours
2 inches	14 hours	10 hours
2½ inches	20 hours	14 hours
3 inches	22 hours	16 hours

Preparation for Hot Mock Smoking

Trout, bluefish, mackerel, shrimp, scallops, and sturgeon can all be smoked. The main reason for smoking fish is to increase its keeping qualities. However, in the process, the fish acquires aromatic flavor and will enhance your menu. Smoked fish can b prepared daily or on short notice.

The equipment you need includes:

- Two full-size 4½-inch-deep alumi num hotel pans nested within eacl other
- One full-size 4½-inch-deep aluminun hotel pan to be used as cover or
- One large, heavy-duty square hea with lid
- Wire rack or glazing rack
- Four metal risers (use tomato past cans)
- Sawdust (hickory, apple, cherry, o pine)
- Masking tape

Sprinkle 2 cups of sawdust or as much as i needed over entire bottom of pan. Place ris ers in pan and top with wire rack. Plac oiled fish carefully on rack. Cover with 4½-inch-deep hotel pan. Seal edges witl masking tape.

Place over high heat until smoke be comes visible. Turn heat to medium anc smoke/roast according to instructions. Re move pan from fire. Rest unopened for 5 tc 10 minutes in an airy space. Uncover, re move fish and chill.

Specific procedures for different types o seafood follow.

Smoked Trout: Use 12–16 oz. trout (bon in). Place into a soft brine (see p. 144) for 2½ hours. Remove and dry. Oil lightly and plac on rack in an aluminum hotel pan. Seal the pan with masking tape when the smok becomes visible. Smoke for 20 to 25 minutes Follow smoking method described above.

Bluefish: Follow basic procedure for trout. Soak in soft brine for 1½ hours. Smoke for 15 to 20 minutes.

Tuna: Cut into 12-ounce pieces. Soak in soft brine for 1½ to 2 hours. Dry. Oi lightly. Place on rack. Smoke for 10 to 15 minutes. Follow smoking method de scribed above.

Boning Smoked Trout.

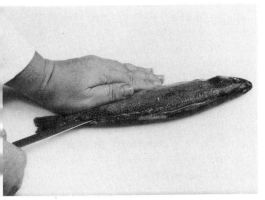

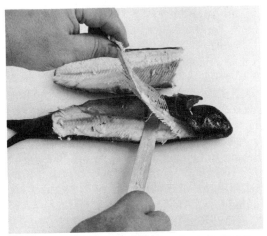

1. Smoked trout should be boned before service. To begin, slice along the backbone and remove fillet.

2. Remove bones by starting at the tail. Holding the bottom fillet in place with the knife, pull the skeleton out carefully with your hand.

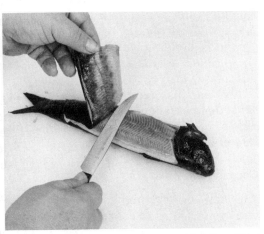

3. Return fillet to top of trout. Holding fillet lightly with knife, pull skin off by hand.

4. For service, remove eyes and replace with Spanish olive. Decorate with marinated zucchini, mushroom, and lemon, or creamed horseradish.

Shrimp, Scallops: Soak for 20 to 30 minutes in soft brine. Smoke for 8 to 12 minutes.

Shellfish

What kinds of shellfish are there?

Shellfish have long been regarded as a luxury, but this attitude is now rapidly disappearing. Some kinds of shellfish can certainly be economical when the supply is plentiful. Shellfish can be obtained fresh, frozen, potted, and canned. The term shellfish includes lobsters, shrimp, crabs, Maryland crabs, crayfish, oysters, clams, mussels, and snails.

Clams: There are several species of clams. Soft clams are found mainly north of Cape Cod. Hard clams are suitable for eating on the half-shell; they are small quahogs called cherrystones. Most clams are marketed alive in the shell, although they are also available canned. The peak season is from June to September. However, fresh clams can be bought all year long.

Crabs: There are several varieties of crabs. The most common are blue crabs, Dungeness crabs, king crabs, and rock crabs. Crabs can be bought alive or ready-cooked. Live crabs are grayish brown, but on boiling they turn a brownish red. They should be well filled, heavy, firm, and should not gurgle when gently shaken. The tails of live or cooked crabs should be firmly closed under the body. Crabs are canned in Alaska and Maryland and in Norway, Russia, and Japan.

Crayfish: A freshwater crustacean, the freshwater crayfish has firm flesh, and it is subtly and delicately flavored. In this country, crayfish are rare in the East but are easily obtainable in the West and Midwest.

Lobsters: Two types of lobster are commonly used: one found in European waters, another in most American waters. Most of the lobsters found on the eastern coast of North America are caught in New England. According to the U.S. Fish and Wildlife Department, a five-year-old lobster measures about 10½ inches and has molted twenty-five times. Lobster is marketed live, boiled, or canned. Almost all the lobster available in the United States is sold live.

Mussels: These edible mollusks are found in oceans all over the world, but they are especially plentiful in cold regions. The species used most often is called the common mussel and are sold as label blue or New Zealand green mussels. It has a long shell with a very slight roughness along the back. Mussels are very often used for seafood salads or cold canapés.

Oysters: Oysters are bivalve mollusks, often eaten raw. Oysters on the Atlantic Coast are in season from September until May and are sold fresh. Oysters coming from certain beds have come to be esteemed as most desirable and have ac-

quired trade names such as Blue Point, Lynnhaven, Belon, and European. Pacific Coast oysters are sold year-round. If oysters are to be used for hot appetizers, buy them in gallons, frozen.

Shrimp: Shrimp vary from the large size found off the Gulf of Mexico that average one dozen to a pound, to the tiny shrimp, averaging forty to a pound. Titi shrimp are caught in Alaska and northern New England. These shrimp are less popular, but have better flavor and are excellent for salads or canapés.

Storage and Handling of Shellfish

Shellfish should be kept for as short a time as possible and should always be stored in a cool place. If it is not fresh when eaten, shellfish can cause serious food poisoning. Fresh shellfish should be alive when purchased. Whether alive or canned, shellfish should have a fresh smell and a clean appearance.

Live shellfish must be rinsed with cold water before using. The shells of clams or oysters should be brushed and rinsed before opening.

Cooking Shellfish

All shellfish, with the exception of clams and oysters, must be cooked. When they are to be used for cold dishes, lobster, crabs, or crayfish should be boiled in salted water with dill and a mirepoix of vegetables. Do not overcook, as they will become tough and lose flavor. Shellfish should be allowed to cool in the liquid they were cooked in.

Cooked lobsters and crabs must always be opened before serving. Mussels, however, should be cooked unopened either in a court bouillon or in their own juices. If they are to be used for cold salads, mussels should be allowed to cool in their own juice.

13

Food Decoration

Food decoration is the art of shaping and arranging raw or cooked food in pleasing designs. Decorations should preferably be made of foodstuffs that combine the patterns, color, and texture of design elements in relation to the kind and size of food to be decorated. Only when a color cannot be found in natural food products is it permissible within reason to resort to artificial food coloring. There is one exception: *blue* is not considered conducive to tantalizing appetites and therefore is not recommended.

Patterns and designs often serve to identify the type of dish that may seem "buried" under a thick coating of chaud-froid sauce. For example, a piece of fish fillet, after being coated, may be decorated with an outline design of the fish from which the fillet was cut. Or the true nature of the coated piece may be indicated by a simple fish figure made of assorted ingredients and put in place with various decorating tools.

When the shape of the food to be decorated is readily recognizable to viewers, as in the case of a whole ham, then the pattern or design used might be geometrical, or the "artist" might choose a subject such as an animal or human figure.

When a theme has been set for an occasion, the food may be decorated with a design appropriate to the theme. If a ham were intended to be displayed on a Dutch or international buffet table, for example, the top of a whole ham might be decorated with a pair of wooden shoes carved from turnips.

How many ways are there to decorate food?

Although there are countless ways to decorate food and food platters, the following two major approaches should be understood before considering the types of materials available to the cook or chef in the garde manger, who is in charge of preparing, decorating, arranging, and displaying cold dishes. These are the classical approach and the commercial approach.

The Classical Approach: Marie-Antoine Carême, called Antonin Carême (1784–1833), was responsible for what is known today as classical cuisine and its application to food decoration. Too poor to finance his education toward a career in architecture, he instead chose to apply architectural principles to food decoration. In his day, food decoration and the general appearance of food platters on buffet tables often exhibited atrocious taste, with heavy use of nonedible materials detracting from the artistry in the *pièces-montées*.

Fish Terrine, Salmon Galantine, Shrimp Salad, and Marinated Cucumber, Quail Egg, and Tomato, arranged for maximum eye appeal.

Different textures of food tempt the appetite. Here, a Headcheese, Veal Galantine, and Smoked Roast Loin of Pork are arranged with a garnish of Pickled Carrot Container Filled with a Cream Cheese (or Horseradish) Rose, Marinated Mushrooms, and a Radish Mushroom.

Carême felt that the decoration of food should be appropriate to the recipe involved and that design elements should be assembled with simplicity and taste. Later, Master Chef Auguste Escoffier (1847–1935) supported Carême's approach by his emphasis on exclusive use of edibles in food decoration. This approach had been abandoned for a while because of a shortage of qualified professionals. However, because of the training provided today in culinary schools and American Culinary Federation–sponsored apprenticeships, today's diners can again enjoy elaborately prepared food at special functions.

The Commercial Approach: There continues to be a great challenge to today's chefs to find feasible methods to decorate food, food platters, and entire buffet tables, and to train others to follow in their steps. The methods stem from the past but must be economically feasible to meet today's marketing conditions.

The methods described and pictured in this book meet modern economic requirements, although on occasion they will be reminiscent of the methods used by Carême and Escoffier. The return to the methods of earlier days occurs only in those situations where old-time results cannot be achieved by new technological means.

What are the edible ingredients used in food decoration?

There are twelve basic ingredients that can be used efficiently and economically in food decoration:

Fresh raw vegetables
Fresh cooked vegetables
Canned or marinated vegetables
Fresh raw fruits
Canned fruits
Candied fruits
Fresh herbs
Aspic sheets
Hard-cooked eggs
Fish roe
Baked goods
Dairy products

How are fresh raw vegetables used in food decoration?

The following are the vegetables chiefly used in food or food platter decoration; however, others not listed here can also be used at the garde manger's discretion, based on experience and imagination:

Carrots
Radishes

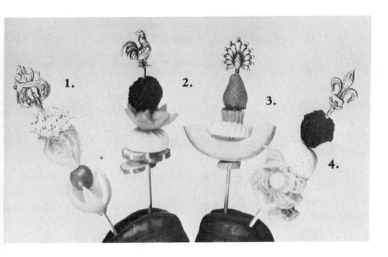

Cucumbers

Leeks

Tomatoes

Red cabbage

Turnips

Celery

Potatoes

These vegetables can be used in three basic ways:

1. Slicing
2. Carving, for instance, into "flowers"
3. Arranging in "bouquet"

Fresh vegetables should always be thoroughly washed.

Decoration Hatelets.

To beautify various foods we suggest using hatelets (decorative silver skewers). These silver skewers can also be used to identify food products like fish, lobster, and chicken.

1. Mum Radish, Boston Lettuce (small heart), Cherry Tomato, Lemon Crown.
2. Mock Truffle, Star Tomato, Fluted Mushroom, Zucchini Slices.
3. Strawberry, Ham Dice or Round Disk, Apple Slice, Melon Wedge, Ham Slices.
4. Mock Truffle, Star Mushroom, Carrot Tiger Lily, Boston Lettuce Leaves.

Vegetable Flowers. From left to right: Apple Bird; Turnip Rose; Carrot Tiger Lily; Leek Daisy.

Slicing. Fresh raw vegetables to be sliced should be blanched and marinated first. Blanching ensures adherence of the slices to other foodstuffs, especially aspic or other coatings, such as chaud-froid sauces. The vegetables can either be peeled or left unpeeled before slicing, depending on the effect desired.

Carving. Fresh vegetables to be used for carving do not need to be blanched or marinated. Beginners who want to learn how to carve vegetables can start developing their skills by carving flowers, since they are relatively simple and do not require much time to create.

Depending on the artistic talent of the preparer, the time available, and the way the selected vegetables hold up through the final stages of carving, designs of all kinds can be fashioned. Among the possibilities are flowers, shoes, chains, fishnets, and other intricate designs.

Bouquet Arrangement. Fresh raw vegetables such as asparagus, string beans, or any other vegetables that can be cut in julienne are usually blanched and marinated, then trimmed (each piece cut to an exact size), and assembled in bunches or bundles. Those that are "loose" (peas, sliced carrots, or other diced vegetables) can be assembled in bunches or bundles by "cradling" them in pastry shells, artichoke bottoms, or other carved foodstuffs. The carving can be as simple or as elaborate as you wish.

Fresh cooked, canned, or marinated vegetables can be used in the same manner as fresh raw vegetables in food decoration.

How are vegetable flowers made?

Vegetable flowers, like those pictured on pages 161 to 167, are colorful and easily made. They can be held for three to four days in a refrigerator when covered with cold water or wrapped first with a moist cloth and then with plastic wrap.

As an example, turnip daisies can be made following these steps:

1. Peel turnip and cut into 1/3-inch-thick slices.
2. Using star cookie cutters in graduated sizes, cut stars from turnips. Cut two or three stars for each flower.
3. Use parisian scoop to form carrot center for daisy.
4. Take an 8- to 10-inch Chinese skewer and put through largest star and one or two smaller stars. Add carrot center last.
5. Push a green scallion stem over skewer.
6. Cut bottom off raw Idaho potato so it stands flat. Push skewer topped with daisy flower into potato.
7. Use skewers of varying lengths for bouquet.
8. Cut leaves of varying sizes from green leek stems. Put toothpick through stem of leek leaf, then push leaf into potato. Use as many leaves as are needed to accompany flowers.

How is fruit used in food decoration?

Fresh raw fruit can be used in exactly the same way as fresh raw vegetables, except that pieces need not be blanched or marinated. However, they should be thoroughly washed, as the fruit is always used unpeeled, and sometimes the peel alone is used.

Large pieces of fresh raw fruit can be carved and used as containers from which other foodstuffs are served. For example, a watermelon can be carved in the shape of a baby carriage and filled with fruit salad. Or a watermelon might be carved into a fish from which shrimp cocktail would be served.

Canned and candied fruits are mostly used *en bordure*, that is, along the edge of a platter or a container made by carving out fresh raw fruits or vegetables.

Carrot Flowers.

Carrot flowers lend a colorful note as part of a floral centerpiece or as an accent on a buffet platter. To make flowers, first peel carrot, then slice lengthwise. Flower will require five thin pieces, 3 to 5 inches long.

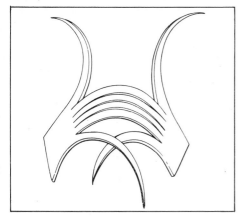

1. Cut lines through carrot slices and shape as shown in diagram.

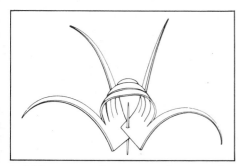

2. Fold first carrot slice over as shown in diagram and insert toothpick to hold it together.

3. Fold next carrot slice and place on same toothpick. Repeat with next two slices. Roll fifth slice and stick on top of carrots.

4. As final step, place a round slice of carrot (ball) into the center of flower to hold it all in place. Place carrot flower into cold water until sides curl.

5. Carrot flower and fish sculpted from butter highlight tray of whole smoked trout decorated with chaud-froid circles.

Apple Bird.

The apple bird, poised for flight on a pineapple perch, provides a conversation-making accent for any food presentation.

1. To make the apple bird, slice off one-third of an apple to be used later for the neck and head. Removing this much of the apple also provides a flat base for the bird to rest on. Next cut out small wedge from apple and start cutting slices around the wedge. Taco-shaped slices will become larger as more slices are cut.
2. Leaving a ridge of apple in place to provide a foundation for the wings and tail, continue to cut taco-shaped slices from either side of the two rims.
3. When enough slices have been cut away to assemble for the wings and tail, pieces can be laid out in the pattern shown.
4. Fit slices together, overlapping them slightly to form wings and tail.
5. Slice off one-third of the apple, if possible on the less colored side. Cut round apple disk in half, then into the bird's head.

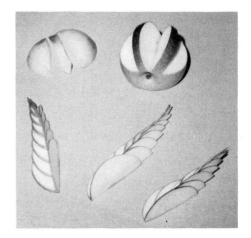

Apple Bird Head.

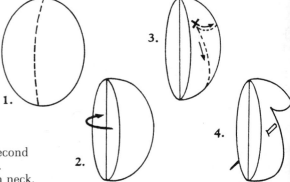

1. Cut saved one-third of apple in half.
2. Fold together.
3. Cut, starting on x, following arrow. Make second cut starting on x and following other arrow.
4. Push toothpick at a 45-degree angle through neck.

Carving Raw Mushrooms.

Leek Daisies.

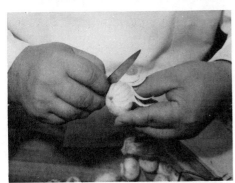

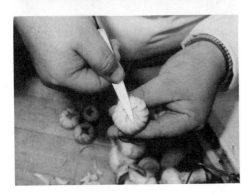

Raw mushrooms to be carved must be firm.
1. Holding the mushroom as shown, insert paring knife and slice off small wedge.
2. Slice from top to bottom.
3. When small wedges have been cut off all around the mushroom, press the tip of the knife into the top of the mushroom to make star.
1. To make flower, cut root off leek. Next cut 2- to 3-inch piece from the white part of the leek. Push toothpick about ½ inch into root end.

2. Holding the leek white by toothpick and root, slice thin strips (⅛ inch) to the center of the leek. Continue cutting similar strips all around the leek.
3. Push a thin carrot circle down over top of toothpick in center of leek. Then press leek lightly against surface of cutting board so strips spread out to create flower. Hold in cold water.

1. For a simple, easy decoration peel the skin from a firm but ripe tomato in one continuous slice.

2. Place the sliced tomato skin on a cutting board or table and roll into a rose shape. Arrange three tomato roses in a cluster and decorate with leaves cut from green peppers and spears cut from leeks.

   Note: These roses can also be cut from apples, oranges, grapefruits, and pears.

Fanned Pickles.

Pickles can make excellent buffet garnishes. The only tool needed is a paring knife.
1. Cut pickle in half lengthwise.
2. Cut pickle half into spears.
3. Remove pickle ends and cut into long slices.
4. Fan pickle ends.
5. Fan pickle halves.
6. Press fanned pickle halves with paring knife lightly to form a reef.

Turnip Roses.

1. To arrange a turnip rose, slice an unpeeled, firm, room-temperature turnip into paper-thin slices. (Do not store the slices in water.) Roll one slice into a tight roll.
2. Surround the rolled center slice with other slices. Use an uneven number of turnip slices until the desired flower shape is achieved.
3. Push two toothpicks through opposite sides of the flower to secure the petals. Drop into cold water to stiffen, and display as shown above.

   Note: For color variations use raw red beets or rutabagas. If potatoes are used, deep-fry after shaping them and serve cold or warm.

Hard-cooked Eggs.

Salmon mousse is piped into hard-cooked egg whites, making an attractive color combination. Stuffed eggs are presented on toasted croutons. The star-shaped cherry tomato shells hold balls of salmon mousse topped with black caviar.

Vegetable Flowers.

1. Setup for making vegetable flowers.
2. Put Chinese skewer through vegetable circle, one or two small stars, large star, and carrot center.
3. Put green scallion over skewer.
4. Slice raw potatoes to use as base. Push flower-topped skewers into potato to make a bouquet.

Purple Cabbage Orchids.

1. Core the cabbage and remove the large outer leaves. Cut the leaves into oval shapes from the bottom (stem portion) or the broad part of the leaf. Turn the leaf upside down and trim the stem to a razor-sharp edge. Prepare the white part of a leek or scallion (shown on page 163, Leek Daisies) without the carrot center.

2. Cut a thin carrot disk and push halfway down a toothpick. Stick one of the cabbage petals on top of the carrot disk, followed by the second and third to complete the orchid.

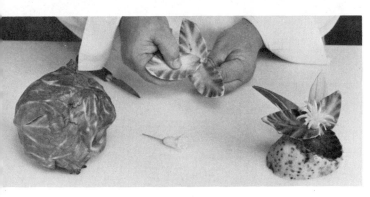

3. To finish the orchid place the prepared leek daisy into its center. Immerse in cold water overnight to stiffen; arrange as needed.
   Note: For color variations use savoy or white cabbage.

How are fresh herbs used in food decoration?

Herbs are generally used to add to the design, the color, or the texture (relief) of a surface to be decorated. Whole leaves are usually used, although sometimes the stems are used too. Fresh herbs work well in the design of trees, flowers, or other floral motifs.

How is aspic used in food decoration?

Although aspic jelly (meat gelatin) is often thought of only as a means of covering or wrapping foodstuffs, in food decoration this material is also used to produce aspic sheets in a wide range of colors.

To make colored sheets of aspic, mix the aspic with natural food coloring (such as yellow from eggs, orange from pimento, green from spinach, black from truffles, red from tomato paste) (see pages 41–43). Pour the colored aspic into a slightly oiled metal or plastic tray in a thin layer and chill until it sets into a solid sheet. When aspic is hard, stamp out decorations, using metal cutters of various shapes and designs.

How are hard-cooked eggs used in food decoration?

Hard-cooked eggs can be used whole, as wedges, sliced, stuffed, or chopped (yolk and/or white). Eggs can be prepared in many ways to serve as decorative additions to platters.

How is fish roe used in food decoration?

Fish roe is used in food decoration primarily for color, but also for texture, and to form designs or patterns of all kinds. Of all the fish roe available, that of salmon (red caviar), sturgeon (black or gray caviar), or lobster (red coral) are usually favored by garde mangers.

14

Cold Sauces—Butter and Cheese Mixtures

The sauce should be the crowning touch for the dish it accompanies. It sometimes seems that there are as many sauces as there are menu items, and a wide variety of sauces is put to good use in the garde manger.

Many of the cold sauces served as accompaniments to garde manger foods are derived from mayonnaise. Chaud-froid sauce (chapter 4) should not be confused with the sauces described in this chapter, since chaud-froid is used as a coating while these sauces add a new complement of flavors to dishes they accompany. They are sometimes presented in separate containers.

MAYONNAISE

Purchasing commercially prepared mayonnaise usually eliminates the need to prepare mayonnaise in the kitchen. However, knowing how to prepare mayonnaise is valuable in many instances.

Mayonnaise is a semisolid emulsion of vegetable oils, eggs (whole or egg yolks only), lemon or vinegar, and salt. It can be prepared by hand or machine.

Eggs and oil must be tempered to room temperature (70°F). Cold ingredients will affect the emulsion process. Cold oil does not easily break into the small fat globules required for emulsion, and the sauce will break.

Mayonnaise is considered a base sauce. Good consistency and neutral flavor give it versatility. It is important that only fresh eggs, vegetable oils, and quality vinegar are used.

To prepare mayonnaise (recipe follows):

1. In the initial preparation step, egg yolks, salt, and some vinegar or lemon juice (optional) are beaten together.
2. Rapid and thorough beating of the eggs and oil in the beginning steps is one of the most important factors in producing the first emulsion.
3. The method of adding the oil is a deciding factor to the stability of the emulsion. Oil must be added slowly in the beginning and in small quantities (drop by drop). Once the emulsion has started, oil may be added more rapidly and in larger volumes, but never exceeding the volume of the emulsion already formed.
4. The vinegar or lemon and water may be added at various intervals during the mixing, alternating with the oil

after a large percentage of the emulsion has been formed. Vinegar/water will thin the emulsion and make it more liquid.

BASIC RECIPE FOR MAYONNAISE

Yield: 1 qt.

Ingredients

Egg yolks	4
Salt	⅓ oz.
White pepper (optional)	to taste
Vinegar or lemon juice	1½ T
Oil	1 qt.
Waters, hot or cold (optional)	2 T

Method

Combine egg yolks, salt, pepper, and a few drops of vinegar or lemon juice (optional) in a noncopper bowl and whisk thoroughly for a few minutes. While beating the eggs, add oil, drop by drop at first, then faster. When mayonnaise begins to thicken, add some vinegar or lemon juice until it is used up.

Note: Auguste Escoffier mentions in his book, *Guide to the Art of Modern Cooking,* that two tablespoons of boiling water can be added to ensure lasting emulsion. Water can also be used in addition to the acid to thin thick mayonnaise.

Broken Mayonnaise

Separate may occur if:

1. Eggs and oil are not tempered to 70°F.
2. Oil is added too fast.
3. Mayonnaise is stored too cold.

To correct:

1. Bring broken mixture to room temperature and beat it bit by bit into one egg yolk. When emulsion occurs, add tempered oil.
2. Beat one egg yolk and gradually add broken mixture.
3. Set broken mayonnaise into a warm water bath and beat until smooth or beat 1 tablespoon of hot water into the broken mayonnaise.

Mayonnaise with Starches

Economic and nutritional considerations may lead us to reduce the amount of either eggs or fat used in mayonnaise. This may be achieved by either stretching or thickening the mayonnaise.

Stretching agents are high-consistency pastes made from oil, flour, starch, and water. Cottage cheese, sour cream, and yogurt are well-known stretchers; however, they may affect the thickness and flavor of the product.

The amount of stretch used depends on individual needs, but as a common rule, we use two-thirds mayonnaise and one-third stretch.

PASTE MADE WITH STARCH

Yield: 1 pt.

Ingredients

Cornstarch	2½ to 3 oz.
Water or chicken stock	16 oz.

Method

Mix cornstarch and cold water. Bring to a boil, constantly stirring. Pour into a bowl and whip until cool. Fold into mayonnaise.

Note: Paste must be folded into mayonnaise while lukewarm. It will be too stiff when cold.

Recipes Based on Mayonnaise

MAYONNAISE SAUCE

Season mayonnaise with lemon juice, Worcestershire sauce, some mustard, salt, and pepper. Depending on taste and use, thin it by adding fonds or essences. Good with salads, vegetables, chicken, fish, seafood, and all kinds of meats.

LAMAZE MAYONNAISE

Yield: 1 qt.
Ingredients

Mayonnaise	¾ qt.
Chili sauce	3 oz.
Lemon juice	to taste
Worchestershire sauce	to taste
Salt and pepper	to taste
Tomato concassée	8 oz.
Shallots, diced and blanched for 2 min.	⅓ oz.
Herbs (parsley, tarragon), chopped	1½ oz.

Method
Combine mayonnaise and chili sauce. Season with lemon juice, Worchestershire sauce, and salt and pepper. Fold in tomato, shallots, and herbs. Good with seafood, fish, eggs, and meat.

RÉMOULADE

Yield: 1 qt.
Ingredients

Pickles	3 oz.
Capers	1 T
Anchovies	2
Parsley	1 oz.
Chervil	⅓ oz.
Tarragon	⅓ oz.
Mustard	1 T
Mayonnaise	1 qt.
Salt and pepper	to taste
Pickle juice	to taste

Method
Finely chop pickles, capers, anchovies, and herbs; fold in mustard and mayonnaise. Season with salt, pepper, and pickle juice. Good with deep-fried fish and cold meats.

PAPRIKA MAYONNAISE

Yield: 1 qt.
Ingredients

Garlic, finely mashed	1 clove
Paprika (Hungarian)	½ tsp.
Mayonnaise	1 qt.
Mustard	⅓ tsp. or to taste
Salt and pepper	to taste
Ham or corned beef, diced small	to garnish

Method
Combine garlic, paprika, and mayonnaise. Fold in mustard, season with salt and pepper, and add diced ham or corned beef. Good with cold egg dishes, artichokes, zucchini, and potatoes.

GREEN GODDESS MAYONNAISE

Yield: 1 qt.
Ingredients

Spinach leaves, blanched	3 oz.
Parsley, blanched	2 oz.
Chervil, tarragon, dill, chives (fresh)	⅓ oz. each
Mayonnaise	1 qt.
Shallot	1
White wine	2 T
Garlic, mashed	to taste
Lemon juice	to taste
Salt and pepper	to taste

Method
Purée spinach and herbs with 3 tablespoons mayonnaise. Dice shallots finely and reduce with wine until all wine is absorbed. Combine all items with remaining mayonnaise. Season with garlic, lemon juice, and salt and pepper.

RUSSIAN MAYONNAISE

Yield: 1 qt.
Ingredients

Mayonnaise	27 oz.
Lemon juice	to taste
Salt and pepper	to taste
Seafood, diced	3 oz.
Caviar	2 oz.
Whipped cream	3 to 4 T

Method

Season mayonnaise with lemon juice, salt, and pepper. Fold in seafood, caviar, and cream. Good with seafood, fish, and vegetables.

TOMATO MAYONNAISE

Yield: 1 qt.
Ingredients

Tomatoes	10 oz.
Tomato paste	3 oz.
Mayonnaise	1¾ pt.
Sugar	to taste
Salt	to taste
Red pepper, blanched and cut into fine julienne	3 oz.

Method

Blanch, peel, and seed tomatoes, and purée with tomato paste and mayonnaise. Season with sugar and salt. Add julienne of red pepper. Good with eggs, cold meats, chicken, turkey, and pork.

CHANTILLY MAYONNAISE

Yield: 1 qt.
Ingredients

Mayonnaise	1¾ pt.
Lemon juice	to taste
Hot pepper sauce	to taste
Salt	to taste
Heavy cream, whipped	¼ pt.

Method

Season mayonnaise with lemon, hot pepper sauce, and salt. Fold in whipped cream. Good with asparagus, artichokes, and cucumbers.

ANDALOUSE SAUCE

Yield: 1½ cups

To 1 cup of mayonnaise, add 3 tablespoons tomato paste and 2 tablespoons diced red pimentos, 1 teaspoon lemon juice, and dash of Worcestershire sauce. This sauce goes well with all meats and poultry.

TARTAR SAUCE

Yield: 1¼ pt.
Ingredients

Eggs, hard-cooked	4
Chives, chopped	1 T
Shallot, chopped	1
Tarragon, chopped	1 tsp.
Chervil, chopped	1 tsp.
Parsley, chopped	1 tsp.
Mayonnaise	1 pt.
Salt, pepper, lemon juice	to taste

Method

Put eggs through food mill. Combine with the herbs and add to the mayonnaise. Season with salt, pepper, and lemon juice to taste.

TYROLIENNE SAUCE

Yield: 1 cup

To 1 cup mayonnaise, add 1 tablespoon chopped parsley, 1 tablespoon chopped chervil, and ¼ cup finely chopped tomatoes. Season with ⅓ teaspoon black pepper, 4 drops Worcestershire sauce, and 1 teaspoon chili sauce. This sauce goes well with seafood, poultry, pork, and veal.

Plate arrangement. From lower left, clockwise: Headcheese; Pâté en Croûte; Lentil Salad; Roast Loin of Veal; Veal Galantine; Broccoli Mousse; and Serbian Garlic Sauce.

SAUCES NOT DERIVED FROM MAYONNAISE

RED PEPPER COULIS

Yield: 1 qt.
Ingredients

Olive oil	1½ oz.
Red peppers, diced	5
Shallots, diced	2 oz.
White wine, dry	1 pt.
Chicken stock	1 pt.
Heavy cream	1 cup
Salt and pepper	to taste

Method
Heat olive oil. Add diced red peppers and cook until tender. Remove peppers and purée. Add diced shallots to the pan and sweat. Deglaze with white wine. Add chicken stock and reduce by half. Add puréed red peppers. Add heavy cream and reduce to coating consistency. Adjust seasoning.

Note: Can be used hot or cold.

TOMATO–BASIL COULIS

Yield: 1½ cups
Ingredients

Olive oil	1 T
Garlic, finely diced	½ tsp.
Shallots, finely diced	½ tsp.
Tomato paste	¼ cup
Tomato concassé	1½ cups
Chicken stock	½ cup
Basil, fresh, chopped	2 tsp.
Cilantro, fresh, chopped	1 tsp.
Oregano, fresh, chopped	1 tsp.

Method
Heat olive oil in a small sauce pot. Add garlic and shallots and sauté for 2 minutes. Add tomato paste and cook for 2 minutes. Add tomato concassé and chicken stock and simmer for approximately 10 minutes. Purée the mixture to a smooth consistency; return it to the pot. Bring coulis to a boil and add chopped herbs. Adjust seasoning.

Note: Can be served hot or cold.

SERBIAN GARLIC SAUCE

Yield: 1 pt.
Ingredients

Garlic	6 cloves
Olive oil	1 T
Mayonnaise with starch	1 pt.
White pepper	pinch
Lemon juice	a few drops

Method
Sauté the garlic in the olive oil until golden brown; remove and cool. Add garlic to mayonnaise and purée in a blender. Season with pepper and lemon juice.

ANCHOVY SAUCE

Yield: 1 cup
Pound four hard-cooked eggs and eight anchovy fillets to a fine paste. Season with

white pepper. Thin to desired thickness with oil and vinegar. Adjust seasoning.

APPLE HORSERADISH SAUCE

Yield: 1 cup

Peel and grate fresh apples. Mix with an equal quantity of grated horseradish. Finish the sauce with a touch of oil, vinegar, salt, sugar, and a small amount of beef stock.

CRANBERRY SAUCE

Yield: 2 cups

Pick over 1 pound of cranberries and wash in cold water. Place in pot and cover with water. Add 8 ounces sugar and juice of one lemon. Bring to a boil; boil for 10 to 15 minutes. Chill and serve cold.

CUMBERLAND SAUCE

Yield: ¾ pt.
Ingredients

Red currant jelly	1 cup
Shallots, chopped	1 T
Orange and lemon zest, blanched	2 T
Ginger, fresh, grated	1 tsp.
English mustard	1 tsp.
Port wine	½ cup
Lemon	juice of 1
Orange	juice of 1
Salt	⅓ tsp.
Cayenne pepper	pinch

Method

Melt red currant jelly; add shallots, julienned orange and lemon zest and fresh, grated ginger. Dissolve mustard in wine and add to currant jelly. Add lemon and orange juice and simmer for 5 to 10 minutes. Season with salt and cayenne.

Note: For Oxford Sauce, add grated orange and lemon peel to this recipe.

FROZEN HORSERADISH SAUCE

Yield: 1 pt.
Ingredients

Whipped cream	1 pt.
Horseradish, grated	3 to 4 T
Vinegar	1 T
Salt	½ tsp. or to taste
Sugar	½ tsp. or to taste
Black pepper, coarsely ground	½ tsp.

Method

Combine whipped cream with horseradish and vinegar. Gently fold all ingredients together. Roll into greased parchment paper and freeze. At service time, cut into slices. This sauce may be served with beef, ham, corned beef, tongue, and smoked fish and seafood.

GRIBICHE SAUCE

Yield: 1¼ pt.
Ingredients

Eggs, hard-cooked	3
Prepared mustard	½ tsp.
Capers, chopped	1 T
Sour pickle, chopped	1 tsp.
Chervil, chopped	½ tsp.
Tarragon, chopped	½ tsp.
Parsley, chopped	½ tsp.
Oil	1 pt.
Vinegar	1½ tsp.
Egg whites, hard-cooked, julienned	2

Method

Put three hard-cooked eggs through sieve. Stir in mustard, capers, pickles, and herbs. Whip in oil and vinegar and fold in julienned egg whites.

APPLE AND PEACH CHUTNEY

Yield: approximately 1 qt.

Ingredients

Apples, peeled and cut into wedges	2 cups
Peaches, peeled and cut into wedges	2 cups
Onions, sliced	2 cups
Sugar	2 cups
Sherry vinegar	1 cup
Orange zest and juice	of 1 orange
Raisins	½ cup
Salt	touch
Cayenne pepper	touch
Nutmeg	touch

Method

Combine all ingredients and bring to a boil. Simmer for 25 minutes and chill.

Note: For a different taste, add 1 tablespoon of grated ginger.

SAUCE ITALIA

Yield: approximately 1 qt.

Ingredients

Pistachio nuts	3 oz.
Almonds	2 oz.
Mayonnaise with starch	1½ pt.
Chopped herbs (tarragon, parsley, chervil, chives)	3 T each
Salt and pepper	to taste

Method

Soak pistachios and almonds in hot water. Peel pistachios and purée together with soaked almonds. Fold herbs and puréed mixture into mayonnaise. Adjust seasoning.

PLAIN HORSERADISH

Yield: 1½ pt.

Ingredients

Fresh horseradish	2 cups
Apple, raw	1 cup
Lemon juice	few drops
Salt	½ tsp.
Pepper	pinch

Method

Peel horseradish and apples; grate fine. Add lemon juice, salt, and pepper.

TOMATO KETCHUP

Yield: approximately 1 qt.

Ingredients

Tomatoes, ripe	8½ lb.
Salt	1 to 1½ oz.
Red pepper	8 oz.
Onions	5½ oz.
Cloves, ground	1 tsp.
Nutmeg, ground	1 tsp.
Pimento, ground	1 tsp.
Ginger, ground	1 tsp.
Black pepper, ground	1 tsp.
Basil leaf, ground	1 tsp.
Savory, ground	1 tsp.
Pumpernickel, chopped	1 tsp.
Hyssop, chopped	½ tsp.
Horseradish, grated	1 T
Brown sugar	7 oz.
White wine vinegar	½ pt.
Preservative (optional)	1 package

Method

Wash tomatoes; core and cut small. Set in a large pot and add salt. Cut red pepper in half; seed and cube. Slice onions thin. Add peppers and onions to the tomatoes and cook for 30 minutes. Strain through a strainer. Return the ketchup to the pot, add all spices, herbs, and horseradish, and simmer over low heat for 45 minutes. Add brown sugar and vinegar and simmer for 20 minutes more. Stir in preservative. Portion into clean bottles. Chill.

CRANBERRY ORANGE RELISH

Yield: 4 lb.

Ingredients

Cranberries, frozen	2 lb.

Apples, whole	4
Oranges, whole	4
Lemons, whole	2
Sugar	1 lb.
Walnuts, chopped	½ cup
Sherry or Madeira (optional)	2 oz.

Method

Grind all fruit through medium plate. Mix with sugar and walnuts. Add wine. Marinate for 24 hours.

ORANGE HORSERADISH SAUCE

Yield: 1 pt.
Ingredients

Apples, fresh, grated	1 cup
Horseradish, fresh grated or prepared	1 cup
Lemon	juice of ½
Orange, grated zest and juice	of 1 orange
Sugar	⅓ tsp.

Method

Mix all ingredients and marinate for 2 hours.

RAVIGOTE SAUCE

Yield: About 2 cups
Ingredients

Fresh parsley, minced	2 tsp.
Fresh chervil, minced	4 tsp.
Fresh tarragon, minced	2 tsp.
Fresh chives, minced	2 tsp.
Vinaigrette sauce (use Basic French)	2 cups
Onions, diced	1½ small
Capers, minced, well drained	2 T
Prepared mustard	1 tsp.

Method

Combine all ingredients and blend them well.

ORANGE MUSTARD SAUCE

Yield: ½ pt.
Ingredients

Orange marmalade	8
Sharp mustard	6
Red wine	4
Onions, chopped, blanched	5

Method

Mix well and rest well.

GREEN PEPPERCORN SAUCE WITH HONEY MUSTARD

Yield: 10 portions
Ingredients

Onion, grated	1
Dijon mustard	4 T
Honey	½ cup
Cider vinegar	¼ cup
Safflower oil	1½ cups
Salt	½ tsp. or to taste
Green peppercorns, crushed	1 tsp.

Method

Combine onion, mustard, honey, vinegar and oil and emulsify. Add salt and green peppercorns.

USE OF COLD SAUCES

Cold sauces make good accompaniment for a large variety of dishes. The following list can certainly be expanded, but it is offered to help menu planners explore the many possibilities for cold sauces.

Asparagus, Artichokes, and Melons
  Chantilly
  Vinaigrette
  Mustard
Egg Dishes
  All sauces derived from mayonnaise

Fish, Shellfish, Poultry, and Veal
  Andalouse
  Italian
  Russian
  Tartar
  Rémoulade
  Green Goddess
  Gribiche
  Anchovy
  Serbian garlic
Game, Beef, and Turkey
  Cumberland
  Oxford
  Cranberry
Meat
  Rémoulade
  Tartar
  Tyrolienne

BUTTER AND CHEESE MIXTURES

Butter and cheese, combined with many ingredients, make spreads that can be used to create a wide variety of canapés. The spreads thus produced enhance the flavor of the canapés; they also provide a flavorful base for other ingredients such as shrimp or olive slices that are used to top canapés make their presentation more appealing.

The following discussion of butter and cheese mixtures can be extended to include various other types of butters; in fact, there is no limit to the variations that can be created.

Remember that through its fine aroma, fresh butter enhances the flavor of food and gives it body.

Cold butter mixtures are used in:

1. Finishing soups and sauces
2. As a garnish for steaks, fish, lobster, and vegetables
3. As an ingredient in a recipe
4. To spread on toasts or croutons

To prepare butter mixtures, set the fresh butter into a stainless steel bowl and bring to room temperature until semisoft, then whip to a creamy consistency. Then add the rest of the ingredients. *Note:* Butter should *not* be melted; it loses its stability. Melted and hardened butter becomes lumpy. Only fresh ingredients give full aroma. Chopped herbs from the day before taste old and should not be used. Whipped, creamy butter and truffle or caviar butter mixtures *should not be refrigerated* but used semisoft. For butter rolls 1 inch in diameter, use moist parchment paper or plastic wrap, then refrigerate. Butter compound rolls should be cut into disks and used with the appropriate food items. For spreads, use in bulk at room temperature.

LOBSTER OR SHRIMP BUTTER

This butter is made from the shells of lobster or shrimp. It is prepared hot. Crush shells and add to a pot with an equal amount of butter and stir over low heat until butter is clear. Then cover evenly with water, bring to a boil, simmer for two hours, strain through cheesecloth, and cool in the refrigerator. Remove the butter, clean well, melt butter, and bring to a boil. Skim well and store in refrigerator.

LOBSTER BUTTER

Yield: 1 lb.
Ingredients

Shells	1 lb.
Butter	1 lb.
Shallots, diced	3
Tomato paste	1½ tsp.
Brandy or white wine	2 oz.

Method
Crush shells and sauté with a little butter. When they color, add diced shallots and tomato paste. Cook for two to three minutes. Deglaze with brandy or wine. Take off heat and stir in slowly 1 pound of cubed butter. Stir until melted, but do not let butter

separate. Strain through a fine sieve or cheesecloth and chill. Store in the refrigerator.

Egg Butter. Blend six cooked egg yolks with 8 ounces of butter and a few drops of olive oil. Put through a fine sieve and add salt and cayenne pepper.

Foie Gras Butter. Blend 4 ounces of cooked foi gras with 4 ounces of butter and put through sieve.

Garlic Butter. Blend five to six cloves of garlic with 1 pound of butter and put through a fine sieve.

Herring Butter. Blend two desalted fillets of smaltz herring with 1 pound of butter and put through a fine sieve.

Horseradish Butter. Mix 2 ounces of grated horseradish with 1 pound butter.

Lobster Butter. Blend 4 ounces of lobster coral and liver with 8 ounces of butter and put through a fine sieve.

Montpellier Butter (green butter). Blanch for 1 to 2 minutes twelve sprigs each of watercress, parsley, chervil, and tarragon, plus two finely diced shallots and twelve small spinach leaves. Remove, shock in ice water, and drain well. Purée in a blender with six anchovy fillets, 1 tablespoon of capers, three cornichons, one clove of garlic, and four hard-cooked eggs. Add ½ pound of soft butter, ¼ pint of olive oil, and ⅓ cup tarragon vinegar. Season well with salt, pepper, and nutmeg to taste.

Moscovite Butter. Blend 8 ounces of butter with 4 ounces of caviar and 2 hard-cooked eggs yolks and put through a very fine sieve. Season with salt and cayenne.

Mustard Butter. Mix 1 tablespoon of English mustard with ½ pound of butter. (This can be made with prepared mustard.)

Nutmeg Butter. Blend grated nutmeg with 1 pound of butter and put through a fine sieve.

Paprika Butter. To a very small onion, chopped and cooked in butter, add 1 tablespoon paprika and sweat a minute or two.

Remove from heat, let cool, and add 1 cup of soft butter. Press through a fine sieve.

Périgourdine Butter. Blend 4 ounces of butter with one-hard cooked egg yolk. Press through a fine sieve and add two medium sized finely chopped truffles. Season with salt and cayenne pepper.

Pimento Butter. Blend 1 ounce of red pimentos with 3 ounces of butter. Put through a fine sieve.

Portuguese Butter. Blend two hard cooked egg yolks with 6 ounces of butter. Add 1 tablespoon of tomato paste, salt, and pepper. Put through a fine sieve.

Ravigote Butter. In a mortar, blend equal quantities of blanched chervil, parsley, tarragon, chives, and garden burnet with three times their quantity in butter. Put through a fine sieve.

Salmon Caviar Butter. Blend 3 ounces of salmon caviar with 6 ounces of butter; add a pinch of mustard and put through a fine sieve.

Smoked Salmon Butter. Blend ½ pound of smoked salmon with 1 pound of butter and put through a fine sieve.

Sardine Butter. Blend twelve sardines without bones, with ¾ pound of butter and put through a fine sieve.

Shrimp Butter. Blend 2 ounces of cooked titi shrimp with 5 ounces of butter and put through a very fine sieve.

Butter for Snails. In a mortar, blend 1 ounce of garlic, 3 ounces of shallots, and 2 pounds of butter; add 2 ounces of chopped parsley, salt, and pepper.

Tarragon Butter. Blend a handful of blanched tarragon leaves with ¾ pound of butter and put through a very fine sieve.

Tuna Butter. Blend 1 ounce of tuna with 3 ounces of butter and put through a sieve. Whipped cream may be substituted for butter but the mixing must be carefully done to prevent curdling.

Cheeses

Crab Cheese. Follow procedure for Lobster Cheese below, substituting crabmeat for lobster.

Lobster Cheese. Blend the meat of one lobster with ½ pound of grated gruyère cheese and 4 ounces of butter. Put through a fine sieve and finish with heavy cream and brandy.

Salmon Cheese. Blend 4 ounces of cooked salmon with 4 ounces of grated gruyère cheese and 2 ounces of butter. Put through a fine sieve and finish with heavy cream and a little port wine.

Truffle Cheese. Blend 4 ounces of truffles with 2 ounces of grated gruyère cheese and 4 ounces of sweet butter. Add ½ ounce of brandy and spices to taste.

Tuna Cheese. Blend 8 ounces of tuna with 3 ounces of grated gruyère cheese and 4 ounces of butter. Put through a fine sieve and finish with heavy cream.

CLASSIC BUTTER MIXTURES

Mixture	Ingredients	Usages
Whipped Butter (Beurre Battu)	lemon, salt, cayenne	fish, seafood, vegetables
Truffle Butter (Beurre de Truffles)	reduction of Madeira, truffle, fond, and glace de viande; diced truffles, cayenne, salt	sauces, fish, seafood, medallion of veal, liverwurst, canapés with veal or chicken
Caviar Butter (Beurre de Caviar)	lemon juice, caviar, whipped cream	fish, seafood
Snail butter (Beurre d'Escargots)	shallots, garlic, parsley, lemon, Worcestershire sauce, pepper, salt, pâté spice	snails
Shallot Butter (Beurre d'Échalotte)	finely chopped shallots (blanched), lemon juice	soups, sauces, fish, seafood, meat, vegetables, mushrooms, potatoes
Bercy Butter (Beurre Bercy)	reduction of white wine, shallots, parsley, lemon, pepper, salt, blanched beef marrow	sauces, fish, meat, vegetables
Colbert Butter (Beurre Colbert)	parsley, glace de viande, lemon, salt, pepper	fish, seafood, meat, roasts, canapés with eggs
Parsley Butter (Beurre Mâitre d'Hôtel)	parsley, lemon, salt, pepper	sauces, fish, seafood, poultry, meat, sausages, roast, canapés
Herb Butter (Beurre Fines Herbes)	puréed parsley, tarragon, chervil, chives, watercress, shallots, lemon, salt, pepper	soups, sauces, fish, seafood, canapés with caviar, roasts
Horseradish Butter (Beurre de Raifort)	grated horseradish, lemon, salt, sugar	fish, meat, canapés of smoked salmon, egg, ham, roast beef, tomato
Red Wine Butter (Beurre Marchand de Vin)	reduction of red wine, shallots, glace de viande, parsley, lemon, salt, pepper	sauces, fish, meat, vegetables, canapés, roasts
Shrimp Butter (Beurre d'Crevette)	crushed shrimp, shells, tomato paste, lemon, salt, pepper	soups, sauces, canapés with eggs, seafood
Lobster Butter (Beurre de Homard)	lobster shells, lobster liver (tomalley), lobster roe (coral), lemon, salt, pepper	soups, sauces, canapés with eggs, seafood

15

Cold Food Presentation for Practical and Culinary Displays

The menu items created in the garde manger are largely classified as cold foods. The successful preparation and presentation of these cold foods depend on the methods and rules explained. Design and arrangement of cold food platters need to be well planned. We suggest using templates, either drawn or put together by cutouts. Always have in mind the initial impression: either to tempt or to distract your guest.

PLATTER

We suggest using cold food mirrors, silver or stainless steel platters, glass or porcelain dishes, or Bonnettef Platters, cast iron coated with rubber/plastic.

All platters and dishes must be clean and have no scratches or chips.

ASPIC JELLY MIRROR

Aspic jelly prevents food from touching the surface of the platter and becoming discolored or losing flavor. Silver and stainless steel platters usually are coated; mirrors need not be coated.

The correct characteristics of an aspic jelly mirror for a platter are:

1. Must be clear
2. Light color for fish
3. Tan color for meat
4. No ripples
5. No bubbles
6. Even thickness
7. Clear edges
8. No smudges

CHAUD FROID MIRRORS

The purpose is the same as aspic mirrors.

The correct characteristics of a chaud froid mirror for a food platter are:

1. Must be clear, no lumps
2. No ripples
3. No bubbles
4. Even thickness
5. Clear edges
6. No smudges
7. Must be colored with natural foods

FLAVOR

As guests tend to remember flavor longer than any other aspect of dining, it is an essential element of the dining experience. All foods should complement each other. For example, pair:

1. Spicy with bland
2. Smoky with sweet
3. Rich with lean
4. Sweet with spicy
5. Sweet and sour

TEXTURE

The texture of various displayed foods can create eye appeal, as well as visibly tempt the palate. For example, you can combine foods that are

1. Smooth
2. Coarse
3. Firm
4. Soft

GLAZING

All foods designed for public display before service should be coated with aspic jelly. This prevents drying out and discoloration and restores the natural sheen.
   Proper glazing techniques:

1. Aspic jelly must be crystal clear
2. Aspic jelly must be clean (no food drippings or fat)
3. No air bubbles
4. No drippings
5. Clean edge
6. Even coating
7. No excessive buildup
8. Proper strength of aspic jelly

ARRANGEMENT

Prepare a template before setting up. Only edible and harmonious foods should be used. Allow some spacing between each food group to give better eye appeal. Plan foods well on platter space; foods should not touch or be placed on borders.

COLOR COMBINATION

Color is one of the most important factor in cold food display. The eye of your gues will pick up clues as to freshness, moistur and proper working techniques. For ex ample:

1. Show a variety of natural colors. Con trast light colors with strong colors for example chicken and beef or to mato and corn.
2. Color should be appropriate to th cooking technique used.
3. Naturally derived food of smooth tex ture may nevertheless at times appea artificial. Colored food items with var ied textures are more appetizing; mos guests taste with the eyes. Add som texture by adding herbs, vegetables or meats to provide the eye with flavo clues.

AMOUNT/PORTION SIZE

The platter size, as well as plates used fo service, will determine the amount and por tion size of foods used. Overloaded foo platters or plates look unappetizing and de stroy the overall impression. The count o sliced food on the paltter is figured on th portion size and the accompanying foo garnitures must equal the portion count.

WORKMANSHIP

Professional workmanship of all foods i imperative. Exactness, consistency, an proper knife skills are a must.

- All foods must be kept cold.
- Knives (machine or hand) must b sharp and well maintained.
- Proper knives for slicing, dicing, o carving should be used.
- Carved foods must be complete, evenl sliced, and have clean edges.

Cold Platter - Covers

Name **Fish and Seafood Variation**

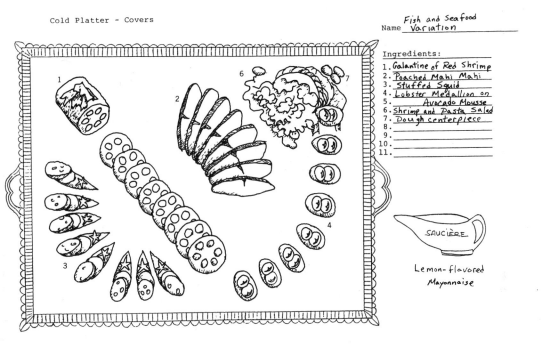

Ingredients:

1. Galantine of Red Shrimp
2. Poached Mahi Mahi
3. Stuffed Squid
4. Lobster Medallion on
5.   Avocado Mousse
6. Shrimp and Pasta Salad
7. Dough centerpiece
8. _____
9. _____
10. _____
11. _____

SAUCIÈRE

Lemon-flavored Mayonnaise

Template of a cold-food platter for eight covers; final platter is shown in photo below.

Cold-food platter ready for display. This platter won high points in competition.

Cold Platter - Covers

Name *Fallow deer – Fall Harvest*

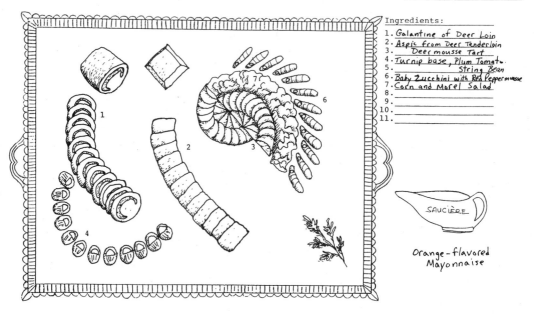

Ingredients:
1. *Galantine of Deer Loin*
2. *Aspic from Deer Tenderloin*
3. *Deer mousse Tart*
4. *Turnip base, Plum Tomato*
5. *String Bean*
6. *Baby Zucchini with Red Peppermousse*
7. *Corn and Morel Salad*
8. _____
9. _____
10. _____
11. _____

SAUCIÈRE

Orange-flavored Mayonnaise

A template for Fallow Deer Variations, a platter for twelve covers; final platter is shown in photo below.

Cold-food platter ready for display. This platter won high points at a recent food show.

- Sliced food must be even and have clean edges and surfaces:
    1. Bias cut
    2. Bevel cut
    3. Straight cut (square)
    4. Clean cut wedge
- Shaping of foods into such styles as tourné, figurines, and parisienne must be exact.
- Dicing as for cubes, brunoise, julienne, or batonnettes, must be done exactly and without bruising.
- Proper cooking techniques are essential for successful acceptance by your guest.
    1. *Roasting:* proper color, white pink, not bloody
    2. *Poaching:* proper temperature, time, cooling, moistness
    3. *Baking:* proper temperature, color, shrinkage, solid texture, moistness
    4. *Sautéing:* amount of fat, heat, even color, moistness, shape
    5. *Smoking:* rich color, proper cure/marination, texture, moistness
    6. *Braising:* not as popular in the cold kitchen, but some meats are braised; for example, boeuf à la mode. Consistency should be moist, not stringy.
    7. *Steaming:* (for example, vegetables) color, shape, texture
    8. *Deep-Fat Frying:* not as popular in the garde manger as in the hot kitchen. However, some foods may be prepared this way, usually in the appetizer service and usually served at room temperature. Greasiness, color, texture.
- *Pâtés en croûte:* These are tempting if properly produced. Consider:
    1. Thickness of crust/and color
    2. Consistency of texture
    3. Color of garnish and size (compatible)
    4. Thickness of slices

    5. Amount of shrinkage
    6. Aspic jelly (color and clearness)
- *Terrines:* Terrines are baked in the vessel, generally in a water bath. Consider:
    1. Lining (fat, meat, vegetables, plastic wrap)
    2. Consistency of texture
    3. Color of garnish and size
    4. Air pockets
    5. Thickness of slices
    6. Aspic jelly coating
- *Galantines:* These molded foods are usually poached in aromatized stock. They are either round, oval, or loaf-shaped. Consider:
    1. Size/evenness
    2. Even seam of casing, especially when natural skin is used.
    3. Moisture
    4. Texture/garnish
    5. Color
    6. Shape
    7. Thickness of slices
    8. Proper coating
- *Mousses:* Excellent for usage of leftover food, this type of food can be used for appetizers, main courses, or garnish. Consider:
    1. Smoothness
    2. Texture
    3. Gelatine amount (firmness)
    4. Color
    5. Shape
    6. Portion size
    7. Proper coating (timbale, mold)

DESIGN OF BUFFET PLATTERS

Buffet platters are more picturesque than the average food arrangement in the hotel and restaurant service. Therefore, it is important that the following rules are followed:

1. Slices are properly shingled (toward the guest)

2. Grosse pièce is of proper size (not figured in portion count)
3. Garnish and slice count are correct
4. Tall food items are toward the rear
5. Portion size of main item and garnishes is correct
6. Garnishes are of proper size
7. No food is hidden by other food items
8. No sauce boat is on food platter
9. No food is on borders
10. Sauce boats, if used, are only two-thirds full
11. If nonedible/edible sculptures (salt, tallow, shortening) are used, no food touches them.

LAYOUT

Today's food platters have various food texture and flavor combinations. For example:

• Grosse pièce or centerpiece might consist of roast, headcheese, and galantine
• Slices without grosse pièce could include sliced ham, roast beef, roast turkey, and pâté
• Necessary garnitures could include stuffed fruit or vegetables, salads, timbales, medallion, or barquette.

BALANCE OF ARRANGEMENT

Various ways to balance the arrangement are:

1. Specially balanced
2. Balance in degree of difficulty
3. Balance of color and texture
4. Balance of food groups (meats, soft or hard, vegetables, fruit, or starch)

FLOW OF FOOD ITEMS

To encourage efficient flow, use:

1. Strong lines
   a. proper sequence of slices
   b. no reversed slices
2. Unidirectional arrangements (bilateral symmetry vs. asymmetry)

For more information for food competitions, see American Culinary Federation Rules and Guidelines for Food Shows (contact the American Culinary Federation, P.O. Box 3466, St. Augustine, FL 32084).

$$16$$

Salads

The word "salad" is derived from the Italian word *insalata*, which originally meant a dish "steeped in salt or brine," or the Latin phrase *Herba Salata* which literally means "salted greens." Today, the term *salad* is widely used for foods marinated or served with a dressing.

Most salads, with the exception of fruit salads, have an acid base. Adding sugar or puréed fruits provides a tart or sweet and sour flavor.

Nearly all foods can be used to make salad. Most salads are made from lettuce and raw vegetable, such as iceberg, Boston, and romaine lettuce, endive, escarole, tomatoes, cucumbers, and radishes. Another large group uses blanched cooked vegetables, such as beans, asparagus, beets, and potatoes.

Salads are also made from meat and fish and from combinations of fruit. These salad arrangements can be served as appetizers, main courses, or desserts, or on buffets, but not as a side dish with other foods.

Salads made from vegetables, or combinations of meat, seafood, rice, noodles, legumes, and vegetables, seasoned with piquant marinades or dressing enhance menus and tempt customers' appetites. Salads must be served fresh; lettuce must be crisp and unblemished. They should appeal to the eye and have a lightly acid, tangy taste.

When we see salad on the menu, we assume it will be fresh, crisp, and healthful; because of this, it is important that we follow the proper guidelines and preparation methods.

Salads that contain tender vegetables that may lose their appeal and crispness should be arranged and marinated just before service. Robust foods such as cabbage or certain meats or fish need to be marinated in advance in order to bring out flavor and texture.

Salads should be interesting, attractive-looking, and consist of at least two different foods. Marinades or dressings must be designed to match or bring out the best in both flavor and appearance.

SALADS FROM RAW INGREDIENTS

Salad Greens

Alfalfa sprouts. Tiny, crisp, succulent sprouts, grassy flavor.

Belgian endive (French endive, witloof chicory). Solid, small tightly-packed spear-like head (average 4 to 6 inches long), yellow to white center, slightly bitter taste.

Bibb or limestone lettuce. Very delicate

Combination Salad. Radicchio, yellow frisée, watercress, and bibb and red oak leaf lettuces garnished with marinated yellow squash and carrot slices and dressed with a shallot vinaigrette.

Combination Salad Variation. Baby red leaf and red oak lettuces, watercress, and julienne of radicchio garnished with marinated zucchini, yellow squash slices, and tomato wedges and dressed with a herb vinaigrette.

flavor, soft pliable leaves that bruise easily, yellow-white center.

Boston lettuce. Same as bibb lettuce.

Cabbage. Tight head of thick, white or purple, sturdy leaves, crisp and durable with a slightly sulfurous taste.

Celery. Fibrous, watery, crunchy texture with a bland flavor.

Chinese cabbage (Napa celery cabbage). Mild, delicate, crisp texture; frilly, pale leaves with celerylike stalks.

Curly endive. Spread-out head, narrow leaves with fine tight curls on heavy stalk. Outer leaves are dark green, spine white, center yellow to white color, slightly bitter taste.

Escarole (broad leaf endive). Sharp, slightly bitter, rough texture, thick green leaves, center pale yellow color.

Frisée. Now available in American markets. A kind of escarole with yellow leaves that are wide and smooth and curled on the ends. Slightly bitter flavor. Available in fall and winter.

Iceberg lettuce. Very crisp, watery, refreshing, with mild flavor.

Mâche. Also known as corn salad, lamb' lettuce, or field salad. Round or spoon shaped dark to medium green leaves, velvet texture, mild flavor. Generally sold in flats or bunches; available from fall to spring.

Mustard greens. Peppery, bitter, frilly leaves.

Parsley. Acid sweet, slightly tough leaves.

Radicchio (wild chicory or red endive). Color generally bright red, white stalk, slightly bitter taste.

Red leaf lettuce. Elongated, tender leaves are green with red tips, white stalk, mild rich flavor.

Romaine. Elongated head with long, narrow leaves, spicy, mild flavor, juicy and crisp.

Scallion or green onions. Sweet with mild piquancy, white end sharper than green.

Simple Color and Flavor Salad Combination. Belgian endive and Boston and Kentucky bibb lettuces garnished with marinated cucumber sliced, tomato wedges, and deviled eggs and dressed with sour cream dressing.

Spring Salad. Marinated asparagus, Belgian endive, and tomato wedges garnished with Boston lettuce, shredded carrots, and stuffed egg and dressed with yogurt dressing.

Spinach. Clean, slightly lemony flavor with a dry aftertaste; thick firm leaves.

Swiss chard. Sturdy, dark green leaves with heavy white stems. Leaves are good for lining bowls.

Watercress. Lively, spicy sweetness to leaves, sharp biting stalk.

Check salad greens thoroughly before use, and remove all limp or discolored leaves and stalks.

Wash greens well in lots of water to remove sand, dirt, and insects, and rinse in fresh water. Remove greens from water as soon as possible; water leaches out important minerals and vitamins. Drain greens and dry thoroughly, using towels or mechanical spin.

Cut or tear large leaves into edible sizes for easy eating and serving.

Marinated julienne of fennel and tomatoes garnished with mâche.

Other Vegetables

Other raw vegetables that can be used in salads include:

Mushrooms

Cucumbers

Peppers (red, yellow, green)

Radishes

Tomatoes

Zucchini

Onions

Uncooked vegetables must be washed well. Tomatoes and cucumbers should be peeled, and peppers cleaned of seeds and membrane. Depending on type, these vegetables can be sliced, diced, or cut into julienne. Cucumbers, tomatoes, and mushrooms should be sliced.

Preparation of Salads from Raw Materials

Prepared greens or vegetables must be evenly coated with a marinade or dressing. This is achieved by tossing both greens/vegetables and dressing/marinade together.

Overdressing (drowning) salads is a common mistake. As a guideline, use 1 to 2 tablespoons of dressing/marinade for each portion of salad.

Salads that contain tender greens and vegetables such as Boston lettuce, cucumbers, and tomatoes, should be tossed immediately before service. Premarination is required for salads made from robust vegetables, such as carrots, cabbage, peppers, and celery. This allows the marinade to be absorbed by the vegetables and gives a stronger flavor.

SALADS FROM COOKED INGREDIENTS

Meat and Seafood

Most meat and seafood used (with the exception of seviche) are cooked, cut into different shapes and sizes, combined with vegetables and fruits, and then marinated or combined with sauces such as mayon-

naise. They offer a good addition to buffets or salad bars. All leftover food, no matter how small in quantity, can be used in these types of salad.

Vegetables

Mushrooms, asparagus, celery, artichokes, broccoli, cauliflower, peas, beans, leeks, carrots, beets, and legumes can all be cooked and used in salads. Vegetables should be cooked to the crunch in slightly salted water, shocked, and immediately removed, dried, and stored. Some vegetables, such as mushrooms, tend to discolor after being cut. Therefore, we suggest tossing them in an acid-based solution (acid/water) before mixing.

Salads made from blanched/cooked vegetables should be premarinated, with the exception of herbs and green vegetables. They should be marinated just shortly before service, or they will lose their color. The marinade should be drained off before service and salads arranged attractively.

Note: If any additional dressing, for example mayonnaise, is added, make sure vegetables are drained well and dried on towels to remove any moisture to ensure good coating.

MARINADES AND DRESSINGS

What is a marinade? What is a dressing? The name depends upon the ingredients used, the style, and the time involved. The word *marinade* is derived from the Latin word *mare*, which means "the sea." Originally it meant steeping food in salt water (brine) to preserve it. Marinating still means to steep foods such as vegetables, meats, and fish in an acid liquid in order to preserve them and add flavor.

Dressing means just what it sounds like —a coating used to enhance the flavor and appearance of a salad. When dressing salads, follow this rule: for robust leaves, se thick dressing; for tender leaves, use liquid dressing.

Major ingredients in dressings/marinades are acids, such as vinegars or lemon, lime, orange, or grapefruit juice; and oils or fats, such as sunflower, olive, or peanut oil, or cream or mayonnaise. Acids add tangy flavor to the dressing. Oils enhance flavor and aroma and loosen fat-soluble vitamins. The consistency of dressings or marinades can be liquid or thick (emulsion).

To reduce the amount of acids or oils, use tofu, fruits, and vegetable purées or pastes in the production of dressing.

Flavor is enhanced by adding herbs and spices, and also pungent ingredients such as shallots, onions, garlic, horseradish, capers, anchovies, or mustards.

Dressings and marinades must be kept refrigerated and must be thoroughly mixed before service.

Most dressings and marinades are to be prepared from basic recipes. However, the professional knowledge and involvement of the chef can expand these basics and create new combinations.

To prevent discoloration of salads and dressing, do not use copper-lined containers, which react with acid. Instead, use stainless steel, porcelain, plastic, or glass.

BASIC RECIPES FOR DRESSINGS AND MARINADES

Oil and Vinegar Vinaigrettes

1. Salt — to taste
   Sugar — pinch
   Vinegar — 1 part
   Oil — 1 to 3 parts
   Pepper — to taste

   Dissolve salt and sugar in vinegar, add oil, season with pepper. Good for all salads.

2. Chicken stock — 1 part
   Vinegar — 1 part
   Salt — to taste
   Pepper — to taste
   Sugar — pinch
   Oil — ½ to 1 part

   Combine chicken stock and vinegar; dissolve salt, pepper, and sugar in the liquids. Add oil. Good for all salads.

3. Salt — to taste
   Vinegar — 1 part
   Oil — 1 to 2 parts
   Pepper — to taste
   Shallots — 1 T per pt.
   Chopped fresh herbs (parsley, chervil, tarragon, chives) — 2 T per pt.

   Dissolve salt in vinegar; add oil, season with pepper, shallots, and herbs. Good for all salads.

4. Garlic — ½ to 1 clove per pt.
   Salt — to taste
   Vinegar — 1 part
   Dijon mustard — 1 tsp. per pt.
   Oil — 1 to 2 parts
   Pepper — to taste

   Mash garlic with salt; dissolve in vinegar, add mustard and slowly whip in oil; season with pepper. Good for all salads.

5. Vinegar — 1 part
   Chicken stock — 1 part
   Salt — to taste
   Sugar — pinch
   Oil — 1 part
   Bacon pieces, warm, dried, crisp — 1 T per pt.
   Pepper — to taste
   Chives — 1 T per pt.

   Combine vinegar and chicken stock; dissolve salt and sugar in this mixture. Add oil and bacon, season with pepper and chives. Good for potato salad, Boston lettuce, and cabbage.

FRESH HERB VINAIGRETTE

Yield: 15 servings
Ingredients

Wine vinegar	3 T
Dijon mustard	½ tsp.
Salt	¼ tsp.
Ground black pepper	⅛ tsp.
Olive oil	⅔ cup
Chives, minced	1 T
Parsley, minced	1 T
Garlic, minced	1 clove
Basil, minced	1 T
Oregano, minced	½ tsp.
Tarragon, minced	½ tsp.

Method
Whisk together the vinegar, mustard, salt, and pepper. While beating, add olive oil. Stir in fresh herbs. The same results can be achieved in a blender.

Emulsified Dressings

EMULSIFIED FRENCH DRESSING

Yield: approximately 1 qt.
Ingredients

Egg, beaten	1
Lemon juice	¾ cup
Worcestershire sauce	1 tsp.
Garlic, mashed fine	¼ tsp.
Salt	1 tsp.
Dry mustard	2 tsp.
Paprika	2 tsp.
Oil	1 qt.

Method
Combine beaten egg, lemon juice, Worcestershire sauce, and garlic. Add dry ingredients. Rest for 15 minutes. Gradually whip in oil.

LOW-CALORIE FRENCH DRESSING

Yield: 3 qt.
Ingredients

Egg, beaten	1
Tomato juice	2 qt.
Lemon juice	4 oz.
Worcestershire sauce	3 T
Hot pepper sauce	¼ tsp.
Garlic, puréed	1 clove
Cider vinegar	2¾ oz
Salad oil	8 oz.

Method
Combine all ingredients except oil. Gradually whip in oil.

CREAMY ITALIAN

Yield: 4 gal.
Ingredients

Eggs, beaten	18
Parsley, chopped	¼ cup
Garlic, minced	¼ cup
Salt	2 oz.
White pepper	2 tsp.
Oregano, fresh, chopped	2 T
Sugar	½ cup
Red wine vinegar	⅓ gal.
Lemon	juice of
Garlic powder	3 T
Worcestershire sauce	2 T
Oil	3 gal.

Method
Combine all ingredients except oil. Gradually whip in oil.

RUSSIAN DRESSING

Yield: 2½ qt.
Ingredients

Mayonnaise	8 cups
Worcestershire sauce	3 T
Horseradish, prepared	⅓ to ½ cup
Chili sauce	2 cups

Onion, blanched, minced ¼ cup
Salt and white pepper to taste
Method
Fold all ingredients into mayonnaise.

BLUE CHEESE DRESSING

Yield: 3½ qt.
Ingredients

Mayonnaise	½ gal.
Buttermilk	1 pt.
Skim milk	½ pt.
Lemon juice	1½ oz.
Worcestershire sauce	1 T
Onion purée	1 T
Garlic purée	1 T
Black pepper	⅓ oz.
Salt	to taste
Blue cheese, crumbled	1 lb.

Method
Mix mayonnaise, buttermilk, skim milk, lemon juice, Worcestershire sauce, onion purée, garlic purée, and black pepper. Adjust seasoning and fold in crumbled blue cheese. Good for robust greens, tomatoes, and vegetables.

DAIRY DRESSINGS

YOGURT AND OIL

Yield: 1 pt.
Ingredients

Yogurt	16 oz.
Orange juice concentrate	1 T
Lemon juice	2 tsp.
Worcestershire sauce	a few drops
Salt	to taste
Pepper	to taste
Oil	8 T

Method
Combine yogurt, orange juice, lemon juice, Worcestershire sauce, salt, and pepper. Whip in oil. Good for all salads.

SOUR CREAM

Ingredients

Sour cream	5 parts
Lemon juice	1 part
Salt	to taste
Sugar	pinch
Dill	1 to 2 T per pt.
Pepper or paprika	to taste

Method
Combine all ingredients. Good for lettuce greens and vegetables.

GARLIC DRESSING

Yield: 24 1-oz. portions
Ingredients

Mayonnaise	1 pt.
Tomato ketchup	1½ oz.
Chicken broth	½ cup
Milk, condensed	3 oz.
Vinegar	½ to 1 oz.
Onions, finely diced, sautéed	1½ oz.
Tomatoes, blanched and cubed	4 oz.
Parsley, chopped	1 T
Garlic	touch of
Salt and pepper	to taste

Method
Combine mayonnaise, ketchup, broth, milk, and vinegar. Stir until smooth. Add onions, tomatoes, and parsley. Adjust seasonings. Excellent with bean salads.

PARSLEY DRESSING

Yield: 24 1½-oz. portions
Ingredients

Mayonnaise	1½ pt.
Milk	½ pt.
Cottage cheese	7 oz.
Lemon juice	1 oz.
Parsley	2 T
Salt, pepper, hot sauce, marjoram	to taste

Method
Combine all ingredients and season to perfection. Goes well with onion salad.

BACON DRESSING

Yield: 24 1-oz. portions
Ingredients
Mayonnaise	1 pt.
Chicken broth	½ cup
Heavy cream	2 oz.
Vinegar	½ to 1 oz.
Bacon, lean, diced and sautéed	2½ oz.
Apples, peeled and diced	4 oz.
Parsley, chopped	½ T
Salt, sugar, and pepper	to taste

Method
Combine mayonnaise, broth, cream, and vinegar and stir until smooth. Add bacon, apples, and parsley, and mix well. Adjust seasonings. Excellent with vegetable salads.

MAYONNAISE AND TOMATOES

Ingredients
Mayonnaise	2 parts
Tomato ketchup	1 part
Brandy or wine	a few drops
Salt, pepper	to taste
Whipped cream	1 to 2 T per pt.

Method
Combine mayonnaise, ketchup, and brandy; season with salt and pepper, fold in whipped cream. Good for robust greens, vegetables, fruit, and seafood.

COMBINATIONS

Ingredients
Mayonnaise	1 part
Yogurt	1 part
Salt	to taste
Pepper	to taste
Worcestershire sauce	a few drops
Chopped herbs (dill, chives, parsley)	1 to 2 T per pt

Method
Combine mayonnaise and yogurt. Season with salt, pepper, Worcestershire sauce and herbs. Good for robust greens and vegetables.

Special Marinades and Dressings

HERB

Yield: 1½ cups
Ingredients
Strong chicken stock	6 oz.
Raspberry vinegar	6 T
Dijon mustard	2 tsp.
Shallots, finely chopped	2
Chopped herbs (dill, parsley, tarragon)	2 T
Salt	to taste
Pepper	to taste
Sugar	pinch
Worcestershire sauce	a few drops
Oil	10 T

Method
Combine stock, vinegar, and all seasonings. Mix well before adding oil. For rice, vegetables, or poultry.

FRUIT

Yield: 1½ cups
Ingredients
Mayonnaise	6 oz.
Peaches, fresh, frozen or canned; puréed	5 halves
Vlasic sweet chips, finely chopped	2 T
Chili sauce	4 to 5 T
Chives, chopped	1 T
Parsley, chopped	1 T
Tarragon vinegar	1 tsp.
Hot pepper sauce	a few drops
Worcestershire sauce	a few drops

alt and pepper | to taste
Vhipped cream | 2 to 4 T

Method

Combine all ingredients but whipped cream. Fold in whipped cream. For poultry nd beef.

RESH GREEN PEPPERCORNS

Yield: 1 cup

Ingredients

Sour cream	4 T
Mayonnaise	6 T
Fresh green peppercorns, chopped coarsely	1 to 2 T
Red currant jelly	2 tsp.
Tomato ketchup	2 to 3 T
Orange concentrate *or*	1 T
Orange juice	2 T
Lemon juice	2 T
Pecans or walnuts, finely chopped	2 T
White wine	3 T
Worcestershire sauce	a few drops
Salt	to taste

Method

Combine all ingredients and season to taste. For poultry and beef. Can also be used as a dressing for radishes or endive.

DILL

Yield: ½ pt.

Ingredients

Sour cream	11 oz.
Mustard	3 oz.
Garlic, mashed	1 clove
Dill, chopped	3 oz.
White wine vinegar	1 to 2 T
t and pepper	to taste
Whipped cream	6 oz.

Method

Combine sour cream, mustard, garlic, dill, and vinegar. Season to taste, then fold in

---

whipped cream. For vegetables, leaf lettuce, fish, seafood.

BANANA

Yield: 2½ pt.

Ingredients

Bananas, large	2 to 3
Lemon juice	3 oz.
Fresh ginger, finely chopped	2 oz.
Yogurt	14 oz.
Madras curry powder (no substitutes)	2 tsp.
Salt	dash
Whipped cream	14 oz.

Method

Purée bananas; add lemon juice, ginger, yogurt, curry, and salt. Fold in whipped cream. For melon, poultry, tossed lettuce.

POTATO SALADS

To prepare a good potato salad, choose potatoes that are not too mealy, for example, Red Bliss potatoes A or B or Yellow Finish.

BASIC POTATO SALAD

Yield: 2½ lb.

Ingredients

Red bliss potatoes	32 oz.
Chicken stock	8 oz.
Onions, finely diced	3½ oz.
White vinegar	4½ oz.
Prepared mustard	½ tsp.
Salt	to taste
White pepper	to taste
Oil	1 oz.
Chives, finely chopped	2 T

Method

Cook potatoes in their jacket until done. Drain and set potatoes on a sheet pan and dry in a 350°F oven for 5 minutes. Peel while warm and slice thin.

Bring chicken stock, onions, vinegar,

mustard, salt, and pepper to a boil. Reduce by half, then add oil and pour over potatoes. Toss gently and marinate for 1 hour. Just before service, sprinkle with chives.

Variations

With bacon: Add 4 oz. bacon, diced and crispy.

With mayonnaise: Use no oil, drain off marinade, and fold 2 to 3 ounces of mayonnaise into salad.

With apple and celeriac: Add 1 peeled apple, sliced, or, for a different taste, add blanched julienne of celeriac and apple in equal amounts. Marinate in lemon juice.

COMBINATION SALADS

WARM LOBSTER SALAD AND CONFIT OF SWEETBREAD

Yield: 3 lb. sweetbread, 16 portions
Ingredients

Sweetbread Confit

Cleaned sweetbreads	4 lb.
Kosher salt	4 T
Black pepper, ground	¼ T
Juniper berries, crushed	2 to 3
Thyme	¼ tsp.
Bay leaf, crushed	1
Garlic, minced	½ T
Duck fat, rendered	3 lb.
Lobster, live	8, 1½ lb. each
Court bouillon	to boil lobsters

Salad

Frisée	4 to 5 heads
Romaine lettuce	1 to 2 heads
Mâche leaves	16
Tomato concassée	16 T
Chives, chopped	1 bunch
Tarragon, chopped	1 T

Dressing

Lemon juice	½ cup
White wine vinegar	⅓ cup
Chicken stock	¾ to 1 cup
Shallots, finely chopped	½ tsp.
Garlic, minced	⅓ tsp.
Salt, pepper, sugar	to taste
Olive oil	½ cup
Safflower oil	½ cup

Method

To make sweetbread confit, combine swee[t]breads with salt, herbs, spices, and garli[c]. Cure for 18 hours, refrigerated. Rinse an[d] dry sweetbreads. Melt duck fat. Add swee[t]bread and stew at 180°F for 25 minutes. Coo[l] in fat. Remove and roll tightly in plast[ic] wrap. Return to duck fat, press lightly, an[d] chill. Remove, unmold, clean off fat, an[d] sear quickly on all sides. Keep warm an[d] slice for service.

Cook lobster in a court bouillon for a[p]proximately 20 minutes. Remove and coo[l]. Break loose tail meat and dice. Break ou[t] lobster claw, remove soft bone.

To make salad, cut frisée, romaine, an[d] mâche into bite-size pieces. Toss with to[-] mato concassée and herbs.

Combine all dressing ingredients. Brin[g] to a boil and emulsify in a blender. Kee[p] hot.

Place salad onto plates. Set two to thre[e] slices of sweetbread next to it. Sprinkle lob[-]ster dices over lettuce. Garnish with lobste[r] claw. Just before service, pour boiling ho[t] dressing over the salad.

CHINESE CABBAGE WITH SMOKED OR MARINATED SALMON

Yield: 8 portions
Ingredients

Chinese cabbage	7 oz.
Ripe tomatoes	4
Eggs, hard-cooked	2
Mustard Vinaigrette (see p. 191, #4)	3 oz.
Juniper berries	2
Shallots	1 oz.
Gin	dash
Salt	to tast[e]

Cooked rice	2 oz.
Smoked or marinated salmon, cut into large sticks	16 oz.
Dill, chopped	1 tsp.
Tarragon, chopped	½ tsp.

Method

Cut Chinese cabbage into julienne. Blanch, skin, and seed tomatoes, then dice coarsely. Peel and slice eggs and add to vinaigrette. Add finely diced juniper berries, finely diced shallots, gin, and salt. Fold rice into dressing and add tomatoes, Chinese cabbage, and egg. Marinate for one hour. Arrange on a plate, garnish with salmon and egg slices, and sprinkle with chopped herbs.

ASPARAGUS MIMOSA

Yield: 20 portions
Ingredients

Asparagus	5 lb.
Vinaigrette	
White wine vinegar	3 T
Shallots, minced	2 T
Dijon mustard	1 T
Salt	½ tsp.
Pepper	¼ tsp.
Vegetable oil	¾ cup
Lettuce leaves, Boston or bibb	2 heads
Eggs, hard-cooked	10
Parsley, chopped	½ cup

Method

Snap off tough ends of asparagus; peel stems if desired. In large deep skillet or shallow saucepan, cook asparagus in batches in boiling water for about 5 minutes or until tender-crisp. Using slotted spoon, transfer asparagus to bowl of ice water; drain and pat dry.

To make the vinaigrette, combine vinegar, shallots, mustard, salt, and pepper; gradually whisk in oil. Combine asparagus with dressing, toss gently to coat; divide among lettuce-lined plates. Press egg yolks

and whites separately through sieve; sprinkle over asparagus. Sprinkle with parsley.

SMOKED SALMON AND MELON SALAD

Yield: 12 portions
Ingredients

Lemon juice	2 oz.
Orange juice	2 oz.
Tomato ketchup	3 T
Olive oil	1 oz.
Salt	to taste
Crushed black peppercorns	to taste
Honeydew melon, cut into balls	1
Cantaloupe melon, cut into balls	1
Grapefruit, cut into cubes	1
Smoked salmon, thinly sliced and cut into squares	24 oz.
Boston lettuce leaves	to line plates

Method

Combine lemon juice, orange juice, ketchup, oil, salt, and pepper. Toss gently with fruit. Fold in salmon. Arrange on a Boston lettuce leaf. Serve immediately.

MODERN SHRIMP SALAD

Yield: 4 portions
Ingredients

Raw shrimp, cut into pieces	12
Salt and pepper	to taste
Oil	4 T
Green pepper, cut in julienne	3 oz.
Madras curry powder (no substitute)	1 tsp.
Tomato concassée	3 oz.
Lichee fruits, fresh, shell removed	6
Garlic, mashed	½ clove
Fish broth	4 T

Lemon juice	2 T
Mango chutney	1 T
Lettuce leaves	to line plates

Method

Season shrimp pieces with salt and pepper. Heat oil, sauté shrimp and green pepper. Dust with curry, add tomatoes. Halve lichees and add, along with garlic, fish broth, and lemon juice. Braise, covered, for 5 minutes. Chill and add chutney. Arrange on lettuce leaves.

FRISÉE SALAD WITH FENNEL, BEET CHIPS, AND ORANGE-PISTACHIO VINAIGRETTE

Yield: 10 portions

Ingredients

Oil, grapeseed or canola	16 oz.
Pistachios, roasted, peeled, chopped finely	2 cups
Beets, medium, peeled, then frozen	20
Vegetable oil	for frying
Salt	to taste
Oranges	juice of 2–3
Lemon	juice of 1
Sugar, salt, freshly ground white pepper	to taste
Frisée	10 cups
Fennel bulbs	30
Parsley, chopped	as needed
Orange	zest of 2–3
Fennel leaves	to garnish

Method

Combine grapeseed or canola oil with 1 cup of the chopped pistachios in a small saucepan and heat gently. When hot, remove from heat and transfer to a glass jar. Cover, shake vigorously, and allow to steep overnight. When the pistachios have settled to the bottom and the oil is perfumed, carefully pour the oil through a coffee filter, leaving the sediment behind. Reserve oil and pistachios separately.

While still frozen, slice beets paper thin on a meat slicer or mandoline. Blot dry on a sheet tray lined with paper towels. Deep fry in 350°F oil until crisp but not browned. Remove with slotted spoon and drain well on paper towels. Sprinkle lightly with salt while still warm.

Combine orange and lemon juices and seasonings. Whisk in pistachio oil; adjust seasoning.

Wash and trim frisée. Dry well. Clean and trim fennel, then shave or grate finely.

To assemble, toss shaved fennel in a little vinaigrette with fresh chopped parsley. Toss frisée separately in vinaigrette. Arrange frisée on plates and top with a small mound of fennel. Garnish with beet chips and orange zest. Sprinkle with chopped pistachios and fresh parsley. Garnish with fennel leaves and serve immediately.

CRAB SALAD IN RADICCHIO CUPS

Yield: 24

Ingredients

Crabmeat	½ lb.
Lemon juice	2 tsp.
Celery, finely chopped	¼ cup
Cayenne pepper	pinch
Salt and pepper	to taste
Mayonnaise	¼ cup
Seafood cocktail sauce	1 T
Radicchio	3 medium

Method

Flake crabmeat and press out any excess moisture. Toss crab with lemon juice, celery, cayenne, and salt and pepper. Blend mayonnaise with seafood sauce; add to crab mixture and toss lightly to mix. Spoon into twenty-four tiny radicchio cups.

RADISH, STRAWBERRY, AND APPLE SALAD

Yield: 4 portions

Ingredients

White radish, peeled	12 oz.

Apple, large red	1
Strawberries	7 oz.
Lemon juice	1 oz.
Oil	½ oz.
Salt	to taste
Sugar	pinch
Hot pepper sauce	1 to 2 drops
Boston lettuce	to line plates

Method

Cut radish and apple into fine julienne. Cut strawberries into thick slices. Combine lemon juice, oil, salt, sugar, and hot pepper sauce. Toss with radish, apple, and strawberries. Arrange on Boston lettuce.

TURKEY SALAD WITH STRAWBERRIES

Yield: 2 portions

Ingredients

Sour cream	3 oz.
Lemon juice	1 T
Salt	to taste
Brandy	½ T
Sugar	½ tsp.
Ginger powder	to taste
Black pepper, coarse	⅓ T
White turkey meat, cooked, cubed	4 oz.
Asparagus, cooked, cubed	4 oz.
Pineapple, cubed	1 slice
Strawberries, halved	4 oz.
Avocado, ripe, cubed	½
Boston lettuce	½ head
Chives, chopped	2 T

Method

Combine sour cream, lemon juice, salt, brandy, sugar, ginger powder, and black pepper and mix well. Add turkey, asparagus, pineapple, strawberries, and avocado and toss to coat. Separate lettuce leaves, divide between two plates, and top with turkey salad. Sprinkle with chives and serve.

CHICKEN SALAD CALIFORNIA

Yield: 4 portions

Ingredients

Chicken legs, cooked	3
Celery	3 oz.
Eggs, hard-cooked	2
Titi shrimp	20
Mayonnaise	3 T
Sour cream	1 T
Shallot, diced, blanched	1
White wine	1 tsp.
Tomato ketchup	2 T
Lemon juice	1 to 2 tsp.
A1 sauce	1 T
Dill, chopped	1 T
Radicchio leaves	to line plates

Method

Cut chicken meat into julienne, cut celery into small pieces, slice eggs, and put all three into a bowl. Add titi shrimp. Combine mayonnaise, sour cream, shallots, white wine, tomato ketchup, lemon juice, A1 sauce, and dill to make a dressing, and toss the salad. Arrange on radicchio leaves.

THAI SPICY LIVER SALAD

Yield: 8 portions

Ingredients

Chicken stock	½ cup
Chicken or turkey liver, sliced rough	24 oz.
Shallots, sliced	3 oz.
Basil, chopped coarse	½ cup
Scallions, sliced thin	6
Lemon or lime juice	½ cup
leftover pilaf rice	4 T
Red chilies, crushed, dried	2–3 T
Fish sauce	4 T
Oil	2 T
Boston lettuce leaves	8 small

Method

Bring chicken stock to a boil. Add chicken liver and cook until medium rare. Remove

from heat and drain well. Add all other ingredients and toss thoroughly. Arrange on
lettuce leaves. Serve at room temperature.

CUCUMBER AND SEAFOOD SALAD

Yield: 6 portions
Ingredients

Shrimp, cooked	8 oz.
Cucumber	1
Wine vinegar	2 T
Salt and white pepper	to taste
Lemon peel, grated	½ tsp.
Sugar	⅓ tsp.
Vegetable oil	¼ cup
Alfalfa sprouts	½ basket

Method

Cut shrimp in half. Cut cucumber in half
lengthwise. Scrape or scoop out seeds,
using a grapefruit spoon or teaspoon, and
slice very thin. In a medium bowl, combine
shrimp and cucumber. In a small bowl, beat
together vinegar, salt, pepper, lemon peel,
and sugar. Add oil. Stir dressing into cucumber mixture. Cover and let stand one
hour. Snip sprouts with kitchen scissors.
Rinse and drain well. To serve, sprinkle
sprouts over salad.

ROASTED EGGPLANT SALAD
THAI STYLE

Yield: 12 portions
Ingredients

Japanese eggplants (approx. 24 oz.)	6
Turkey or chicken, ground	2 oz.
Peanut oil	6 T
Shrimp, peeled, halved	12 medium
Shallots, finely sliced	4 oz.
Green chilies, small, chopped coarse	6
Lime juice	5 T
Salt	to taste
Cucumber, peeled, sliced, and marinated	1

Method

Dry roast eggplants in a 400°F oven or over
a gas flame for 15 to 20 minutes or until
soft. Cool, remove skin, and slice into
1-inch-thick slices.

Over high heat, sauté ground turkey in
peanut oil. Add shallots and shrimp and
cook for 5 minutes. Add eggplant and fresh
chilies, season with salt and lime juice, toss,
and chill.

Arrange sliced marinated cucumbers on
a platter or individual plates, placing turkey
and eggplant mixture in the center.

FRISÉE AND MÂCHE SALAD WITH
PEARS AND DEEP-FRIED WALNUTS

Yield: 4 portions
Ingredients

Pears, fresh	2 lb.
Lemon juice	2 T
Pear juice (or light syrup)	3 T
Walnuts, stir-fried	2 oz.
Frisée	½ head
Mâche	4 bunchlets
Vinaigrette (vinegar, salt, pepper, oil, and walnut oil)	to toss
Deep-fried Walnuts (see recipe below)	1 lb.

Method

Peel pears and cut into wedges, removing
seeds. Sprinkle with lemon juice. Poach
pear wedges for one minute in pear juice or
light syrup, remove, and cool. Toss cut frisée and mâche with vinaigrette and arrange
with pears and walnuts.

DEEP-FRIED WALNUTS

Yield: 1 lb.
Ingredients

Water	½ gal.
Cornstarch	2 T
Sugar	2 T
Walnuts	1 lb.

| Honey | 1 T |
| Oil | to deep-fry |

Method
Bring water to a boil. Dilute cornstarch with cold water and add to boiling water together with sugar. Add walnuts and boil for 3 to 4 minutes. Drain and dry, mix with honey, and rest for 1 hour. Deep-fry at 260 to 280°F for 4 to 5 minutes, until crisp.

RADICCHIO AND SPINACH SALAD

Yield: 6 portions
Ingredients

Red endive, medium head	1
Young spinach	8 oz.
Artichoke hearts	½ of a 14-oz. can
Onions	2
Garlic	1 clove
Egg, hard-cooked	1
Olive oil	6 T
Wine vinegar	¼ cup
Salt and white pepper	to taste

Method
Remove outer endive leaves and discard. Slice off endive stem and shred stem. Separate remaining endive leaves. Remove long stems from spinach. Drain artichoke hearts and cut each in half. Slice onions into thin rings. Cut garlic clove in half. Using the cut side, rub garlic around the inside of a salad bowl. Combine endive, spinach, and artichoke hearts in a salad bowl. Scatter onion rings over greens. Chop hard-cooked egg. In a small bowl, beat together oil, vinegar, salt, pepper, and shredded endive stem, and pour over salad. Sprinkle with chopped egg before serving.

MARINATED SALAD

Yield: 6 to 8 portions
Ingredients

Ripe tomatoes, peeled, seeded, and chopped	1¼ lb.
Cucumbers, peeled, seeded, and chopped	2 med.
Green bell peppers, chopped	2
Red onion, chopped	½
Oil- or brine-cured black olives, pitted and cut into slivers	½ cup
Fresh parsley, chopped	½ cup
Fresh mint, chopped	¼ cup
Olive oil	⅔ cup
Red wine vinegar, preferably balsamic	⅓ cup
Garlic cloves, minced	2
Salt	½ tsp.
Black pepper, freshly ground	½ tsp. or to taste
Cumin, ground	¼ tsp.

Method
In a large bowl, combine the chopped tomatoes, cucumbers, green peppers, onion, olives, parsley, and mint. In a small bowl, whisk the olive oil, vinegar, garlic, salt, black pepper, and cumin until blended. Pour the dressing over the vegetables and mix. Refrigerate, covered, for several hours or overnight. Stir before serving.

LEEK SALAD

Yield: 8 portions
Ingredients

Leek, white and mild green part only, thinly sliced	1 cup
Boiling water	2 cups
Celery, chopped	1 cup
Frozen peas, thawed	1 cup (5 oz.)
Fresh mint or fennel leaves, finely chopped	1 T

Chicory, torn into bite-size pieces	about ½ lb.
Red onion, thin rounds, separated into rings	4 or 5
Navel orange, peeled and cut into thin rounds	1 small
Vegetable oil	6 T
Cider vinegar	2 T
Dijon mustard	1 tsp.
Fresh dill, minced *or*	1 tsp.
Dried dill weed	½ tsp.
Sugar	¼ tsp.
Paprika	¼ tsp.
Salt	¼ tsp.
Pepper, freshly ground	⅛ tsp.

Method

Place the sliced leek in a colander. Pour 2 cups of boiling water over it, rinse under cold water, and drain well. In a medium bowl, combine the leek, celery, peas, and mint. Toss together and place on a bed of chicory. Arrange the onion rings and orange slices on top. In a small bowl, whisk the oil, vinegar, mustard, dill, sugar, paprika, salt, and pepper until blended (or place in a small jar, cover, and shake well). Drizzle the dressing over the salad.

CLEREMONT SALAD

Yield: 9 lb.

Ingredients

Cabbage	6 lb.
Carrots	6
Green peppers	6
Cucumbers	6
Red onions	to garnish
Marinade	
Sugar	2 cups
Tarragon vinegar	2 cups
Wine vinegar	2 cups
Water	1 cup
Oil	2 cups
Salt	⅓ cup
Garlic powder	2 T

Method

Shred cabbage, peel carrots, seed pepper and cut into julienne. Peel cucumber, remove seeds, and cut into thin slices. Combine vegetables with marinade and marinate 1 hour or overnight. Garnish with red onion slices.

TABBOULEH

Yield: 2½ lb.

Ingredients

Bulgur wheat	2 cups
Boiling water	1 cup
Parsley, chopped	2 cups
Scallions, chopped	1 cup
Mint, chopped	2 T
Fresh tomatoes, medium	4
Lemon juice	¾ cup
Olive oil	1 cup
Salt	½ tsp.
Black pepper, freshly ground	½ tsp.
Paprika	1 tsp.

Method

Mix wheat with water in a bowl and refrigerate for an hour. Add all remaining ingredients. Mix well. Refrigerate at least an hour. Before serving, mix again. Check for seasonings.

PASTA SALADS

GREEN NOODLE SALAD BOLOGNAISE

Yield: 3 lb.

Ingredients

Green noodles, cooked al dente	1 lb.
Ham, finely julienned	6 oz.
Salami, finely julienned	6 oz.
Red pepper *or* red pimento, finely julienned	3 oz.
Tomatoes, blanched, peeled, seeded, and diced	4

Garlic, mashed	1 clove
Black olives, cut in half	30
White vinegar	2 to 3 oz.
Water or chicken stock	2 to 3 oz.
Oil (if possible, olive)	2 oz.
Eggs, hard-cooked, chopped coarsely	3 to 4
Salt and pepper	to taste
Radicchio	to line plates

Method
Combine all ingredients, toss well, and adjust seasoning and vinegar. Serve on a small leaf of radicchio lettuce.

VEGETABLE PASTA SALAD

Yield: 6 portions
Ingredients

Fresh basil, chopped	¼ cup
Fresh parsley, chopped	¼ cup
Garlic clove, minced	1
Olive oil	¼ cup
Lemon juice	½ cup
Parmesan cheese, grated	2 T
Dijon mustard	2 T
Fusilli	12 oz.
Zucchini, sliced	1½ cups
Carrots, shredded	1 cup
Fresh mushrooms, sliced	1 cup
Tomatoes, seeded, diced	2 small
Salt and pepper	to taste

Method
To make the dressing, combine herbs and garlic in a mixing bowl. Whisk in oil; stir in lemon juice, cheese, and mustard. Cook pasta according to package directions. Drain in colander. In a large bowl, toss hot pasta with dressing. Blend in vegetables. Season to taste with salt and pepper. Cover and refrigerate 4 to 6 hours before serving.

SPAGHETTI SALAD

Yield: 2 lb.
Ingredients

Spaghetti, cooked	10 oz.
Ham	8 oz.
Pimentos	6 oz.
Pickles	6 oz.
Oil and vinegar dressing	1 cup
Parsley, chopped	1 T

Method
Cut spaghetti and ham into small pieces. Cut pimentos and pickles into fine julienne. Toss with dressing and marinate for 1 hour. Sprinkle with parsley.

TORTELLINI SALAD

Yield: 6 lb.
Ingredients

Tortellini	2 lb.
Italian dressing	½ qt.
Pesto	1 cup
Genoa salami	1½ lb.
Red onions	8 oz.
Celery	8 oz.
Red peppers or pimentos	8 oz.
Green peppers	8 oz.
Tomatoes, peeled, seeded, diced	10
Chicory	to line plates

Method
Put tortellini in boiling water and cook al dente. Drain and immerse in Italian dressing immediately. Chop salami and vegetables uniformly. Use #10 scoop for portions. Serve at room temperature on a base of chicory.

RICE SALADS

Rice salads should be served at room temperature.

INDIAN RICE SALAD

Yield: 5 cups

Ingredients

Rice	1 cup
Saffron	⅓ tsp.
Olives (Spanish/stuffed)	1 oz.
Olives (black)	1 oz.
Pimento	1
Green pepper	1
Salt	⅓ tsp.
Pepper, freshly ground	2 to 3 grinds
Worcestershire sauce	½ tsp.
Basic French dressing	1 cup

Method

Make a pilaf of rice, using the saffron. Cool and mix with sliced olives, diced julienne of pimentos, and diced green pepper, and season with salt, pepper, and Worcestershire sauce. Mix well with the French dressing.

CURRY RICE PATRICIA

Yield: 5 cups

Ingredients

Onions, diced	9½ oz.
Butter	¼ lb.
Curry powder	1½ T
White wine	½ cup
Vinegar	¼ cup
Converted rice	1 cup
Water	2½ cups
Ham, diced	4½ oz.
Apples, diced	2
Oil	¼ cup
Salt and white pepper	to taste

Method

Sauté onions in butter; add curry powder, wine, and vinegar. Reduce until onions are translucent. Cook rice in water for 20 minutes or until done. Mix ham, rice, and apples, then incorporate onion mixture and oil. Add salt and pepper to taste.

RICE SALAD WITH CURRY

Yield: 8 to 9 cups

Ingredients

Rice	2 cups
Salt	1 tsp.
Oil	1 T
Bananas	2
Red peppers	2
Titi shrimp, cooked	8 oz.
Cashews, toasted	2 oz.
Curry powder	1 tsp.
Thousand Island dressing	1 to 1½ cups

Method

Cook rice in salt water and shock with cold water. Drain well and sprinkle with oil. Peel bananas and cut into slices. Cut red peppers in half, remove seeds, and cut into cubes. Toss bananas, peppers, shrimp, and cashews with rice. Mix curry powder with Thousand Island dressing and fold into the salad. Marinate for 20 minutes.

RICE SALAD BOMBAY

Yield: 4 cups

Ingredients

Cooked rice	1 cup
Red peppers, diced	2
Mango, fresh or canned, cubed	1
Boston lettuce	1 head
Sugar	1 tsp.
Oil and vinegar dressing	1 cup

Method

Combine rice, diced red peppers, and cubed mangoes. Clean Boston lettuce and line a bowl. Set rice salad in center. Mix sugar with dressing and pour over salad. Marinate for 5 minutes before serving.

MEAT SALADS

LEFTOVER-BEEF SALAD WITH RICE

Yield: 8 portions

Ingredients

Leftover cooked beef	8 oz.
Red peppers	2
Pickle	1
Onion	1
Boiled rice	4 oz.
Oil and vinegar dressing	3 oz.
Salt	to taste
Pepper	to taste
Cayenne pepper	to taste
Tomatoes	8 medium
Lemon wedges	8
Parsley	to garnish

Method

Dice beef, red peppers, pickle, and onion, and blanch. Mix with rice and dressing and season. Hollow out tomatoes and fill with salad. Decorate with lemon wedge and parsley.

SAUSAGE SALAD

Yield: 1 lb.

Ingredients

Knockwurst	12 oz.
Vinegar	2 to 3 oz.
Water	1 to 2 oz.
Salt	to taste
Sugar	to taste
Oil	1 to 2 oz.
Onions, finely sliced	3 to 4 oz.
Pepper	to taste
Lettuce leaves	to line plates

Method

Skin sausage and slice. Combine vinegar, water, dissolve salt and sugar, and add oil. Stir into sliced sausage and onion and season with pepper. Marinate for one hour. Arrange on lettuce leaf. Serve with rye or pumpernickel bread.

VARIATION I

Yield: 1½ lb.

Ingredients

Knockwurst, sliced	10 oz.
Kosher pickle, cut into julienne	1
Carrots, blanched and shredded	3 oz.
Onion, thinly sliced	2 oz.
Apple, peeled, cored, cut into julienne	1
Italian dressing	3 oz.
Chopped chives	to garnish

VARIATION II

Yield: 1 lb.

Ingredients

Tomatoes, blanched, peeled, seeded, and cubed	16 oz.
Red onions, thinly sliced	3 oz.
Garlic, finely mashed	1 to 2 cloves
Green pepper, cut into julienne	1
Kielbasa or garlic sausage, sliced	7 oz.
Lemon juice	1 oz.
Olive oil	2 oz.
Salt	to taste
Pepper	to taste
Mustard	1 T

TONGUE SALAD

Yield: 2½ lb.

Ingredients

Ox tongue, cooked	24 oz.
Pickled cucumber	1
Pimento	2 oz.
Belgian endive	2
Truffle	1
French dressing	1 cup
Paprika	1 tsp.

Method
Cut ox tongue, pickled cucumber, pimento, endive, and truffle into julienne strips. Combine all ingredients with dressing and paprika and mix.

GAME SALAD

Yield: 17 oz.
Ingredients

Leftover game (venison, pheasant, hare)	10 oz.
Mayonnaise	⅓ cup
English mustard	1 tsp.
Red currant jelly	¼ cup
Orange, cut into wedges	1 small
Walnuts, chopped	2 T

Method
Cut game into julienne strips. Mix mayonnaise with mustard and red currant jelly. Combine game and orange with mayonnaise mixture and sprinkle with walnuts.

AMERICAN SALAD

Yield: 24 oz. (5 to 6 portions)
Ingredients

Frankfurters	8 oz.
Swiss cheese	8 oz.
Mayonnaise	1 cup
French mustard	1 T
Shallots, chopped, sautéed	1 T
Salt	1 tsp.
Pepper	½ tsp.
Vinegar	¼ cup
Chives, chopped	2 T

Method
Cut frankfurters on a bias into ½-inch pieces. Cut cheese into julienne strips. Mix mayonnaise with mustard. Add sautéed shallots, salt, pepper, and vinegar to the sauce. Combine frankfurters, cheese, and sauce. Mix all ingredients with chives.

ITALIAN MEAT SALAD

Yield: 24 oz.
Ingredients

Salami, veal, or bologna	8 oz.
Pickles	2 oz.
Apple	1 oz.
Mayonnaise	½ cup
Worcestershire sauce	½ tsp.
Anchovies, chopped	½ oz.
Eggs, hard-cooked, chopped	2
Pickles, chopped	1 T

Method
Cut salami, veal, or bologna in fine julienne strips. Cut pickles and apple into julienne. Combine these ingredients with mayonnaise; blend well. Add Worcestershire sauce and chopped anchovies. Mix all ingredients well. Decorate salad with chopped egg and chopped pickle.

CHICKEN SALAD

Yield: 1½ lb.
Ingredients

Chicken, cooked, diced	12 oz.
Celery stalks, diced	2
Pecans, toasted	20
Shallot, diced	1
Eggs, hard-cooked, diced	2
Lemon juice	1 tsp.
Mayonnaise	2 to 3 oz.
Salt	to taste
Pepper	to taste
Lettuce Leaves	to line plate

Method
Combine chicken, celery, nuts, shallots, egg, and lemon juice. Fold in mayonnaise and season with salt and pepper. Serve on lettuce leaf.

VARIATION I

Yield: 2 lb.

Ingredients

Chicken meat, diced	10 oz.
Apple, peeled and shredded	1
Lemon	juice of 1
Pineapple, diced	4 rings
Kernel corn	8 oz.
Mayonnaise	8 oz.
Salt	to taste
Pepper	to taste

VARIATION II

Yield: 1½ lb.

Ingredients

Chicken meat, diced	12 oz.
Celery stalks, diced	2
Shallot, diced	1
Almonds, toasted	3 oz.
Mayonnaise	3 oz.
Brandy	1 T
Salt	to taste
Pepper	to taste
Hot pepper sauce	2 drops
Hard-cooked egg, apples, capers, and Boston lettuce	to garnish

VARIATION III

Yield: 1¾ lb.

Ingredients

Chicken meat, diced	12 oz.
Celery, diced	5 oz.
Orange, cut into wedges	1
Green seedless grapes, cut in half	2 oz.
Walnuts, coarsely chopped and toasted	1 oz.
Ripe banana, sliced	1
Mayonnaise	3 oz.
Sour cream	1 oz.
Salt	to taste
Black pepper	to taste

BEEF SALAD #1

Yield: 1¾ lb.

Ingredients

Cooked beef, cut into julienne	16 oz.
Mayonnaise	8 oz.
Apples, braised in white wine, *or* applesauce	2
Madras curry powder	2 to 4 tsp.
Mango chutney	2 T
Salt	
White pepper	
Shredded coconut	2 tsp.
Toasted almond sticks	2 tsp.

Method

Combine beef, mayonnaise, apples, curry powder, and chutney. Season with salt and pepper. Garnish with coconut and almonds.

BEEF SALAD #2

Yield: 1 lb.

Ingredients

Beef, cooked	8 oz.
Pickles	1 oz.
Tomatoes	1 oz.
Celery	1 oz.
Basic French dressing	¼ cup
Salt	⅓ tsp.
Pepper	½ tsp.
Garlic powder	⅓ tsp.
Prepared mustard	1 T
Parsley, chopped	1 tsp.
Tarragon, chopped	1 tsp.
Chives, chopped	1 tsp.
Green olives	1 T
Egg, hard-cooked, sliced	1

Method

Cut beef, pickles, tomato, and celery into julienne. Marinate in dressing containing salt, pepper, garlic powder, prepared mustard, parsley, tarragon, and chives. Before serving, decorate dish with sliced egg and sliced olives.

COMBINATION SALAD

Yield: 12 portions
Ingredients

Potatoes, baked or boiled, diced	32 oz.
Chicken, turkey, *or* beef, cooked, diced	16 oz. (3 cups)
Zucchini, diced	4 medium
Eggs, hard-cooked, coarsely diced	6
Chopped herbs (chervil, parsley, chives)	2 to 3 tablespoons
Mayonnaise	1 cup
Heavy cream *or* chicken stock	¼ cup
Vinegar	1 to 2 T
Salt	¾ tsp. or to taste
White pepper	¼ tsp. or to taste

Method
Combine potatoes, chicken, zucchini, eggs, and herbs. Combine mayonnaise, heavy cream or stock, vinegar, white pepper, and salt (if needed). Fold in potato/chicken mixture. Toss well. Marinate for 1 hour. Adjust seasoning. Serve salad at room temperature.

VEGETABLE SALADS

LEEKS IN ORANGE TARRAGON VINAIGRETTE

Yield: 8 portions
Ingredients

Leeks	8 medium
Orange	1
Olive oil	¾ cup
Vinegar, white	2 T
Orange juice	3 T
Garlic, minced	1 tsp.
Tarragon, fresh	1 T

Method
Clean leeks thoroughly in cold water. Cut leeks diagonally into 2-inch pieces and boil, steam, or microwave until tender. Cool. Remove rind from orange with a vegetable peeler and cut into fine strips. Blanch in boiling water for two minutes; cool and drain. To make the orange vinaigrette, combine oil, vinegar, and orange juice in a bowl. Stir in garlic and tarragon. Serve the leeks with orange vinaigrette and top with rind.

KASHI VEGETABLE SALAD

Yield: 4 portions
Ingredients

Kashi, cooked and chilled	2 cups
Mushrooms, sliced	½ cup
Green pepper, diced	¼ cup
Red pepper, diced	¼ cup
Waterchestnuts, sliced	8 oz.
Parsley, chopped	¼ cup
Green onions, diced	¼ cup
Celery, diced	¼ cup
Tomatoes, diced	¼ cup
Vegetable oil	⅓ cup
Soy sauce	⅓ cup
Wine vinegar	2 T
Dijon mustard	1 T
Radicchio leaves	4

Method
In a mixing bowl, combine kashi, mushrooms, peppers, waterchestnuts, parsley, green onions, celery, and tomatoes. In another bowl, stir together the oil, soy sauce, vinegar, and mustard. Pour the dressing over the kashi salad and toss. Refrigerate until thoroughly chilled. Arrange radicchio leaves on cold plates. Spoon the kashi salad over the lettuce. Serve cold.

   Note: Kashi is a blend of whole grains (oats, brown rice, rye, wheat, triticale, buckwheat, and barley) and sesame seeds.

BEET SALAD

Yield: 15 oz.

Ingredients

Beets	1 lb.
Heavy cream	½ cup
English mustard	1 tsp.
Lemons	juice of 2
Sugar	1 tsp.
Salt	1 to 1½ tsp.
Pepper	⅓ to ½ tsp.

Method

Wash beets and cook in boiling water till tender. Cool and slice. Blend heavy cream, mustard, lemon juice, sugar, salt, and pepper and combine with beets.

BOSTON LETTUCE, HARICOT VERT, AND TOMATO SALAD

Yield: 6 portions

Ingredients

Boston lettuce	2 heads
Haricots verts	10 oz.
Tomatoes	3 medium
Dressing	
White wine	2 oz.
Chicken stock	2 oz.
Shallots, diced	1½ oz.
White wine vinegar	2 to 3 T
Salt and pepper	to taste
Walnut oil	1½ oz.
Chervil, finely chopped	1 T
Parsley, finely chopped	1 T
Chives, finely chopped	1 T

Method

Clean Boston lettuce and separate leaves. Blanch haricots verts to the crunch, shock, and drain. Blanch tomatoes, peel, cut into wedges, remove seeds. Arrange on a plate.

Prepare dressing by reducing white wine, chicken stock, and shallots by three-quarters; add vinegar, salt, and pepper.

Chill; add chopped herbs and oil. Sprinkle over salad before service.

CARROT SALAD

Yield: 15 oz.

Ingredients

Carrots, fresh (or a 14-oz. can of Belgian carrots)	1 lb.
French mustard	2 T
Garlic, finely chopped	1 clove
Oil	½ cup
Vinegar	¼ cup
Salt	½ to 1 tsp.
Pepper	⅓ tsp.
Chives, chopped	2 tsp.

Method

Peel fresh carrots, cook until tender, and slice. If using canned carrots, drain before using. Combine all remaining ingredients and hold for 30 minutes before serving.

BASIC CUCUMBER SALAD

Yield: 8 to 10 portions

Ingredients

Cucumbers, peeled and sliced	3
Onion, finely diced	1 small
Dill, fresh, chopped, or	3 T
Dill, freeze-dried	2 T
Salt	1 tsp. or to taste
Sugar	1 tsp.
Chicken vinaigrette	½ cup

Method

Combine cucumbers, onions, dill, salt, and sugar. Add vinaigrette and toss well. Marinate for 1 hour. Chill. Adjust seasonings and serve.

Note: For a Russian cucumber salad, drain and add sour cream. This cucumber salad is also good for mixing, half and half, with potato salad, especially in summer.

GREEN BEAN SALAD

Yield: 2 lb.
Ingredients

Green beans, fresh or frozen	1 lb.
Pimento, diced	½ cup
Bacon, diced, cooked crisp	4 oz.
Garlic powder	⅓ tsp.
Salt	½ to 1 tsp.
Pepper	½ tsp.
Basic French dressing	½ cup

Method
If using fresh beans, cut tips from both ends and cut into 2-inch pieces. Cook beans in boiling salted water until done. Drain thoroughly and cool. If using frozen beans, cook according to directions. Combine pimento, bacon, and seasonings with dressing. Add cooked beans to dressing. Mix well.

CAULIFLOWER SALAD

Yield: 20 to 25 oz.
Ingredients

Cauliflower	1 medium, 16 to 20 oz.
Basic French dressing	1 cup
Prepared mustard	1 T
Lemon	juice of 1
Garlic, chopped	1 clove
Egg yolks, hard-cooked, chopped	3

Method
Wash cauliflower and cook in boiling water until done. Cool and cut into small pieces. Combine remaining ingredients and mix with cauliflower. Marinate for 1 hour in refrigerator.

WALDORF SALAD

Yield: 1 lb. 14 oz.
Ingredients

Apples	1 lb.
Celeriac, blanched	4 oz.
Walnuts, toasted	2 oz.
Mayonnaise	¼ cup
Sour cream or whipped cream	¼ cup
Lemon	juice of 1
Salt (optional)	⅓ tsp.

Method
Dice apples, celeriac, and walnuts. Combine mayonnaise, sour cream or whipped cream, and lemon juice. Blend apples, celeriac, and walnuts into mayonnaise mixture.

SALAD MARIE-LOUISE

Yield: 2 portions
Ingredients

Banana	1
Celery	1 stalk
Apple	1
Truffle	1
Mayonnaise	½ cup

Method
Peel and slice banana; peel and dice apple; peel and dice celery. Combine all ingredients with mayonnaise and arrange on platter with a slice of truffle on top.

FISH SALADS

The following recipes can be made using any leftover fish.

HEALTHY TUNA SALAD

Yield: 6 portions
Ingredients

Yogurt, plain low-fat	8 oz.

Parsley, chopped	¼ cup
White onion, minced	½ tsp.
Fresh dill, chopped	1 tsp.
Green beans	2 cups
Boston lettuce	1 medium
American cheese, cubed	½ cup
Tomato, cubed	1 large
Tuna, water-packed, drained	12 oz.
Cucumber slices	12
Parsley	for garnish

Method

In a bowl, combine yogurt, parsley, onion, and dill. Cover and chill. Cook green beans in salted boiling water until done and drain. Chill quickly in ice water and drain well. Clean and dry lettuce. Cut into bite-sized pieces. In a large bowl, combine lettuce, green beans, and cheese. Spoon dressing over salad and toss. Add tomato. Flake tuna into the salad bowl. Gently toss salad. Garnish salad with cucumber slices and parsley.

HERRING SALAD

Yield: 18 oz.

Ingredients

Bismarck herring	8 oz.
Apples	2 oz.
Beets, cooked	2 oz.
Potatoes, cooked	2 oz.
Basic French dressing	½ cup
Salt	⅓ tsp.
Pepper	2 to 3 grinds

Method

Soak herring in water. Dice apples, beets, and potatoes. Drain herring and dice. Combine all ingredients. Add dressing, salt, and pepper. Refrigerate for 1 hour.

SMOKED SALMON WITH ENDIVE AND ZUCCHINI

Yield: 4 portions

Ingredients

Belgian endive	2 large heads
Zucchini	2 small
Vinaigrette	¼ cup
Smoked salmon, sliced	8 oz.
Parsley sprigs	to garnish

Method

Cut endive in half lengthwise. Remove cores and slice leaves into very fine julienne. Slice the zucchini lengthwise into thin slices. Cut into julienne. Place zucchini and endive in a mixing bowl and toss with vinaigrette. Divide salad evenly among four plates. Arrange smoked salmon slices on top of salad. Garnish with sprigs of parsley. Serve cold.

LOBSTER SALAD

Yield: 21 oz.

Ingredients

Lobster meat	8 oz.
Eggs, hard-cooked	2
Mayonnaise	½ cup
Lemon	juice of 1
Mustard	1 T
Salt	⅓ tsp.
Pepper	2 to 3 grinds
Lettuce	1 leaf
Parsley, chopped	1 tsp.
Lobster coral	1 tsp.

Method

Dice lobster meat; combine with chopped egg. Blend mayonnaise with lemon juice, mustard, salt, and pepper and combine with lobster and egg. Place salad on lettuce leaf. Sprinkle with chopped parsley and coral.

KING CRAB SALAD

Use same procedure and amounts of ingredients as for Lobster Salad, substituting crabmeat for lobster.

SALAD OF LEFTOVER FISH

Yield: 23 oz.
Ingredients
Shallots, chopped	1 T
Olive oil	¼ cup
Capers	2 tsp.
Green olives, sliced	2 oz.
Cèpes (wild mushrooms)	4 oz.
Garlic, chopped	2 cloves
White wine	½ cup
Pickles, diced	2 oz.
Tarragon, fresh	1 T
Chili sauce	¼ cup
Salt	1 tsp.
Pepper	½ tsp.
Lemon	juice of 2
Fish, leftover, flaked	8 oz.

Method
Sauté chopped shallots in oil until transparent. Add capers, green olives, cèpes, and garlic and heat through. Deglaze pan with white wine. Add pickles, tarragon, chili sauce, salt, pepper, and lemon juice. Cook for 5 minutes. Pour sauce over fish, mix, and cool for 2 hours before serving.

MUSSEL SALAD

Yield: 9 oz.
Ingredients
Mussels, cooked, cleaned	4 oz.
Asparagus tips	1 oz.
Green beans, French-cut, cooked	1 oz.
Tomato, peeled, diced	1 oz.
Onion, chopped	1 T
Horseradish, grated	1 tsp.
Basic French dressing	½ cup
Salt	⅓ tsp.
Pepper	⅓ tsp.

Method
Combine all ingredients. Refrigerate for 1 hour before serving.

SHRIMP, MANGO, AND AVOCADO SALAD

Yield: 6 portions
Ingredients
Avocados	3 medium
Mangoes, peeled	2 medium
Shrimps, cooked, peeled, and deveined	1½ lb.
Button mushrooms, sliced	4 oz.
Fresh ginger, grated	1 tsp.
Salad oil	½ cup
White vinegar	2 T
Honey	1 tsp.
Mustard (with seeds)	1 tsp.
Lemon juice	1 T
Fresh chives, chopped	1 T
Fresh dill, chopped	1 T

Method
Cut avocados in half lengthwise. Remove seeds and spoon flesh out of shells. Save shells. Cut avocado flesh into medium chunks. Slice and dice mangoes into medium pieces. Combine avocado, mango, shrimp, and mushrooms in a large bowl and set aside. In a mixing bowl, combine ginger, oil, vinegar, honey, mustard, lemon juice, and herbs. Add dressing to avocado/mango mixture; toss lightly. Serve salad in avocado shells.

SOUTH AMERICAN SALAD

Yield: 6 portions
Ingredients
Bananas	3 large
Celery	1 stalk
Seedless green grapes or blue grapes	4 oz.
Mayonnaise, flavored with lemon juice	½ cup
Pistachio nuts	1 oz.
Apple, cut into 12 wedges	1 medium

Method

Cut bananas into half lengthwise. Slice bananas and celery into ⅓-inch pieces and combine with grapes. Blend mayonnaise into mixture. Sprinkle salad with pistachios and decorate with apple wedges.

MACEDOINE OF FRUITS

Yield: 4 lb.
Ingredients

Apples	2
Pears	2
Peaches	2
Pineapple	1 medium
Bananas	2
Oranges	2
Sugar	as needed
Walnuts	1 oz.
Pistachio nuts	1 oz.
Maraschino brandy (optional)	

Method

Peel fruit and slice or dice. Combine all fruit and mix well; add sugar if necessary. Serve chilled in a crystal bowl or in individual portions in champagne glasses. Top servings with chopped walnuts and pistachio nuts. Maraschino brandy can be added.

CANTALOUPE STUFFED WITH CHICKEN, LOBSTER, OR CRABMEAT

Yield: 4 portions
Ingredients

Cantaloupes	2
Chicken, lobster, or crab-meat	8 oz.
Pickles, diced	4 oz.
Mayonnaise	½ cup
Lemon juice	1 tsp.
Tarragon, chopped	1 tsp.

Method

Cut cantaloupes in half and remove melon from shells. Dice melon and combine with chicken, lobster, or crab, and pickles. Combine mayonnaise, lemon juice, and chopped tarragon and blend into mixture. Fill melon halves with salad, chill, and serve on crushed ice.

STUFFED PEACHES

Yield: 4 portions
Ingredients

Lobster meat	4 oz.
Pears	4 oz.
Salt	¼ tsp.
Pepper, freshly ground	4 grinds
Orange juice	¼ cup
Peach halves	4

Method

Dice lobster meat and pears. Season with salt and pepper and mix with the orange juice. Stuff peach halves with mixture and chill. Serve with mayonnaise and lemon juice.

STUFFED TOMATOES #1

Yield: 6 portions
Ingredients

Cooked chicken meat	4 oz.
Pineapple	2 oz.
Chutney, chopped	1 oz.
Chili sauce	1 oz.
Oil	2 T
Lemon	juice of 1
Salt	⅓ tsp.
Pepper	⅓ tsp.
Tomatoes, cut in half, with pulp scooped out	6 medium

Method

Dice chicken and pineapple, then combine with remaining ingredients. Stuff tomatoes with mixture and serve cold.

STUFFED TOMATOES #2

Yield: 6 portions
Ingredients

King crabmeat	12 oz.
Mushrooms, cooked	6 oz.
Oil	¼ cup
Lemons	juice of 2
Chili sauce	2 oz.
Salt	⅓ tsp.
Tomatoes, cut in half, with pulp scooped out	6 medium

Method

Dice crabmeat and mushrooms. Season with oil, lemon juice, chili sauce, and salt. Stuff tomato halves and serve cold.

STUFFED TOMATOES #3

Yield: 8 portions
Ingredients

Artichoke bottoms	4
Green beans	8 oz.
Basic French dressing	¼ cup
Parsley, chopped	1 T
Tarragon, chopped	1 tsp.
Tomatoes, cut in half, with pulp scooped out	4 medium

Method

Cut artichokes into julienne strips. Combine with beans and season with dressing. Stuff tomato halves and sprinkle with tarragon and parsley.

Cheeses

Only by knowing how various cheeses taste and how they are made can the chef blend each kind of cheese successfully with other ingredients in cooking and select the proper cheese as the finishing touch for a successful dinner.

Cheese is made in a variety of ways. Usually, rennet, an extract taken from newborn calves, is added to whole milk. The rennet causes the milk solids to coagulate into curds; the remaining liquid is whey. The whey is drained from the curds by straining through linen cloth. The curds are then molded into different shapes and sizes and ripened into cheese. The different cheese-making regions add a variety of molds and bacteria to the rennet, based on tradition, to give their cheeses distinctive flavor.

Every country and, in some countries, every district, has its own unique cheese. Many local cheeses have become famous as menu items and are considered "kings" in their own right. Among the kings of cheesedom are Cheddar, an English cheese that was first made in the village of Cheddar from the milk of Ayrshire cows; Emmenthaler cheese, named after the Emmenthal Valley in the canton of Bern in Switzerland; Roquefort, a cheese from France, named after the village where it is made.

As time has passed, many cheeses, origi-nally made only in one specific place, are now being made elsewhere as well. For example, today there are American cheddars, brie from Wisconsin, and bleu cheese from Denmark. These cheeses are known as variants of the originals and are sold as such.

What are the varieties of cheeses?

1. Fresh cheese (unfermented, made from raw curds)
2. Fermented cheeses, usually divided into two types:
   a. Soft cheese (Brie)
   b. Hard cheese (Cheddar)
3. Cheeses made from scalded curds (Emmenthaler or Parmesan), also called rennet cheeses
4. Semi-soft cheese (Bel Paese, Muenster)
5. Blue mold cheese (Roquefort, Stilton)
6. White mold cheese (Camembert)
7. Sour milk cheeses
   a. Fresh sour milk cheese (cream cheese)
   b. Stored sour milk cheese (basket cheese)

The following list describes the cheeses most often used.

Bel Paese. This Italian cheese is semisoft in consistency and of milk flavor.

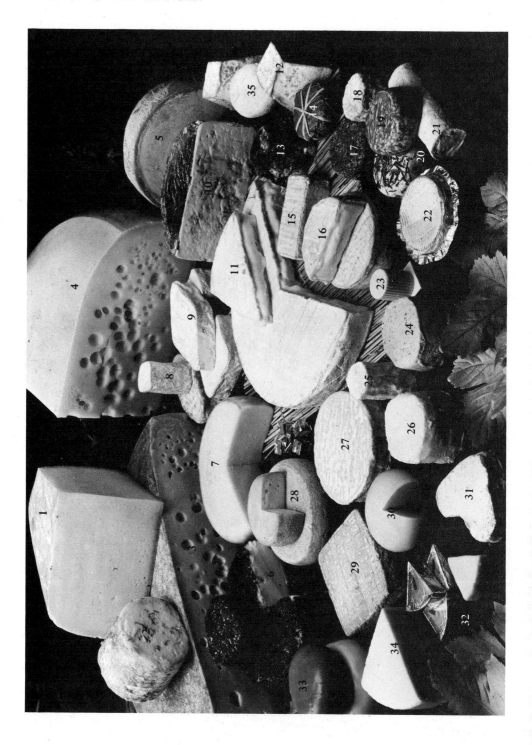

Among the many cheeses that may be used in the garde manger department are: 1. Cantal (French Cheddar); 2. Bleu de Bresse; 3. Comté; 4. Emmenthaler; 5. Beaumont; 6. Fromage au Marc de Raisin; 7. Port Salut; 8. Chabichou; 9. Reblochon; 10. Roquefort; 11. Brie de Meaux; 12. Valençay (Pyramid Goat Cheese); 13. Selle sur Cher; 14. Baron de Provence; 15. Baguette d' Avènes; 16. Colommiers; 17. Poivre Doux; 18. Triple Crème (Boursin); 19. Livarot; 20. Ascot; 21. Saint Maure; 22. Camembert; 23. Petit Suisse; 24. Montréal; 25. Bellétoile Triplecrème; 26. Chaource; 27. Brillat-Savarin; 28. Muenster; 29. Fromage de Cure; 30. Guerbigny; 31. Angelot; 32. Gervaise; 33. Edam; 34. Tomme de Savoie; 35. Reblochon. (*Courtesy* Foods of France)

Brie. This French white mold cheese has a soft consistency and a fine, mild aroma. The cheese is round and flat, about 1 to 1½ inch thick, and sold on a straw matting. Brie remains in perfect condition for only a short time, during which the rind is firm and thin and the inside mellow and soft in texture.

Camembert. This white mold cheese is from Normandy; a similar cheese is produced and sold under the same label in this country. Camembert reaches maturity after one month. The consistency is waxy and semisoft; the crust is white. As the cheese continues to ripen, the skin becomes brownish-red.

Cheddar. This cheese is generally available in large cylinders, weighing 50 to 100 pounds. It is wrapped in cheesecloth and stored at a low temperature for six to twelve months. A good Cheddar should be uniformly colored and free of holes, and there should be no cracks in the rind.

Danish Bleu Cheese. Made from cow's milk, Danish bleu looks somewhat like Roquefort but the taste is sharper and the consistency smoother. Danish bleu cheese ripens very quickly. It must always be listed as bleu cheese.

Edam. All Dutch cheeses have a characteristic appearance. They are spherical, with an outer covering of red wax, and weigh 2 to 4 pounds. A smaller variety, weighing 1 pound, is known as baby edam. Edam is slightly flattened in shape and wrapped in red cellophane. Edam cheese is light golden in color. The taste is mildly sour and rather salty. Storage time is two to four months.

Emmenthaler. This cheese originated in Switzerland but is now produced in the United States and the rest of the world. Emmenthaler cheese takes from seven to twelve months to ripen. When ripe, it has a firm, dry texture with large tunnels or holes that contain a clear liquid. The cheese is made in the shape of wheels that measure about a yard in diameter and weigh up to 200 pounds.

Gouda. This Dutch cow's-milk cheese resembles edam but contains more fat. It is pressed in cloth-lined molds, cured in brine, and ripened for one year. Gouda has a straw yellow color, a fairly hard texture, and a strong but pleasing flavor.

Gruyère. Gruyère resembles Emmenthaler cheese but is made in smaller sizes. It is stored in cellars having high humidity, and as a result a puttylike layer is formed on the outer surface, giving the cheese a strong flavor and aroma. The period of aging is eight to twelve months.

Parmesan. A cheese that belongs to the group of Italian grand cheeses, Parmesan is used grated or shredded in cooking. The storage period is two to five years; the texture is hard and brittle. The flavor is mild but pronounced. The characteristic black surface of the cheese is achieved by smearing it with oil containing lamb fat.

Roquefort. This French blue-veined cheese is made from sheep's milk. A salty cheese, it is stored in caves near the town of Roquefort under special conditions of temperature and humidity. The cheese is cylindrical and wrapped in tin foil.

Stilton. This is a blue mold cheese of high fat content with a brown wrinkled surface and a whitish-yellow inside. The flavor is strong, aromatic, and salty.

STORING CHEESE

All cheeses require cool storage. If the room is too warm and moist, cheeses ripen too fast; if it is too dry, they become hard. Small pieces of cheese may be stored under cheese covers, rolled aluminum foil, or a damp cloth. Larger pieces of cheese should be folded in cheesecloth that has been soaked in strong brine.

Soft cheeses, like brie or camembert, are difficult to store. These types of cheeses should be bought when just ripe and should be used as soon as possible. Leftover pieces that have become hard can be grated, ground, or dried and stored in a screw-top jar in the refrigerator to be used in salads or other dishes.

How should cheese be served?
Man invented cheese by accident, but it has always served faithfully as a nutritious food that refreshes the palate. Today,

cheese is still in demand on most buffets and in à la carte setups.

If cheese has been stored in the refrigerator, it must be taken out at least one-half hour before serving to give it a chance to breathe. Cheese is always served before the dessert, following the main course or with the salad. Cheese is served on separate plates, if served individually, or on a cheese board, for variety or more dramatic presentation.

Butter can be served with the cheese; however, connoisseurs will reject it. Among the breads that are excellent as accompaniments to cheese are Russian pumpernickel, Knaeke-Brot, various crackers, rye bread, toast, croutons, and French or Italian bread. For extra color and flavor, radishes and celery can be added to cheese servings. Sticks of celery, tomato wedges, olives, or bulb fennel also make very good accompaniments to cheese, as do all kinds of noncitrus fruits.

What wines should be served with cheese?
Cheeses, especially strong ones, can be served with all wines, except sparkling and sweet wines. Strong cheeses demand red wine; lighter cheeses demand light wines.

CREAM CHEESE SPREAD

Yield: 16 oz.
Ingredients

Cream cheese	10 oz.
Butter	4 oz.
Salt	to taste
Heavy cream, whipped	1 to 2 oz.

Method
Press cream cheese through a flour sieve. Whip butter until creamy. Mix with cream cheese. Season with salt. Fold whipped heavy cream into cream cheese—butter mixture.

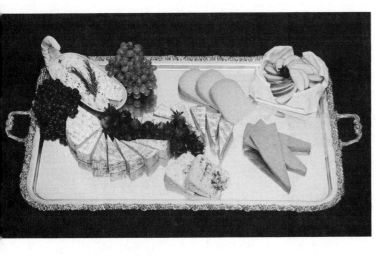

Assorted cheeses and fruit. Cheese is displayed on a sheet of Plexiglass to protect the silver tray.

For other flavor combinations, before adding whipped cream, add 1 tablespoon dill; 1 teaspoon sweet paprika and 1 tablespoon chopped chives; or 1 cup of fresh chopped herbs.

Interesting service suggestions include enveloping grapes or nuts in the spread or rolling a ball of the spread in fresh chopped herbs.

HOT COTTAGE CHEESE PUDDING

Yield: 4 portions

Ingredients

Large eggs	4
Butter, soft	3 oz.
Cottage cheese	17½ oz.
Semolina	2 oz.
Baking powder	1 tsp.
Fresh mushrooms or chanterelles *or* cèpes	9 oz.
Onion	1 medium
Garlic, minced	3 cloves
Parsley	½ bunch
Red or green pepper	7 oz.
Sausage meat	9 oz.
Pepper, salt, soy sauce, Worcestershire sauce	to taste
Grated lemon peel	from ½ lemon
Butter	to grease mold
Red Wine Sauce (see below)	approximately 1½ pt.

Method

Separate eggs. Whip butter and egg yolks till creamy. Fold in cottage cheese, then semolina and baking powder. Slice mushrooms; dice the onion and garlic fine; chop parsley fine. Remove seeds from pepper and slice. Sauté onions and garlic in butter. Add all other raw ingredients and sausage meat. Saute for 5 minutes. Season and cool. Combine cottage cheese/sausage mixture. Whip egg whites stiff and fold into mixture. Grease soufflé mold. Set in a preheated 400°F oven, covered, for 25 minutes. Remove cover and bake for 10 more minutes. Serve immediately with tomato sauce or Red Wine Sauce and crisp, tossed salad greens.

RED WINE SAUCE

Ingredients

Dried cèpes	1 oz.
Butter or olive oil	¾ to 1 oz.
Bacon, diced	12 oz.
Onion, diced	1
Garlic, mashed	1 clove
Red wine, dry	½ bottle
Veal fond	1 cup

(continued)

Red Wine Sauce (continued)

Salt, pepper	to taste
Parsley, chopped	3 to 4 T
Heavy cream	½ cup

Method

Soak mushrooms in boiling water for 1 hour and drain. Heat butter or oil. Sauté bacon, onion and garlic. Add cèpes and brown lightly. Add wine and fond and reduce by half to a syrupy consistency. Purée in a blender. Season. Fold in heavy cream and chopped parsley.

Note: Any type of mushrooms can be used instead of cèpes.

CHEDDAR CHEESE BISCUITS

Yield: 16 to 20 biscuits

Ingredients

Flour, all-purpose	1 cup
Cheddar cheese, sharp, grated	1 cup
Milk	½ cup
Butter, softened	¼ cup
Salt	½ tsp.
Baking powder	2 tsp.

Method

Combine all ingredients into a smooth paste, shape into a cylinder, roll into plastic wrap, and refrigerate until firm. Cut into ½-inch-thick slices. Bake at 350°F for 10 to 15 minutes.

CHEESE CIGARETTES

Yield: 8 portions

Ingredients

White bread	8 slices
Swiss cheese	1 cup
Heavy cream	⅓ cup

Method

Roll the bread with a rolling pin. Melt the cheese with the cream. Cool and spread over bread. Roll the bread into a cigarette shape. Deep-fry at 370°F until golden brown. Cut into halves or quarters. Serve hot.

GOUGÈRE BOURGUIGNONNE

Yield: 7 portions

Ingredients

Water	1 cup
Butter	4 oz.
Salt	¼ tsp
Flour	1 cup
Eggs	4
Swiss cheese, grated	4 oz.

Method

Boil water, butter, and salt. Add flour and mix well over medium heat to form a smooth paste. Stir in the eggs, one at a time. Finally fold the cheese into the mixture. Spoon or pipe small amounts onto a baking sheet. Brush with egg. Bake at 375°F for 10 to 15 minutes. May be served with a cheese sauce.

MUFFINS WITH BRIE

Yield: 4 portions

Ingredients

English muffins	2
Brie cheese	4 oz
Ham, chopped	2 oz

Method

Cut the muffins in half and toast. Melt the cheese over low heat and mix in the ham. Spread the cheese mixture over the muffins. Cut into bite-size portions. Broil and serve warm.

PARMESAN TOAST

Yield: 12 rounds

Ingredients

Mayonnaise	½ cup
Parmesan cheese, grated	½ cup
Onion, minced	1 medium

Toast, round	1 dozen
Paprika	1 tsp.

Method

Combine mayonnaise and cheese. Add the minced onion. Spread on small toast rounds. Sprinkle with paprika. Broil until lightly brown. Serve hot.

ROQUEFORT CHEESE BALLS

Yield: 16 cheese balls

Ingredients

Cream cheese	8 oz.
Roquefort	4 oz.
Green grapes, small	16
Walnuts, finely chopped	4 oz.

Method

Blend cheeses until smooth. Flatten the mixture and wrap each grape in the cheese. Roll balls into walnuts until well coated.

WALNUT CHEESE LOG

Yield: 1½ lb. spread

Ingredients

Cheddar cheese, grated	1 lb.
Cream cheese, softened	8 oz.
Butter, soft	¼ cup
Salt	1 tsp.
Walnuts, chopped	1½ cups
Pimento, chopped	2 T
Ripe olives, chopped	2 T

Method

Beat cheeses, butter, and salt together until smooth. Stir in half the walnuts and all the pimento and olives. Chill mixture for easy handling; shape into log or ball. Roll in remaining walnuts and chill until firm. Serve with crackers.

Note: If desired, 2 tablespoons of sherry may be substituted for soft butter.

PISTACHIO LOG

Yield: 12 oz.

Ingredients

Gorgonzola	½ lb.
White cheddar, grated	½ lb.
Cream cheese	¾ lb.
Pistachio nuts, chopped	½ cup

Method

Mix all cheeses into a paste. Shape into a large cylinder. Roll in pistachio nuts. Chill for several hours. Serve with crackers.

COTTAGE CHEESE MUSHROOMS

Yield: 1 lb.

Ingredients

Cottage cheese	8 oz.
Cheese (Camembert, bleu, Roquefort)	8 oz.
Fresh herbs (chives, chervil), finely chopped	2 T each
Salt and white pepper	to taste
Marinated mushroom buttons	32

Method

Purée cottage cheese and cheese in food processor or press through a fine sieve. Add herbs, salt, and white pepper and mix well. Spoon into a pastry bag with a plain tube. Pipe into mushrooms and chill. Sprinkle with sweet paprika and top with small cheese circles.

CHEESE CRACKERS WITH BLEU CHEESE

Yield: 12 portions

Ingredients

Flour	10 oz.
Grated Swiss cheese	7 oz.
Butter, soft	3 oz.

(continued)

Cheese Crackers with Bleu Cheese (continued)

Salt	to taste
Egg	1
Buttermilk	as needed

Topping

Bleu cheese	4 oz.
Butter, soft	2 oz.
Chopped herbs (parsley, dill, chervil)	2 T
Chopped chives	to garnish

Method

Combine flour and cheese. Add butter and salt. Add egg and knead to a dough (if too firm, add some buttermilk). Let rest for 2 hours in the refrigerator. Roll out ½-inch thick, cut into round circles, brush with egg white, and bake at 350°F to a light color. Cool. Prepare topping from bleu cheese and butter, pressed through a fine sieve or puréed in food processor. Mix in the finely chopped herbs. Pipe a small rosette on each cheese cracker. Sprinkle with chopped chives.

PARTY CREAM CHEESE SPREAD

Yield: 1 lb.

Ingredients

Butter, soft	7 oz.
Cream cheese	7 oz.
Mustard	1 tsp.
Onion, finely chopped	2 T
Chives, chopped	2 T
Caraway seeds	½ T
Hungarian sweet paprika	1 T
Beer, dark	4 T
Salt and white pepper	to taste

Method

Whip butter till creamy. Fold in cream cheese. Fold in all other ingredients. Mix well. Serve with crackers or pumpernickel or rye bread. Excellent with beer.

18

Nonedible Displays

Although food holds the spotlight in all buffet presentation—and the objective of buffet planning must be to achieve visual beauty both in the artistic presentation of each item of edible food and in the arrangement of the many dishes on the buffet table—nothing heightens the beauty of the buffet more than an outstanding centerpiece made of ice, tallow, or other nonedible materials.

The guest should be able to identify the theme of the buffet at a glance, just by observing the nonedible decorations that provide an eye-catching background for the presentation. A nonedible decorative display piece should be a work of art, always in good taste, whether the figure is made of ice, sugar, tallow, or any other material.

The garde manger staff can use various methods and materials to enhance the presentation of a buffet. The list of possibilities would include:

1. Ice carvings
2. Tallow displays
3. Salt carvings or sculptures
4. Decorative touches created with miscellaneous items that can be either made or assembled (flowers; styrofoam figures; boats made of bread, fruits, and vegetables; candles; wine bottles; flags made of wax leaves and

similar items). China, posters, and appropriate items from antique shops can be rented.

ICE CARVING

The ice sculpture is the highlight of any buffet, the artistic touch, the focal point. Ice can be carved in any shape, size, or figure that fits the theme or occasion. For example, for Christmas, there could be a Santa Claus; for an anniversary, a heart; for an Easter buffet, a bunny.

Before starting an ice carving, the following items should be assembled:

1. A 100- to 300-pound block of ice, 40 inches high by 20 inches wide by 10 inches thick. Blocks like this can be purchased.
2. A pair of ice tongs for moving and handling the ice.
3. An ice shaver with three to six prongs, used to carve out the details and do the small cutting on the block of ice.
4. An ice pick, used to split the block into smaller pieces.
5. A hand saw, used to remove large cuts of ice or to make rough outlines.
6. Wood chisels ranging in size from $1/2$ to 2 inches.

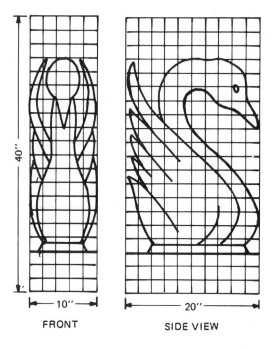

FRONT   SIDE VIEW

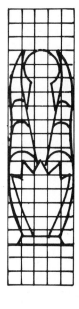

BACK

40"

←— 10" —→   ←——— 20" ———→

Before starting work on an ice car-
ing, draw the figure to scale on
piece of graph paper. This patter
is called a template.

7. A compass for drawing circles.
8. An electric chain saw; when working
   with this type of saw, it is important
   to have the saw grounded to prevent
   accidents.
9. A template, made on graph paper, of
   the shape of the ice carving that is to
   be made.

The best temperature for ice carving is
28°F or less. An ice block will melt at the
rate of ½ to 1 inch per hour at room temperature.

Each ice carving must have a base that is
at least 4 to 5 inches high. In other words,
when planning the carving, deduct 5
inches from the total height for the base. Be
sure to draw the template accurately.

If a piece of ice breaks off, dip each broken edge into salt and press pieces back
together for a few minutes; the length of
time will depend on the size and weight of
the broken pieces. With the salt added, the
broken pieces will freeze together and hold.

How to Display the Ice Carving
on a Buffet

1. The table used for the carving must b
   sturdy and strong enough to suppo
   the weight of the ice.
2. The carved ice block should b
   placed in a specially constructe
   metal pan, wider than the base of th
   carving; wooden blocks should fir
   be placed in the bottom of the pa
   and the carving should rest securel
   on top of the blocks.
3. Colored rotating lights and newly de
   signed display units can produce
   dramatic effect; this is especially e
   fective when the lights themselve
   cannot be seen.
4. The pan under the ice sculpture ca
   be decorated with a linen clotl
   flowers, ferns, or other decorative ma
   terial.

For additional assistance in plannir
and producing ice carvings, refer to th

Tallow sculpture—Sherlock Holmes —from the 1976 International Culinary Cooking Competition.

Tallow bust of August Escoffier.

An ice carving provides an elegant centerpiece to heighten the beauty and set the theme of a buffet. Proper lighting can enhance the effectiveness of a carving. This swan was produced from the templates in the previous illustration.

book *Ice Carving Made Easy* by Joseph Amendola, published by Van Nostrand Reinhold.

TALLOW AND SALT DISPLAYS

When deciding on the selection of a pattern for a tallow or salt display piece, it is essential that the display piece chosen match the theme of the food design or buffet. It is even more desirable, however, to select a pattern that may also fit into the decor theme of other buffets at a later date. Creating an eye-catching tallow or salt piece is always time-consuming and should be planned well in advance.

A French restaurant serving a French buffet would add effectiveness to the presentation by displaying a bust of Napoleon or Escoffier or the Eiffel Tower. Such displays can be used over and over, but they should be covered with transparent wrap when not in use as dust tends to stick to them.

Pictured are two tallow displays executed with the assistance of students. All have been displayed on our buffets, at exhibitions, and at private parties.

To be successful in the execution of a tallow or salt display, it is essential that certain rules be followed. The person making the tallow or salt display should have a photograph or model of the piece to be made. This is especially helpful in creating busts, as it helps to keep the proportions right. Architectural blueprints and photographs have been used to reproduce individuals and objects accurately in tallow.

The composition of the material used in making a tallow or salt display depends upon the piece to be made. In general, a formula made up in the following proportions works well in tallow or salt displays:

⅓ beeswax

⅓ paraffin

⅓ beef fat

These ingredients should be melted together in a pot. The beef fat should be rendered and strained. The quantity of fat can be increased if a more pliable and workable mixture is needed, especially if the working area is cool, that is, below 65°F. Most of the tallow illustrations in this book have been made with the above formula and can stand temperatures up to 90°F.

Preparing the Tallow

In a large pot, melt:
5 lb. of beeswax
5 lb. of paraffin
5 lb. of rendered beef fat (adjustable)

Salt-dough sculpture: mix salt dough with various spices and food colorings.

The preferred method of melting the mixture is in a water bath, although that is not absolutely necessary. However, it is dangerous to melt paraffin over a flame; do it very carefully. When the wax and fat are melted, pour the mixture into empty milk cartons or other containers that can be opened. Allow to cool at room temperature, not under refrigeration. When the tallow is completely cold, figures can be carved from the solid block. Great care should be exercised while carving, as the tallow is brittle and may break.

The tallow can also be grated and then molded like clay. When grating large amounts, use the coarse plate of the meat grinder.

A solid structure and base for the tallow or salt piece must be created, especially if the finished piece has to be transported. A wooden base with dowels and a rough structure made of styrofoam, metal armature, and aluminum foil have been used in the illustrations.

Salt-dough cutouts: roll out salt dough, cut into desired shapes, dry and arrange.

Salt-dough sculpture: this sculpture was colored by dusting with dried powdered herbs and spices.

Note: For fat sculptures, any type of commercial shortening can be used instead of tallow.

Basic Salt Dough for Sculptures

This dough is used by The United States Culinary Olympic Teams. The method of working with it is the same as that for working with tallow. Use the following formula:

  1 cup cold water

  1 cup cornstarch

  2 cups warm popcorn salt

Combine the water and cornstarch. Mix well over medium heat, stirring constantly, to a very thick paste. Knead 2 cups of popcorn salt into hot cornstarch mixture (for best results, use a mixing machine).

For brown color, add some soy sauce to the water. To make brown paint, brown cornstarch to various shades of light and dark brown and mix with water and some gin. When sculpture is finished, use a brush to paint it with the cornstarch mixture.

Salt-dough sculpture: this sculpture was colored with powdered
spices and food coloring.

For natural color, use fine ground spices and freeze-dried herbs. Prepare a liquid spice or herb paint and brush onto the dry salt sculpture. Then, with a brush, dust with dry herbs and spices.

To create successful sculptures:

1. For large salt-dough sculptures, a good solid metal armature is needed to support the weight of the sculpture.
2. Cover the armature with aluminum foil to create desired shape.
3. Cover aluminum foil with thin sheets of salt dough. Dry. Repeat and dry again.
4. Finish details on the third layer of salt dough. Dry and paint with brown cornstarch color or dust with herbs and spices.

WILLY SPRY'S SALTILLAGE

Yield: 5 lb.
Ingredients

Plain powdered gelatin	6 oz.
Boiling water	1¼ pt.
Cornstarch	3 lb.
Salt (table)	1 lb.

Colorings: turmeric, paprika, vegetable or confectioners' colors, spices, dried herbs, poppy or caraway seeds, finely chopped nuts

Method

Dissolve the gelatin in boiling water; make sure it is well dissolved. Use extra heat if necessary, but do not boil. Strain the liquid through cheesecloth or filter paper and let cool.

Place cornstarch and salt in mixing bowl and stir in liquid gelatin a little at a time until you get a smooth paste. When you notice that the saltillage clears the sides of the mixing bowl, it is ready. Add desired colorings. Roll into clear plastic and store in an airtight container.

Saltillage has the same appearance and texture as pastillage. It dries quickly and for some reason tends to crack easily. Do not make large pieces out of this paste unless you have a base; a styrofoam sculpture that you may wish to cover will do. Any small animals or birds, flowers, mushrooms, umbrellas, wheelbarrows, chef's hats, or other decorations that you already have made out of marzipan or pastillage can also be made of saltillage. The rest is left to the imagination.

SALT CARVING

Yield: 25 lb.
Ingredients

Coarse salt (kosher)	25 lb.
Cornstarch	½ lb.
Egg whites	12

Method

Mix salt, cornstarch, and egg whites well and pack in a square or cylindrical mold. Pack well. Bake in a 350°F oven for 2 hours or until dry. Remove and cool. Carefully unmold.

This salt mixture is very brittle, like sandstone, and can be carved into any shape required with a sharp paring knife or wood knife.

Note: Commercial white salt lick can be carved like stone into various shapes and sizes, using chisels, drills, or dremel tools.

19

Healthy Foods for à la Carte Service and Buffets

Let thy kitchen be thy apothecary
and
Let food be thy medicine
Hippocrates

Nutritionists and scientists have been telling Americans for several years that they should cut their consumption of animal fats and sugar. It appears that many have been listening. A recent report issued by the U.S. Department of Agriculture shows that Americans have increased their intake of crop-based foods at a greater rate than their consumption of animal-based foods. And public awareness is responsible for most of the changes. Ultimately, the goal is to improve health.

The foods that have gained in popularity are predictable: we are consuming more broccoli, low-fat milk and yogurt, pasta products, and poultry. The losers are whole milk, refined sugar, coffee, and eggs. The demand for poultry products keeps increasing and may soon surpass the consumption of beef. The consumption of seafood has also dramatically increased.

The food industry has a lesson to learn from these changes: it is obvious that tomorrow's chef and foodservice operator will have to take into account the changes that are occurring in our society. The public is becoming more and more health conscious and it is the obligation of the foodservice industry to respond to its needs.

Yet, there is something paradoxical about this new health consciousness. Despite the general trend toward eating nutritious foods, there is still a national tendency to obesity. This is because the fat consumption in the United States surpasses that of Italy and France, even though so-called heavy foods and sauces are perceived as the norms in those countries. One of the reasons is our preoccupation with taste. The American public wants more taste, smell, and texture in its food today than it did twenty years ago.

Today's chef does not have to become a dietician or food scientist to understand the changes in our eating habits. With a little imagination, it is possible to create, arrange, and display low-calorie, low-cholesterol, and low sodium foods for buffet and à la carte service.

As we know, the temptation of eating

food from buffets is great and people tend to overeat, especially if the buffet is self-service. Brillat-Savarin, an eighteenth-century French expert on food and cooking, once said: "It is a cook's duty to tempt the appetite, and it is the guest's duty to curb it." Today, the world has changed drastically, and although it is still the guest's duty to curb his or her appetite, the burden falls on the cook to tempt it but with healthy and nutritious foods, reducing calories and cholesterol and often sodium.

This chapter will not cover nutritional and physiological details, as this information is available in specialty books. However, some advice and recipes are presented in order to assist in preparing buffets and food arrangements in accordance with the majority of the public's liking. Remember that the basic principles of cooking must be followed when preparing low-calorie and healthy nutritious foods. And well-decorated foods still play an important role in à la carte and buffet presentation; moreover, accurate portion sizes should be observed. For details on decorative ideas and food presentations, see *Elegant and Easy*, by John F. Nicolas, published by Van Nostrand Reinhold.

The following represent a repertoire of low-calorie and low-cholesterol recipes. It is possible to create additional recipes to achieve a specific dietetic goal by a simple substitution or removal of particular ingredients.

Among the numerous salad recipes in chapter 16, the following are considered low in calories and/or cholesterol:

Fresh Herb Vinaigrette
Low Calorie French Dressing
Herb Marinade and Dressing
Iceberg and Fruits. Substitute sour cream
    with low fat yogurt
Smoked Salmon and melon salad
Shrimp Salad Modern

Sicilian Salad
Cucumber and Seafood Salad
Marinated Salad
Leek Salad
Tabbouleh
Rice Salad Bombay
Turkey Salad with Fruit
Red Cabbage Salad #1
Carrot Salad
Basic Cucumber Salad
Tuna Salad #2
Salad of Leftover Fish
Macedoine of Fruits
Stuffed Peaches
Stuffed Tomatoes, #1, #2

LOW-CALORIE SALADS

Low-calorie salads are made from seafood, poultry, uncooked vegetables, or fruit and are high in vitamins and minerals. They are a welcome addition to our menu structure.

Preparation

Fresh vegetables and fruits are available throughout the year. Only top-quality products should be used. All raw vegetables and fruits must be well washed before preparation.

To aid in both eating and digestion, these foods should be cut into small pieces by:

- tearing (leaf lettuce)
- slicing (radishes, cucumbers)
- shredding (vegetables of robust structure, such as cabbage)
- grating (horseradish, ginger, nuts)
- dicing/chopping (fruits and some vegetables)

In the preparation of these salads, a variety of seasonings and other ingredients can be used:

- polyunsaturated or monosaturated oils: sunflower, soy, olive, corn
- low-calorie dairy products: cottage cheese, low-fat yogurt, buttermilk
- acids: lemon, lime, orange, grapefruit, red currants, vinegars (white, wine, balsamic, flavored with herbs)
- seasonings: herbs, horseradish, garlic, shallots, mustards
- fresh or diced fruit: raisins, dates, figs, apricots, peaches, apples, prunes
- other ingredients: wheat germ, oatmeal, granola, tofu

Plating

As with all salads, these must be well seasoned, colorful, and tasty. They should be arranged attractively, on plates, in glass bowls or cocktail glasses, or in carved fruits or vegetable containers. These salads can be decorated with lemon slices, orange or grapefruit wedges, tomato fans, sliced or carved radishes, cucumber or zucchini, watercress, parsley, or dill.

AUTUMN SALAD

Yield: 6 portions
Ingredients

Cucumber	1 small
Salt	1 tsp.
Sugar	½ tsp.
Tomatoes, peeled	2 medium
Potatoes, small	8 oz.
Green pepper, diced	1 small
Onion, diced	1 small
Green olives, stuffed	12
Yogurt dressing	¾ cup
Sardines	7 oz.
Eggs, hard-cooked	2

Method

Peel cucumber. Cut in half lengthwise and slice thinly. Sprinkle with salt and sugar and allow to set for 30 minutes. Drain, squeezing out all liquid.

Dice tomatoes. Boil potatoes in their jackets; cool, peel, and dice. Chop the olives. Mix all vegetables. Combine with the dressing.

Place in a mold. Invert on a serving platter. Decorate top with sardines and chopped eggs.

CAULIFLOWER SALAD

Yield: 6 portions
Ingredients

Cauliflower	1 lb.
Vinegar, red wine	1 T
Mayonnaise	¼ cup
Paprika, sweet	2 tsp.
Ketchup	1 T
Salt	½ tsp.
White pepper, ground	¼ tsp.
Radishes	4

Method

Cut small florets from the cauliflower. Cook in salted boiling water until al dente. Cool under cold water. Drain. Make the dressing by mixing vinegar, mayonnaise, paprika, ketchup, salt, and pepper.

Blend the dressing with the cauliflower. Chill. Before serving, grate radishes over the cauliflower.

SQUID SALAD

Yield: 4 portions
Ingredients

Squid cones, small, cleaned	12 oz.
Salad oil	2 T
Carrots, grated	4 oz.
Onions, chopped	2 T
Mint leaves, chopped	4
Lemon juice	2 T
Water	1 T
Osyter sauce	1 T
Sugar	1 tsp.
Garlic, minced	1 clove

Cayenne pepper	¼ tsp.
Lettuce leaves	4

Method

Use the smallest squid cones available. Cut the squid into small rings. Fry in hot oil for 15 to 20 seconds. Remove immediately from the heat. Combine squid with carrots, onions, and mint. Prepare dressing by mixing lemon juice, water, oyster sauce, sugar, garlic, and cayenne. Blend dressing into squid salad. Marinate for one hour. Arrange lettuce leaves in plates. Spoon squid salad over lettuce.

SALADE NIÇOISE

Yield: 4 portions

Ingredients

Potatoes, new	1 lb.
Vinaigrette	½ cup
Onion, sliced	1
String beans, small	1 lb.
Eggs	4
Lettuce	1 small head
Tomatoes, sliced	2 medium
Tuna, canned	8 oz.
Capers	2 T
Black olives	12 small
Parsley, chopped	3 T
Anchovy fillets	4

Method

Boil potatoes in their jackets. Cool, peel, and slice while warm. Mix ¼ cup vinaigrette with the potatoes; add onions.

Snap string beans and cook in boiling water until al dente. Cool under cold water. Drain well. Boil eggs for 10 minutes. Shell.

Arrange clean lettuce leaves in bottom of bowl. Place a ring of potatoes on lettuce. Top with string beans, quartered eggs, tomato slices, tuna chunks, capers, olives, parsley, and anchovy fillets. Pour remaining vinaigrette over or serve separately.

JELLIED BEET SALAD

Yield: 10 portions

Ingredients

Beets, fresh	1 lb.
Salt	2 tsp.
Red wine vinegar	½ cup
Bay leaf	1
Sugar	2 oz.
Peppercorns	1 tsp.
Unflavored gelatin	1 envelope
Water	2 T
Lettuce, shredded	to garnish

Method

Cook beets in salted boiling water until tender. Drain, reserving cooking liquid. Allow beets to cool. Skin and dice beets.

Simmer 1½ cups of the cooking liquid with vinegar, bay leaf, sugar, and peppercorns.

Dissolve gelatin in cold water in a mold. Strain cooking liquid over gelatin. Stir well. Add the diced beets. Chill until set. Serve over shredded lettuce.

Note: Individual molds are easier to handle than one large mold.

MIXED SHREDDED SALAD

Yield: 8 portions

Ingredients

Chinese cabbage	3 cups
Red cabbage	2 cups
Onion, chopped	1 small
Vegetable oil	1 cup
Sesame oil	1 T
Garlic, minced	1 clove
Soy sauce	1 T
Red wine vinegar	2 T
Carrots, grated	2 medium
White radish, grated	1
Alfalfa sprouts	½ cup

Method

Shred the Chinese and red cabbages separately. Mix half of the onion with the

Chinese cabbage and the other half with the red cabbage.

Blend the oils, garlic, soy sauce, and vinegar to make the dressing. Pour some of the dressing over each cabbage. Toss and arrange separately on serving platter. Top with remaining vegetables. Serve with remaining dressing.

TURKEY AND SWISS SALAD

Yield: 12 portions
Ingredients

Elbow macaroni, cooked	2½ cups
Turkey, cooked, cubed	2 cups
Swiss cheese, julienned	2 cups
Carrots, sliced thinly	1 cup
Celery, diced	½ cup
Green pepper, diced	½ cup
Scallion, chopped	¼ cup
Pimento, chopped	2 oz.
Basic vinaigrette	1 cup
Lettuce leaves	to garnish

Method
In a large bowl, combine all ingredients. Toss lightly. Cover, then chill to blend flavors. Serve on a bed of lettuce leaves.

ITALIAN GARDEN SALAD

Yield: 6 cups
Ingredients

Tarragon vinegar	3 T
Oil	2 T
Dill weed	1 tsp.
Salt	¾ tsp.
Dry mustard	¼ tsp.
White pepper	⅛ tsp.
Garlic, minced	1 small clove
Elbow macaroni, cooked	1½ cups
Tomato, chopped	1 cup
Zucchini, sliced	1 cup
Olives, pitted	1 cup

Method
In small bowl, combine vinegar, oil, dill weed, salt, mustard, pepper, and garlic.

Combine cooked macaroni, tomato, zucchini, and olives.

Pour dressing over salad mixture; toss well to combine ingredients. Chill at least one hour to blend flavors.

MUSHROOM ASPARAGUS SALAD

Yield: 4 portions
Ingredients

Asparagus, fresh	½ lb.
Lemon juice	3 T
Salt	½ tsp.
Black pepper	pinch
Nutmeg	pinch
Olive oil	2 tsp.
Mushrooms, sliced	½ lb.

Method
Cut asparagus into 1-inch pieces and cook just until tender; drain and chill. In a small bowl, mix lemon juice, salt, pepper, and nutmeg. Beat in oil. Toss mushrooms and asparagus with dressing until well coated. Chill.

CAESAR SALAD

Yield: 4 portions
Ingredients

Egg	1
Anchovy fillets	4
Dijon mustard	1 tsp.
Salt	½ tsp.
White pepper	1 tsp.
Oil	½ cup
Red wine vinegar	¼ cup
Romaine lettuce	1 medium head
Parmesan cheese, grated	1 T
Croutons	½ cup

Method

Scald egg in boiling water for 1 minute. Shock in ice water.

In a bowl, mix anchovies to a paste. Add mustard, salt, and pepper, and mix well. Stir in oil and vinegar; then mix in the egg until sauce is smooth and creamy. Add the cleaned romaine lettuce leaves. Sprinkle with parmesan cheese and croutons. Toss well before serving.

TOMATO-MUSHROOM SALAD

Yield: 8 portions
Ingredients

Tomatoes, blanched	1 lb.
Mushrooms, fresh	1 lb.
Green peppers	8 oz.
Lemon juice	2 oz.
Oil	2 oz.
Salt and pepper	to taste
Lettuce leaves	8
Parsley, chopped	1 T
Chives, chopped	1 T

Method

Dice the tomatoes. Slice the mushrooms. Cut the green peppers into julienne. Combine the vegetables with lemon juice and oil. Season with salt and pepper. Marinate for an hour.

Arrange salad on plates covered with lettuce leaves. Sprinkle with herbs and serve cold.

APPLE-CARROT SALAD

Yield: 8 portions
Ingredients

Carrots, grated	1 lb.
Apples, peeled and diced	12 oz.
Orange juice	½ cup
Pecans, chopped	2 oz.

Method

Combine carrots and apples with orange juice. Arrange in orange cups or cocktail glasses. Sprinkle pecans over top. Serve chilled.

SAFFRON RICE SALAD

Yield: 8 portions
Ingredients

Long-grain rice	1½ cups
Saffron	½ tsp.
Red wine vinegar	4 T
Salt	¼ T
Olive oil	¼ cup
Vegetable oil	2 T
Black pepper	¼ tsp.
Red pepper, diced	½
Green pepper, diced	½
Tomato, chopped	½ medium
Chick-peas, cooked	1 cup
Green peas, cooked	1 cup
Black olives, chopped	⅓ cup

Method

Put the rice in a saucepan. Add twice the volume of boiling water. Stir in the saffron, and simmer for 20 minutes, until rice is tender and water is absorbed.

Make the vinaigrette with vinegar, salt, oils, and pepper. Pour over warm rice. Add the red and green peppers, tomato, chick-peas, green peas, and black olives. Toss well to blend. Serve at room temperature or slightly chilled.

BEAN SPROUT SALAD

Yield: 2 portions
Ingredients

Bean sprouts	2 cups
Soy sauce	2 T
Sesame seeds	1 T
Pimento, diced	¼ cup
Scallion, chopped	¼ cup
White vinegar	1 T
Garlic, minced	1 small clove

Method

Combine all ingredients in a salad bowl. Mix well. Refrigerate for one hour before serving.

BEET SALAD #3

Yield: 3 portions
Ingredients

Beets, fresh	1 lb.
Yogurt, low-fat	½ cup
Mustard, prepared	1 tsp.
Lemons	juice of 2
Sugar	1 tsp.
Salt	½ tsp.
White pepper	¼ tsp.

Method

Wash beets and cook in boiling water until tender. Cool, peel, and slice. Blend remaining ingredients and combine with beets. Allow to marinate for an hour before serving.

SALAD ALICE

Yield: 4 portions
Ingredients

Apples	4 large
Lemon juice	1 T
Almonds, sliced	3 T
Red currant jelly	3 T
Yogurt	½ cup
Salt	¼ tsp.
Sugar	½ tsp.
Lettuce leaves	4 medium

Method

Slice the stem-side tops from the apples, leaving stems attached. Set aside tops. Scoop all fruit from the apples. Remove all seeds and core. Dice remaining fruit, then pour lemon juice over diced apples.

Combine diced apples with almonds and melted currant jelly. Mix well. Add yogurt, salt, and sugar. Fill hollowed apple and re-place tops over. Serve on cleaned lettuce leaves.

RED CABBAGE SALAD #2

Yield: 4 portions
Ingredients

Red cabbage, shredded	1 medium head
White vinegar	⅓ cup
Onion, diced	1 medium
Salt	½ tsp.

Method

Combine all ingredients in a salad bowl and toss together. Marinate for 24 hours or more before serving.

ZUCCHINI SALAD

Yield: 4 portions
Ingredients

Zucchini	4 medium
Tomato, peeled	1 small
Garlic, crushed	1 clove
Olive oil	4 T
Red wine vinegar	1 T
Salt	½ tsp.
White pepper	¼ tsp.

Method

Blanch zucchini until slightly tender. Cool under cold water. Drain well. Cut off both ends of the zucchini, then slice each lengthwise. Allow to drain well.

Cut tomato in half. Squeeze seeds out, then cut tomato pulp into small dice. Combine tomato dice with garlic, oil, and vinegar. Mix well. Season with salt and pepper.

Place zucchini on serving platter. Pour dressing over. Marinate for an hour before serving.

DRESSINGS

YOGURT-SESAME DRESSING

Yield: 1 cup
Ingredients

Yogurt, low-fat	⅔ cup
Sesame seeds, toasted	3 T
Cider vinegar	2 T
Honey	2 T

Method

Mix all ingredients well. Store covered in refrigerator. Toss with mixed greens just before serving.

Note: To toast sesame seeds, cook and stir in a heavy frying pan over medium heat until light brown.

Other salad suggestions that can be featured in a buffet for dieters include the following.

Artichoke bottoms. Clean fresh artichoke bottoms and cook in water and lemon juice. Serve cold with 2 ounces of low-fat cottage cheese per artichoke.

Asparagus. Peel and boil 4 ounces of fresh asparagus. Marinate for a short time in ½ teaspoon of lemon juice to avoid discoloration. Serve with 2 ounces of low-fat cottage cheese.

Bananas and radishes. Peel and slice a medium banana. Slice an equal amount of white radishes. Combine the juice of half an orange with 1 teaspoon lemon juice. Mix all ingredients and serve on a lettuce leaf.

Beets, apples, and horseradish. Cut 4 ounces of peeled, cooked, fresh beets into julienne strips and 1 ounce of fresh apples into julienne; combine and add a grating or two of fresh horseradish. Mix with ½ teaspoon of lemon juice and ½ teaspoon of honey. Serve on lettuce leaves. Garnish with three to four toasted sliced almonds sprinkled on top.

Belgian endive with ginger. Dice 2 ounces of fresh endive, ½ ounce of tomato, ½ ounce of fresh pineapple, and 1 ounce of fresh orange sections. Mix all ingredients with 1 ounce of low-fat cottage cheese and 1 to 2 teaspoons of lemon juice. Serve on lettuce leaves. Grate ¼ teaspoon of fresh ginger over the salads.

Celery and fresh pineapple. Mix 4 ounces of diced celery, 2 ounces of diced apple, 1 ounce of diced pineapple, and 1 ounce of fresh mandarin oranges with 2 ounces of low-fat yogurt and 1 tablespoon of orange juice. Decorate with celery leaves.

Melon. Mix 2 ounces of cantaloupe cut into julienne with 2 ounces of red peppers cut into julienne; add 1 teaspoon of lemon juice.

Mushrooms and spinach. Mix 2 ounces of fresh spinach, cut into julienne, 1 ounce of sliced mushrooms, and 1 ounce of diced apples with 2 ounces of low-fat cottage cheese. Season with 1 tablespoon of orange juice and ½ teaspoon of honey.

Mushrooms and tomato. Mix 2 ounces of sliced raw mushrooms, 2 ounces of diced tomatoes, 2 ounces of diced apples, and 2 ounces of diced melon and 4 ounces of low-fat cottage cheese, 2 teaspoons of orange juice, and 1 teaspoon of lemon juice. Garnish with watercress.

Radishes. Mix 2 ounces of sliced, fresh radishes with ½ teaspoon of orange juice. Serve with shredded lettuce and herbal dressing.

Red cabbage. Combine 4 ounces of red cabbage cut into julienne and 1 ounce of apple cut into julienne with a vinaigrette.

Sauerkraut. Mix 1 cup fresh sauerkraut with ¼ cup grated apple and ¼ cup diced fresh pineapple; serve on lettuce.

HEALTHY COCKTAILS

MILD SAUERKRAUT JUICE

Yield: 1 portion
Ingredients

Sauerkraut juice	2 oz.
Orange juice	2 oz.
Honey	2 tsp.
Onions, chopped	1 tsp.

Method
Combine all ingredients and chill.

TOMATO AND CELERY JUICE

Yield: 1 portion
Ingredients

Tomato juice	2 oz.
Celery juice	1½ oz.
Lemon juice	1 tsp.
Sour cream	2 T
Salt, pepper, mild paprika	touch
Parsley, chopped	1 tsp.

Method
Combine all ingredients and chill.

CUCUMBER COCKTAIL

Yield: 1 portion
Ingredients

Cucumber juice	2 oz.
Apple juice	2 oz.
Celery juice	¾ oz.
Lemon juice	1 tsp.
Salt, freshly ground black pepper	touch
Parsley, chopped	1 tsp.

Method
Combine all ingredients and chill.

CARROT-APPLE JUICE

Yield: 1 portion
Ingredients

Carrot juice	2 oz.
Apple juice	3 oz.
Lemon juice	1 tsp.
Salt, pepper	touch
Dill, chopped	1 tsp.

Method
Combine all ingredients and chill.

COLD SOUPS

Cold soups are delightful, a welcome refreshment generally served during the summer months. These soups are nutritious, and low in calories and cholesterol. Cold soups can be vegetable or fruit based.

Cold Vegetable Soups

For the preparation of these soups, the use of butter is not recommended. Aside from its high cholesterol level, it does not incorporate well in chilled soups. Polyunsaturated oil can be used as a substitute.

AVOCADO SOUP

Yield: 6 portions
Ingredients

Chicken stock, strong	4 cups
Avocado, peeled	1 large
Yogurt, plain, low-fat	1 cup
Onion powder	¼ tsp.
Salt	½ tsp.
White pepper	¼ tsp.

Method
Combine all ingredients in a food processor and purée. Strain and chill. Serve cold.

GAZPACHO ANDALUSIA

Yield: 10 portions
Ingredients

Beef consommé	2 cups
Water	2 cups
Tomato juice	1 cup
Green peppers, seeded	2
Tomatoes	8 oz.

Cucumbers	8 oz.
Garlic	1½ cloves
White pepper	¼ tsp.
Tarragon, chopped	¼ tsp.

Method

Purée consommé, water, tomato juice, half of the vegetables, garlic, pepper, and tarragon. Strain; dice the remaining diced vegetables and use as garnish. Serve well chilled.

COLD BROCCOLI SOUP

Yield: 6 portions
Ingredients

Potatoes	4 medium
Onions, chopped	4 medium
Chicken stock	1½ quart
Broccoli, chopped	2 cups
Yogurt, low-fat	½ cup
Lemon juice	1 T
Salt	1 tsp.
White pepper	¼ tsp.
Lemon slices	to garnish

Method

Cook the potatoes and onions in the chicken stock until tender. Add broccoli and continue cooking for 10 minutes. Purée in a blender or processor until smooth. Refrigerate for several hours or until thoroughly chilled.

At serving time, stir in yogurt, lemon juice, salt, and pepper. Garnish soup with lemon slices.

COLD HERB SOUP

Yield: 20 portions
Ingredients

Leek, white part, diced	8 oz.
Onion, diced	8 oz.
Vegetable oil	2 oz.
Potatoes	2 lb.
Flour	3 oz.
Chicken broth	3 qt.

White wine	1 cup
Sorrel, fresh	8 oz.
Watercress	5 oz.
Chervil, fresh	5 oz.
Yogurt, low-fat	1½ cups
Salt	½ tsp.
White pepper	¼ tsp.

Method

Sauté the leek and onion in oil over low heat. Add potatoes. Stir in the flour. Add broth. Stir well. Simmer for 30 minutes. Purée in blender. Add wine. Strain and chill.

Chop the herbs and vegetables. Blend herbs and yogurt and add to the purée. Season and chill before serving.

VICHYSSOISE   *Cold Potato leek soup*

Yield: 20 portions
Ingredients

Celery	20 oz.
Leek, white part	14 oz.
Potatoes, peeled	2 lb.
Chicken broth	3 qt.
Nutmeg, ground	¼ tsp.
Salt	½ tsp.
White pepper	¼ tsp.
Light cream	½ cup
Yogurt, low-fat	¾ cup
Chives, chopped	¼ cup

Method

Dice celery, leek, and potatoes. Wash in cold water and drain. Cook in chicken broth for 30 minutes. Season with nutmeg, salt, and pepper. Purée in blender. Add cream, yogurt, and chives. Chill and serve.

Note: This base, minus the chives, can be used for: curry soup, cucumber soup, or zucchini soup.

COLD ZUCCHINI SOUP

Yield: 4 portions
Ingredients

Chicken broth	2 cups
Zucchini, sliced	2 medium
Onions, chopped	2 medium
Garlic, minced	1 clove
Salt	½ tsp.
White pepper	¼ tsp.
Yogurt, low-fat	1 cup
Lemon juice	1 tsp.
Nutmeg, ground	⅛ tsp.
Lemon slices	to garnish

Method

Place chicken broth, zucchini, onions, garlic, salt, and pepper in a saucepan. Bring to a boil. Reduce heat to low, cover and simmer until vegetables are tender. Cool. Purée in a blender or food processor until smooth. Stir in remaining ingredients. Cover and chill. Garnish with lemon slices.

Cold Fruit-based Soups

The main ingredients for cold fruit-based soups are fresh or frozen fruits or fruit juices. These soups should not be prepared too long before serving, as exposure to air causes various fruits to change color. The eye appeal, taste, and aroma may then be altered or compromised, particularly with apples, pears, peaches, and bananas. The use of lemon, lime, pineapple, or orange juice can help prevent the loss of color and aroma.

BASIC FRUIT SOUP

Yield: 8 portions
Ingredients

Fruit, puréed	2 cups
Water	1 qt.
Sugar	3 oz.
Cornstarch	½ oz.

Method

Combine fruit purée and one-half of the water. Bring to a boil. Add sugar. Dissolve cornstarch in remaining water. Stir in the fruit purée. Simmer over low heat to thicken. Strain through a fine china cap. Chill. Garnish with diced fruit before serving.

COLD STRAWBERRY SOUP

Yield: 12 portions
Ingredients

Strawberries, sliced	3 cups
White wine	3 cups
Water	3 cups
Lemon zest	1 tsp.
Lemon juice	1 T
Sugar	3 oz.
Cornstarch	1 oz.
Strawberries, sliced	8 oz.

Method

Purée 3 cups of strawberries with wine. Strain through a fine strainer.

Combine water, lemon zest and juice, sugar, and cornstarch. Bring to a boil, stirring constantly. Cool. Add strawberry mixture. Garnish with remaining strawberries before serving.

COLD ORANGE SOUP

Yield: 8 portions
Ingredients

Water	1 qt.
Sugar	5 oz.
Orange zest	of 2 oranges
Cornstarch	1 oz.
Orange juice	1½ cups
Lemon juice	¼ cup
White wine	¼ cup
Orange sections	16

Method

Combine water, sugar, orange zest, and cornstarch. Bring to a boil and stir to thicken. Add orange and lemon juices. Stir in wine and orange sections. Chill.

COLD PINEAPPLE SOUP

Yield: 5 portions
Ingredients

Pineapple, peeled	1 lb.
Soda water	1 cup
Lemon juice	1 T
Kirschwasser	1 oz.
Mint leaves	5

Method
Purée pineapple in blender. Add soda water, lemon juice, and Kirschwasser. Chill. Serve in chilled glass bowl. Garnish with mint leaves.

Terrible

MID-HUDSON APPLE SOUP

Yield: 8 portions
Ingredients

Apples	1 lb.
Lemon juice	of 1 lemon
Water	1 qt.
Sugar	3 oz.
Cinnamon, ground	½ tsp.
Cornstarch	½ oz.
Lemon zest	from 1 lemon
Apple	1 medium
Raisins	1 oz.
Sugar	1 tsp.
Water	2 oz.
White wine	2 oz.
Pound cake croutons	4 oz.

Method
Peel, core, and slice 1 pound of apples. Blend in the lemon juice. Add one-half of the water to apples. Bring to a boil. Mix in the sugar and cinnamon. Purée.

Stir cornstarch into remaining water. Add to puréed apples. Simmer over medium heat until thickened. Add lemon zest. Allow to cool.

To prepare garnish: core and dice the re-

maining apple. Combine raisins, sugar, water, and wine. Bring to a quick boil. Stir apple/raisin mix into cold soup. Serve with cake croutons.

RHUBARB SOUP

Yield: 7 portions
Ingredients

Rhubarb, peeled	1 lb.
Sugar	3 oz.
Water	3 cups
Cornstarch	½ oz.
Cinnamon, ground	½ tsp.
White wine	½ cup

Method
Dice rhubarb. Combine rhubarb with sugar and one-half the water in a saucepan. Bring to a boil. Skim the top.

Combine the remaining water with the cornstarch. Stir in the rhubarb mixture. Bring to a boil to thicken. Purée and strain. Add cinnamon and white wine. Chill before serving.

Note: Add more sugar if soup seems too sour.

MELON SOUP #1

Yield: 8 portions
Ingredients

Melon, peeled	1 lb.
Orange juice	of 2 oranges
Lemon juice	of 1 lemon
Water	3 cups
Sugar	2 oz.
Orange zest	¼ tsp.
Lemon zest	¼ tsp.
Cornstarch	½ oz.
Melon balls	4 oz.
Pound cake croutons	3 oz.

Method
Dice 1 pound of melon. Remove seeds. Purée in a blender with the orange and lemon juices. Chill.

Combine water, sugar, orange zest, and cornstarch. Bring to a boil and simmer until thick. Add melon purée. Chill. Garnish with melon balls and cake croutons.

MELON SOUP #2

Yield: 8 portions

Ingredients

Melon, peeled	1 lb.
Soda water	8 oz.
Red port wine	1 oz.
Orange slices	8
Melon balls	4 oz.

Method

Dice, seed, and purée melon in a blender. Chill. Add soda water and port wine. Mix well. Serve with orange slices and melon balls.

OTHER HEALTHY DISHES

VEGETABLE TERRINE

Yield: 8 portions

Ingredients

Green beans, snapped	10 oz.
Artichoke bottoms	6
Carrots, sliced	6 small
Green peas	12 oz.
Chicken, ground twice	16 oz.
Whole eggs	2
Olive oil	3 oz.
Lemon juice	up to 2 oz.
Glace de volaille (optional)	up to 2 oz.
Salt	½ to 1 tsp.
Black pepper	½ tsp.
Cold Tomato Sauce (see recipe below)	2 cups

Method

Blanch vegetables, drain and cool. Place chicken into a food processor, add eggs, and purée. Gradually add oil, lemon juice, and

Salad of Scallops Seviche wth Marinated Tomato Slices and Avocado Purée.

glace de volaille. Season with salt and pepper.

Line a terrine with plastic wrap. Spread a thin layer of the chicken forcemeat in bottom. Garnish with a layer of carrots. Add more forcemeat, then a layer of beans. Continue the same procedure, using the forcemeat, the peas, the forcemeat, and the artichokes.

Cover the mold with plastic wrap. Bake in a water bath for 45 minutes or until the terrine reaches an internal temperature of 160°F. Chill for 6 to 8 hours before serving. Slice and serve with Cold Tomato Sauce.

CHICKEN TERRINE

Yield: 12 portions
Ingredients

Chicken breast, skinned	8 oz.
Egg whites	2
Light cream, chilled	4 oz.
Salt	1½ tsp.
Dill, chopped	1 T
Basil, chopped	1 T
White pepper	¼ tsp.
Carrots, cubed	8 oz.
Zucchini, cubed	4 oz.
Artichoke bottoms	4 oz.
Red peppers, julienned	8 oz.
Spinach leaves	8 oz.
Cépes, canned, julienned	4 oz.
Cold Tomato Sauce (see recipe on this page)	2 cups

Method

Bone and grind chicken breasts. Place in a food processor and purée to a fine paste. Add egg whites and mix well. Slowly add the chilled cream. Mix in salt, dill, basil, and pepper. Refrigerate.

Cook carrots till tender, then cool in ice cold water and drain. Cook zucchini, diced artichokes, and julienned red peppers al dente in separate pots. Blanch spinach in boiling water, shock in ice water, and drain well. Cut spinach and cépes into julienne.

Fold all vegetables into chicken mixture. Line a 12-inch terrine with plastic wrap. Fill with mixture; press well. Enclose with plastic wrap and cover.

Bake in a water bath in a 300°F oven to an internal temperature of 150°F. Cool and refrigerate. Serve with Cold Tomato Sauce.

COLD TOMATO SAUCE

Yield: 2 cups
Ingredients

Tomatoes, fresh	1 lb.
Tomato paste	1 T
Red wine vinegar	1 T
Olive oil	2 T
Salt	½ tsp.
White pepper	¼ tsp.
Tarragon, chopped	1 T

Method

Peel and quarter tomatoes. Purée in a blender and strain through a fine strainer. Chill. Add the tomato paste and gradually stir in the vinegar and olive oil. Season to taste with salt, pepper, and tarragon.

OYSTERS IN MUSTARD SAUCE

Yield: 12 portions
Ingredients

Oysters	12
White wine, dry	¼ cup
Water	¼ cup
Watercress	1 small bunch
Radicchio	¼ small head
Low-fat yogurt	2 T
Mayonnaise	1 T
Dijon mustard	1½ tsp.

Method

Shuck oysters; save bottom shells. Bring wine and water to a boil. Add oysters, return to boiling for 1 minute. Remove oysters. Reduce liquid by one-third. Chill.

Shred watercress and radicchio. Place in reserved oyster shells. In bowl, mix low-fat yogurt, mayonnaise, mustard, and cooking liquid. Arrange oysters on greens in shells. Top with sauce.

20

Charcuterie

One of the tasks facing today's chef is making good use of leftover foods. Charcuterie—the art of sausage making—offers ways to transform many kinds of meat, poultry, and fish into old and new food creations.

The art of charcuterie is one of the oldest professions. Sausage making was known in Babylonia, Rome, ancient Greece, and ancient China. This chapter will give you some ideas and methods of how to prepare these food morsels, to be served either hot, cold, or as a salad.

POACHED SAUSAGE

Sausages for poaching include bratwurst, skinless bratwurst, frankfurter, turkey sausage, Bavarian weisswurst, cooked salami, kielbasa, and leberkäse.

Depending on the texture of sausage desired, meat should be cut into cubes, coarsely ground, and finished in a mixing machine or a food processor. Salt is added first, followed slowly and gradually by shaved ice, cold water or stock, and spices. The consistency of the brat (forcemeat) should be doughlike, either coarse or fine. The brat can be stuffed into natural or collagen casings, prepared skinless, or used to fill loaf molds. These products can be smoked, poached, or baked.

Basic Emulsified Preparation of Poached Sausage

Meat can be veal, pork, beef, or chicken. For best results, use tougher parts such as shank, butt, shoulder, or any trimmings you might have available.

Bone and trim meats, cut into cubes, and chill well. Season meat with salt (approximately ⅓ ounce per pound based on total weight to meat, fat, and ice) and grind through large plate.

If curing salt is needed, add 0.04 ounce (1 gram) and 2 grams of sugar per pound.

Trim and skin fatback or use pork jowls. Cut into cubes and grind through large plate.

Note: Never season fat.

To make brat (forcemeat):

1. Place prepared meat in a food processor bowl.
2. Run food processor for 2 to 3 seconds to break loose the protein (binder).
3. While machine is working, gradually add the ice one-third at a time, or according to formula. When desired consistency is reached, remove two-thirds of the mixture and reserve.
4. Place ground fat in the bowl. Mix well with the remaining one-third of the brat to a smooth consistency. Add reserved brat to the fat emulsion. Mix for 2 minutes.

5. Add prepared spice mixture according to the recipe specifications and some ice water and mix well for 1 minute. Remove and keep cool.

To stuff sausage:

1. Select a casing (natural or collagen).
2. Clean natural casing well in a solution of water and vinegar. If collagen casing is used, soak in warm water.
3. Select a sausage nozzle (size depending on type of sausage).
4. Fit the casing onto the moistened nozzle of the sausage stuffer.
5. Stuff casing evenly without air pockets by applying even pressure through rotation of handle.
6. Tie into size.

To smoke sausage:

1. Dry sausages well.
2. Hang in smoke chamber.
3. Smoke either hot or cold (70 to 100°F), according to recipe.
4. Remove from chamber and poach.

Note: Smokehouses are available commercially. If no smokehouse is available, use liquid smoke or smoked seasoning. For liquid smoke, use 2 ounces per 50 pounds of mixture, for smoked seasoning, use 4 ounces per 50 pounds.

To poach sausage:

1. Blanch sausages at 170°F to an internal temperature of 150°F.
2. Chill in ice water.
3. Refrigerate; keep moist.

FRESH SAUSAGE

Put meat and fat through a meat grinder using various plates for coarse or fine texture. Then fold water, salt, and spices as specified into the mixture. By hand or machine, stuff the mixture into natural casing or wrap in plastic wrap or pig's caul (crépinette).

Note: This type of sausage is not cooked. It needs to be used immediately, as it is highly perishable. For longer storage freeze.

COOKED SAUSAGE

Prepare this type of sausage with partially cooked or blanched food materials. Poach, starting with the poaching liquid at 180° to 185°F (simmer), then turn it down to 170°F and cook to an internal temperature of 150°F. Cool slowly in tempered water and refrigerate.

SAUSAGE CASING

Animal casings are made from the intestines of hogs, sheep, and cattle.

Hog Casing

Small hog casings have three commonly accepted grades: narrow, medium, and wide. These grades are often modified by manufacturers, who receive demands for such widths as narrow medium and extra wide.

Grade	Size in Millimeters	Size in Inches
Narrow	28 and under	1⅛ and under
Narrow Medium	28 to 32	1⅛ to 1¼
Regular Medium	32 to 35	1¼ to 1⅜
English Medium	35 to 38	1⅜ to 1½
Wide	38 to 44	1½ to 1¾
Extra Wide	44 and over	1¾ and over

Hog casing packed in salt is sold as follows.

Grade	Hank (yd.)	Strands	Stuff Capacity (lb.)
Narrow	100	16	90 lb
Narrow Medium	100	18	100
Regular Medium	100	16	115
English Medium	100	16	125
Wide	100	15	135
Extra	100	15	145

Sheep Casing

Sheep casing is among the most valuable of animal casings and is produced from the small intestine. Sheep casing is used mainly for frankfurters and pork sausages. Sheep casing is first thoroughly cleaned, then graded by quality, measured for diameter and length, salted, and packed according to specifications required by the trade. It is sold by hanks or strands. Like pork casing, sheep casing is also purchased in hanks of 100 yards each.

Grade	Diameter (mm)	Capacity (lb.)
Narrow	16–18	34–36
Standard Medium	18–20	38–41
Medium Wide	20–22	47–52
Special Wide	24–26	60–64
Extra Wide	26+	64–70

Instead of being packed in salt, sheep casing can also be prepackaged in a specially prepared solution. The solution acts as a preservative, keeping the casing soft and pliable for immediate filling. A problem with this style of casing is that the solution will last for only a few months, while salted casing lasts indefinitely.

Beef Casing

Beef rounds derive their name from their "ring" or "round" characteristic. There are two general classifications: Export and Domestic. Beef rounds are used for ring bologna, ring liver sausage, mettwurst, Polish sausage, kishka, blood sausage, and Holsteiner.

Grade	Average Diameter (mm)	Average Capacity per Set (lb.)
Extra Wide Domestic	44+	85–95
Wide Domestic	40–44	75–85
Medium Domestic	40 or less	60–70
Extra Wide Export	44+	85–95
Wide Export	40–44	75–85

Grade	Average Diameter (mm)	Average Capacity per Set (lb.)
Special Wide Export	37–40	70–80
Medium Export	36–38	65–70
Narrow Export	28–35	55–65

Beef rounds are purchased in sets of 100 feet each.

Beef rounds are considered among the finest casings on the market because they are liberally measured, accurately calibrated, cleaned, and fatted and all waste material is removed.

Beef middle is used satisfactorily for Leona-style sausage, all other types of bologna, cooked salami, and veal sausage. Beef middles are purchased in sets of 57 feet.

Grade	Diameter (in.)	Capacity per Set (lb.)
Extra Wide	2½ +	90–100
Special Wide	2¼–2½	80–90
Medium	2–2¼	55–65
Narrow	2 and less	45–55

Other types of beef casing include *beef bung* and *beef bladder*. Beef bung has a capacity of 9 to 15 pounds and is used for large bologna and cooked salami. The casing has a curve in it. Beef bladder is oval and has a capacity of 5 to 14 pounds. It is used chiefly for mortadella and for square- and pear-shaped molds.

Caul Fat

Caul fat is a strong, nearly transparent membrane studded with fat that encloses the digestive organs of hogs. When spread out, it has a lacy appearance. Because of the strength of the membrane and the amount of fat, caul is ideal to wrap around dishes that benefit from basting, such as roasts, pâtés, and sausages.

Caul can be frozen. Check for odor and wash before using. If it has a strong odor, soak in one part vinegar to nine parts water; rinse and squeeze dry before using.

Manufactured Casings

Manufactured casings are divided into two types.

Cellulose: The base raw material used to manufacture cellulose casing is cotton. Cotton liners are first dissolved and subsequently regenerated into casings of various sizes. During the cooking and smoking process, a "skin" is formed on the surface of the sausage under the casing. This skin results from the coagulation of protein. When the casing is removed, this skin remains intact and has the appearance of casing. Cellulose casing is not harmful if eaten, but it is not considered palatable. There are different types for different sausages. Some, which are specially treated, shrink with the product. Cellulose casing requires careful storage. Humidity is particularly critical in the case of the small-diameter casing, since cellulose becomes quite brittle when very dry.

Check the temperature of the forcemeat to ensure a good final product.

Maintain an even pressure while stuffing sausages.

Fibrous Casings: These are made of special paper impregnated with cellulose. There are four types: regular, easy release, moisture impermeable, and dry sausage fibrous casing.

Check the internal temperature of the sausage to make sure cooking is complete.

Regenerated Collagen Casing

These casings, called simply collagen casing, were developed to be edible but are sometimes tough and rubbery and unpleasant to eat.

Collagen casing is made from the corium layer of split beef hides. This material is ground, swelled in acid, filtered, and finally extruded.

All collagen casing should be stored at temperatures of 50°F or below. The opened box should be put in the cooler. If they dry out, they will be brittle. Large-diameter collagen casing is usually soaked in warm water before using.

SALT

Salt performs various jobs in the preparation of sausages. It not only gives the meat flavor, but it also preserves it by removing the moisture bacteria need to live. It also furthers the emulsion process and helps to absorb added water/ice. The use of fine salt rather than coarse salt is suggested because it is absorbed more easily. The suggested amount of salt per pound is ⅓ ounce, or according to recipe. Note that salt is always added according to the total amount of meat, fat, and ice.

Curing Salt

The curing salt usually used is 94 percent salt and 6 percent sodium nitrite. It is pink (to differentiate it from ordinary salt). Its proper usage is 4 ounces per 100 pounds of meat.

Nitrite salt mixtures are added because they:

1. Inhibit the growth of bacteria, especially *Clostridium botulism*
2. Stabilize the color of meat
3. Contribute to flavor
4. Lengthen shelf life

Nitrites are suspected carcinogens and health warnings have been issued about them. Because no alternative bacteria inhibitors are available at this time, however, their ability to control bacteria outweighs their possible cancer-causing attributes, and so they must be used. Efforts are being made to find substitutes for them.

HERBS AND SPICES

Any food, but especially sausages, prepared without herbs and spices, is not worth mentioning. These aroma givers are needed to lend the final touch to a successful product. And herbs and spices add not only flavor or aroma, but have other impor-

tant functions as well. They stimulate appetite or digestion, and can help constrain bacteria growth (juniper berries) and preserve sausages to some degree (pepper, nutmeg). Only good-quality herbs and spices should be used. If dried, they must be kept dry and in a well-sealed container. Fresh herbs should not be discolored. They should be chopped or minced with a sharp knife, placed in cheesecloth, rinsed under cold water, and dried. Fresh herbs are generally more potent than dried, and so less of them should be used.

The term spice covers five general areas.

- *True spices*: product of tropical plants (bark, roots, flowers, buds)
- *Herbs*: leaves of plants mostly grown in gardens (thyme, chervil, marjoram, oregano, tarragon)
- *Seeds*: of any plant (cardamom, celery, dill, caraway)
- *Freeze-dried*: any type of prepared vegetable seasoning (parsley, dill, onions, garlic)
- *Spice blends*: ground and chopped flavor combinations of spices, herbs, seeds, and freeze-dried seasoning (Italian, frankfurter, Greek)

For successful products, it is imperative to measure all fresh or dehydrated herbs and spices exactly, as only slight deviations will alter the taste, aroma, and appearance of your charcuterie items.

RECIPES FOR POACHED SAUSAGES

BASIC FORCEMEAT

Yield: 16 lb.
Ingredients

Veal or pork or beef, cut into sticks and coarsely ground	11 lb.
Salt	6 to 7 oz.

Ice	4 to 5 lb.
Fatback, coarsely ground	5½ lb.

Method

Put meat in a food processor. Run three to five rounds, until sticky. Add the salt and ice. Run machine until ice is absorbed and forcemeat feels sticky. Remove forcemeat, leaving a little behind.

Add ground fat to machine and run until mixture is as smooth as velvet; add forcemeat. Mix well. If color change is desired, curing salt may be added.

FINE BRATWURST

Yield: 16 lb.

Ingredients

Basic Forcemeat (see above)	
White pepper	¾ to 1 oz.
Grated lemon peel (optional)	⅓ oz.
Grated onions	2½ oz.
Nutmeg	⅕ oz.

Method

Combine all ingredients. Use mixture to fill pork or sheep casing. Tie. Blanch at 170°F to internal temperature of 160°F. Cool in ice water.

COARSE BRATWURST

Yield: 10 lb.

Ingredients

Lean pork	5½ lb.
Salt	1 oz.
Basic veal forcemeat	4½ lb.
Pepper	12 grinds
Coriander	6 grinds
Nutmeg	6 grinds
Lemon peel, grated	6 grinds

Method

Grind pork through a medium (⅙-inch) plate. Season with salt. Combine ground

pork with forcemeat. Add spices and lemon peel and mix well. Fill pork casing with mixture; tie into 5-ounce links and blanch. *Note:* Sausage may be dipped in milk before browning.

PORK LUNCHEON BRATWURST

Yield: 14 lb.

Ingredients

Lean pork butt, shoulder, or trimmings	11 lb.
Salt	2 to 2½ oz.
White pepper	½ oz.
Marjoram	¼ oz.
Caraway	½ oz.
Mace	¼ oz.
Lemon peel, grated	¼ oz.
Onion, blanched	1 oz.
Basic brat/forcemeat	3 lb.

Method

Coarsely grind pork. Mix salt, spices, lemon peel, and onion with pork. Fold in forcemeat. Use to fill sheep casings; tie into links. Blanch in 170°F water to 160°F internal temperature. Chill in cold water.

Sauté sausage until golden brown. Serve with sauerkraut or potato salad.

SKINLESS BRATWURST

Yield: 20 lb.

Ingredients

Veal or fresh turkey breast, well chilled	11 lb.
Fatback	3½ lb.
Salt	6½ oz.
Frozen milk or ice	5 lb.
Eggs	6 to 8
Pepper	½ to ¾ oz.
Mace	⅓ oz.
Lemon peel, grated	⅓ oz.
Onions, blanched	⅓ oz.
Cardamom, optional	to taste
Butter	to sauté

Method

Grind veal or turkey coarsely. Grind fatback coarsely. Place veal or turkey in food processor, add salt and run for 2 to 3 seconds until sticky. Add ice slowly until absorbed. Remove three-fourths of brat/forcemeat. Add fatback and mix with meat mixture to a smooth consistency. Return brat/forcemeat and combine.

Add remaining ingredients. Blend and mix well.

Put into pastry bag, pipe into 104°F water, and bring to 170°F. Slowly cool under running water. Chill.

Sauté in butter. Good with potato salad.

TURKEY BASIC BRAT/FORCEMEAT

Yield: 22 lb.

Ingredients

Turkey breast, cubed	5½ lb.
Pork butt (trimmings), cubed	5½ lb.
Pork fat (trimmings or fatback)	5½ lb.
Salt	7 oz.
Curing salt	½ oz.
Shaved ice	5½ lb.
White pepper	½ oz.
Allspice	⅙ oz.
Mace	⅓ oz.
Nutmeg	⅓ oz.
Ginger	⅓ oz.
Monosodium glutamate (optional)	⅓ oz.

Method

Mix turkey and pork with salt and curing salt. Chill well. Grind coarsely. Grind fat coarsely. Place turkey and pork in food processor and run two to three rounds until mixture is sticky.

Slowly add all the ice until absorbed (56°F). Add fat and mix well. Add spices and mix well.

Make dumpling test (poach in seasoned water). Fill casings (beef middle or hog) tie.

Poach at 170°F to an internal temperature of 160°F. Chill in ice water.

Cold smoke for 4 to 6 hours (optional).

BEER SAUSAGE

Yield: 22 lb.

Ingredients

Salt	3 oz.
Curing Salt	⅓ oz.
White Pepper	⅙ oz.
Nutmeg	⅓ oz.
Ginger	⅙ oz.
Sugar	½ oz.
Turkey legs, cubed	11 lb.
Basic forcemeat	11 lb.

Method

Combine salts and spices with cubed turkey legs. Mix well and cure overnight. Knead until sticky. Fold in 11 pounds of basic forcemeat. Mix well. Stuff into casings; tie.

Poach at 170°F to an internal temperature of 160°F. Chill in ice water.

Cold smoke for 4 to 6 hours (optional).

Note: For Hunter Sausage, grind turkey legs coarsely.

NEAPOLITAN SAUSAGE

Yield: 12 lb.

Ingredients

Fatback, cubed small	1½ lb.
Pistachio nuts	½ lb.
Smoked beef tongue, cooked, cubed small	2 lb.
Coriander	3 g.
Pepper	3 g.
Garlic	to taste
Madeira	⅓ to ⅔ oz.
Basic forcemeat	7 lb.

Method
Blanch fatback and chill. Peel pistachio nuts. Combine cubed fat, tongue, and pistachio nuts, and mix with spices and wine. Fold into basic forcemeat. Use to fill beef middle or loaf mold.

Poach at 170°F to an internal temperature of 160°F. Chill.

Cold smoke 4 to 6 hours (optional).

Note: For loaf mold, bake in a water bath at 250°F.

BASIC BRAT/FORCEMEAT FOR BOLOGNA

Yield: 15 lb.

Ingredients

Veal *or* turkey	3 lb.
Pork butt	3 lb.
Beef shank	3 lb.
Salt	3 oz.
Curing salt	2 tsp.
Fatback *or* jowl fat	3 lb.
Ice	3 to 4 lb.
White pepper	½ oz.
Caraway, ground	1/7 oz.
Nutmeg	½ oz.
Onion, diced and blanched	1½ oz.
Sugar	1 oz.

Method
Cut veal, pork, and beef in cubes. Add salt and curing salt. Place in refrigerator overnight. Next day, grind the beef, veal, and pork, using a medium plate. Grind fatback or jowl fat using a medium plate. Place meat in food processor. Run 30 seconds until sticky. Add ice slowly, a handful at a time. Add fat and combine. Add spices, onion, and sugar, and blend for 30 seconds.

Use mixture to fill beef middle casing, approximately 15 inches long. Let set in a cooler for two hours, to dry.

Cold smoke for 2 to 3 hours.

Blanch at 170°F to an internal temperature of 150°F. Shock in ice and remove water.

Note: This recipe can be used as a basic forcemeat before spices are added. To use it for frankfurters, substitute frankfurter spices for those in the recipe.

COOKED SALAMI

(Pennsylvania Pork Sausage)

Yield: 15 lb.

Ingredients

Salt	3½ oz.
Curing salt	2 tsp.
Pork butt, 1-inch cubes	10 lb.
Beef, lean, 1-inch cubes	4½ lb.
Pepper	1 oz.
Coriander	1/3 oz.
Garlic powder	1/3 oz.
Caraway	1/3 oz.
Paprika	1/3 oz.
Bologna forcemeat (see above)	4½ lb.

Method
Mix salts into cubed meat. Cure for 24 hours in refrigerator.

After curing, combine spices with meat. Grind through a medium die; mix well. Mix into bologna forcemeat.

Put into beef middle casing (approximately 14 inches long). Smoke for four hours.

Poach in 170°F water to an internal temperature of 150°F. Shock in ice water.

FARMER'S SAUSAGE

Yield: 8 lb.

Ingredients

Pig's head	1 12-lb.
Brine	to cover pig's head
Mirepoix (onion, celery, carrot)	2 lb.
Bologna forcemeat	4½ lb.
Pepper	4 grams (1 tsp.)
Nutmeg	4 grams (1 tsp.)
Celery seeds	2 grams (½ tsp.)
Salt	to taste

Method

Remove jowls (1½ lb.) from pig's head and freeze for later use. Brine pig's head for four days.

Add mirepoix and cook for approximately 3 hours. Remove and cool. Remove all meat, fat, and skin, approximately 3 lb., and save. Cut meat large; cut fat small; chill. Add bologna forcemeat and mix well. Add pepper, nutmeg, celery seeds, and salt. Stuff into beef middle casing, approximately 15 inches long, and tie. Smoke for 3 to 4 hours, using cold smoke (100°F). Poach at 170°F, to an internal temperature of 150°F. Remove. Shock with cold water, then refrigerate.

FRANKFURTERS

Yield: 12 lb.

Ingredients

Beef shank, cubed	2 lb.
Pork butt, cubed	4 lb.
Salt	3 oz.
Curing salt	2 tsp.
Pig jowls or fatback, cubed	3 lb.
Ice	3 to 4 lb.
White pepper	⅓ oz.
Coriander, powdered	¼ oz.
Nutmeg	¼ oz.
Onion powder	2 T
Garlic powder	½ tsp.

Method

Mix meat cubes with salts. Cure overnight in refrigerator.

Grind fat through medium plate. Set aside. Grind meat through medium plate and place in food processor. Run for 30 seconds until mixture is sticky. Add ice slowly, a handful at a time. Run machine until ice is absorbed.

Remove three-fourths of brat/forcemeat and add fat. Blend well. Combine with brat left in machine and mix well. Add spices.

Fill sheep casing. Twist into 6-inch links. Place into preheated 165° to 170°F smoke house and smoke for 2 hours. Remove and poach in 170°F water to an internal temperature of 160°F. Chill in ice water.

WEISSWURST (Bavarian Style)

Yield: 22 lb.

Ingredients

Veal or fresh turkey breast, ground coarsely	5½ lb.
Pork butt, ground coarsely	5½ lb.
Salt	7 oz.
Ice	6½ lb.
Pig jowls or fatback, ground coarsely	5½ lb.
White pepper	34 g. (2¾ T)
Mace	7 g. (1½ tsp.)
Ginger	7 g. (1½ tsp.)
Lemon peel, grated	to taste
Pork skin or calf's head, boiled, ground coarsely	35 oz.
Onions, diced, blanched, ground coarsely	10½ oz.
Parsley, chopped	4 to 5 T

Method

Place veal and pork in a food processor. Sprinkle meat with salt. Run machine two or three times until mixture is sticky. Add 4 pounds of ice slowly until absorbed. Remove three-fourths of mixture and save. Add fat and blend to a smooth, velvet, consistency.

Add reserved brat/forcemeat and combine. Add pepper, mace, ginger, and lemon peel. Add the rest of the ice slowly until absorbed. Add ground pork skin or calf's head, onions, and parsley and fold into mixture. Run machine on slow a few times to remove air from mixture.

Fill pork casing, tie and poach in 170°F water for 20 to 25 minutes or to 150°F internal temperature. Cool slowly under running water.

Serve for breakfast, lunch, or midnight snack.

LEBERKÄSE BAVARIAN LOAF

Yield: 3 to 5 loaves

Ingredients

Jowl fat or fatback	4½ lb.
Beef shin, lean	5½ lb.
Pork butt	5½ lb.
Salt	5 oz.
Curing salt	2 tsp.
Shaved ice	6 lb.
Sugar	1 T
Marjoram	1 T
Ginger	1 tsp.
Mustard, ground	1 T
Nutmeg	2 T
Black pepper, ground	2 T
Maggi seasoning	¾ oz.
Onion, diced, blanched	½ cup

Method

Cube fat and grind through a medium die. Set aside. Cube beef and pork; add salts. Place meat in a food processor and run for approximately 30 seconds, until sticky. Add ice slowly, running machine until it is absorbed. Add fat and run machine until mixture is smooth. Add sugar, spices, maggi, and onion.

Oil pans or molds well. Place molds on sheet pans. Fill molds with loaf mixture. Place in water bath, and bake/poach in a 350°F oven to an internal temperature of 160°F.

Note: This sausage can be used hot or cold. For cold use, cubed Swiss cheese may be added.

POLISH KIELBASI

(Saucission Cuit)

Yield: 3 lb.

Ingredients

Lean beef	2 lb.
Salt	½ oz.
Curing salt	⅒ oz.
Ground pepper	½ tsp.
Paprika	1 pinch
Potato starch (diluted in ice water)	2 to 3 oz.
Garlic, mashed	1 clove
Fatback, chopped medium	8 oz.

Method

Grind beef very finely. Place in mixer with seasoning; beat at medium speed, adding the water and potato starch gradually. Add garlic. Add more water if necessary. Add very cold fatback.

Stuff in beef rounds, tie both ends together, leaving enough string so they can be hung in a cold smoke box. Smoke for about 6 hours.

Place sausages in 170°F water, reduce heat, and poach slowly for about 25 minutes.

These sausages can be eaten cold or slightly warm, with a warm potato salad.

CHORIZO

Yield: 8 lb.

Ingredients

Garlic, chopped	¾ oz.
Spanish paprika	1⅛ oz.
Crushed red pepper	¾ oz.
Coarse black pepper	⅓ oz.
Oregano	⅓ oz.
Fresh pork butt, cubed	5 lb.
Jowl fat	2½ lb.
Salt	2 oz.
Curing salt	⅓ oz.
Cold water	4 oz.
Red wine vinegar	2¼ oz.

Method

Combine garlic, paprika, peppers, and oregano. Mix with pork, jowl fat, and salts.

Grind meat into mixing bowl, using medium die or plate. Mix water with vinegar, pour mixture into meat and mix with paddle.

Stuff into pork casing and twist into 4½-inch long sausages. Use dry-cure method: place on plastic tray for approximately 24 hours. Smoke using cold smoke 4 to 5 hours. If you wish, blanch at 170°F to an internal temperature of 160°F.

RECIPES FOR FRESH SAUSAGES

ANDOUILLES SAUSAGE

Yield: 25 lb.
Ingredients

Pork butt	25 lb.
Onion, chopped, blanched	5 lb.
Garlic, fresh	5 oz.
Cayenne	2½ oz.
Salt	6¼ oz.
Curing salt	1¼ tsp.
Thyme, ground	5 tsp.
Mace, ground	1¼ tsp.
Cloves, ground	1¼ tsp.
Allspice, ground	1¼ tsp.
Marjoram, ground	5 tsp.

Method

Bone and cube pork butt. Mix in all remaining ingredients. Grind once through fine die using ⅛-inch plate, and mix well.

Stuff into sheep casing, twisting to make six sausages, each 6 to 8 inches long. Cold smoke for 12 to 14 hours.

BREAKFAST SAUSAGE

Yield: 8 lb.
Ingredients

Pork butt (25% fat, 75% lean)	8 lb.
Salt	2 oz.
Ground white pepper	½ oz.
Poultry seasoning	⅓ oz.
Ice cold water	12 oz.

Method

Grind pork through a medium-size plate. Add salt, pepper, seasoning, and ice water and mix in mixing machine until water is absorbed and mixture is sticky.

Stuff into sheep casing; twist or tie. For storage, freeze.

ITALIAN SAUSAGE

Yield: 10 lb.
Ingredients

Pork butt (25% fat, 75% lean)	10 lb.
Black pepper, coarsely ground	1 oz.
Salt	3 oz.
Paprika	¼ oz.
Fennel seeds, whole	1½ oz.
Ice cold water	1 pt.

Method

Grind pork butt coarsely. Place into a mixing bowl. Add remaining ingredients and mix until water is absorbed and forcemeat has sticky consistency. Stuff into pork casing. Twist or tie. For storage, freeze.

GAME SAUSAGES

Yield: 5 lb.
Ingredients

Lean pheasant *or* venison meat	2 lb.
Lean pork	1¼ lb.
Fresh pork fat	1¾ lb.
Salt	1 oz.
Ground white pepper	¼ oz.
Onion powder	½ T
Curing salt	¼ oz.
Sugar	1 T
Poultry seasoning	1 T
White wine	2 oz.

Method

Grind game meat, lean pork, and pork fat through a ³⁄₁₆-inch plate. Add all other ingredients and mix well. Stuff into sheep casings, making links 4 inches long. Rinse

n hot tap water. Hang to dry in refrigerator
for 12 to 24 hours. Cold smoke for 6 to 7
hours.

RECIPES FOR COOKED SAUSAGE

PAPA METZ LIVERWURST

Yield: 12 lb.

Ingredients

Pig jowls	6 lb.
Pork butt	5 lb.
Pork liver	53 oz.
Onions, diced	3 lb.
Butter	8 oz.
White pepper	½ oz.
Ginger	½ oz.
Cardamom	½ oz.
Marjoram	¾ to 1 oz.
Salt	5 oz.

Method

Cook pig jowls and pork butt in boiling salt
water approximately 1 to 1½ hours, and
chill. Scald whole liver in boiling water.
Cut into thick ¼- to ½-inch slices and
scald again; chill.

Cut half of the liver into small cubes. Cut
pork butt into small cubes.

Sauté onions in butter to a golden color.
Grind rest of liver, pork jowls, and onions
through a medium plate. Mix well; add seasonings, and cubed pork butt and liver.

Stuff into beef middle casings. Blanch 45
minutes in 170°F water. Remove and cool,
starting in warm water and gradually adding ice to chill.

If smoke is desired, smoke 7 hours in
cold smoke. Refrigerate.

KASSLER LIVERWURST

Yield: 6 lb.

Ingredients

Pork, cubed	3 lb.
Pork liver	2 lb.
Jowl fat	1 lb.
Onions	½ cup
Salt	½ oz.
Curing salt	½ tsp.
Monosodium glutamate (optional)	1 tsp.
Potato starch	6 oz.
White wine	½ cup
Eggs	6
Ground white pepper	1 tsp.
Pâté spice	1 tsp.
Chopped truffle (optional)	2 oz.
Pistachio nuts, peeled, chopped	½ cup

Method

Grind pork coarsely and liver, jowl fat, and
onions finely. Add salt and curing salt. Mix
potato starch and white wine. Place meat
in a mixer and mix well using a paddle.
Add potato starch mixture and eggs and mix
well. Fold in spices, truffle, and pistachio
nuts. Stuff into beef middle and tie. Poach
at 170°F to an internal temperature of
160°F.

Cold smoke for 3 to 4 hours.

BLOOD SAUSAGE

(*Boudin Noir*)

Yield: 8 lb.

Ingredients

Leaf lard	1 lb.
Onions, diced	10 lb.
Butter	½ lb.
Heavy cream	1 qt.
Salt and pepper	to taste
Pâté spice	1 T
Beef blood	½ gal.

Method

Remove skin from leaf lard and dice.
Smother onions well in butter, cool, add

leaf lard. Add all other ingredients, stirring carefully when blood is introduced.

Using a funnel, fill pork casings and twist to desired size.

Drop sausages into boiling water, lowering the heat immediately to prevent bursting.

Using a small pot or ladle, keep the simmering water (170°F) in motion. Cook the sausages for about 25 minutes.

Using a needle or toothpick, pierce one sausage; if no blood comes out, the sausages are ready.

Remove from water and lay on sheet pans lined with side towels.

BLACK PUDDING

Yield: 8 lb.
Ingredients

Fatback, diced	1 lb.
Pork kidneys, fresh	3 lb.
Pork heart, fresh	1 lb.
Pork butt, smoked	1 lb.
Pork skins, soft cooked (reserve stock)	1 lb.
Beef blood	1 qt.
Cloves	1/10 oz.
Marjoram	1/3 oz.
Black pepper	1/3 oz.
Salt	3 oz.

Method
Dice fatback, kidneys, and heart small and blanch for 5 minutes. Dice smoked port butt. Grind cooked pork skins through a fine plate, and combine with some of the cooking broth, beef blood, spices, and salt, and heat slowly over a water bath to sabayon consistency. Fold in fat, kidney, heart, and smoked butt. Stuff into beef middle and tie well.

Blanch in 180°F water to an internal temperature of 170°F. Rinse with warm water; slowly cool under running water.

Smoke for 3 to 4 hours cold (99°F) smok (optional).

Chill well.

Note: This sausage is excellent for buf fets, cold cut platters, and sandwiches, o with home-fried potatoes.

SEAFOOD SAUSAGE

Yield: 9 lb. (36 to 40 links)
Ingredients

White bread, diced	5 oz.
Egg whites	10
Heavy cream	1 qt.
Pike Fillet, skinned, cubed and chilled, *or*	3 lb.
Flounder fillet *and*	2 lb.
scallops	1 lb.
Salt	to taste
Paprika	1 tsp.
Coriander	1 tsp.
Cayenne pepper	1/3 tsp.

Garnish

Shrimp, peeled and diced	1 lb.
Bay scallops, whole	1 lb.
King crab meat	1 lb.
Truffles *or* pistachio nuts	3 oz.
Chervil *or* parsley, chopped	2 to 3

Method
Combine the bread and egg whites with little of the heavy cream to make a panada Chill the soaked mixture.

Put the cubed fish into a food chopper o processor with a little ice, and purée. Ad the panada to the fish and mix well. Ad the salt and spices, then add the remainde of the heavy cream very slowly. Make a tes dumpling by poaching in lightly simmerin seasoned water. Adjust seasonings if neces sary.

Fold in the garnish ingredients and stu the mixture into pork casing, using a sau sage stuffer or piping bag. Tie the casin into links and blanch in 170°F water to a internal temperature of 150°F. Remove the sausage; shock in ice water and refrigerate.

The sausage may be served poached, sautéed, or grilled. Sauce Béarnaise and glazed carrots are ideal accompaniments.

RECIPES FOR SPECIALTY SAUSAGE

THÜRINGER ROTWURST

Yield: 9 lb.

Ingredients

Pork butt, large cubed	8 lb.
Salt	2½ oz.
Curing salt	¼ oz.
Pork skin, cooked	18 oz.
Pork liver, ½-inch cubes	9 oz.
Beef blood	18 oz.
Broth from pork skin	9 oz.
Onion, blanched	1 oz.
Allspice	⅓ oz.
Cinnamon	pinch
Caraway seeds	⅓ oz.
Black pepper	⅓ oz.
Marjoram	½ oz.

Method

Mix cubed pork with salt and curing salt; rest overnight. Simmer in water for 30 minutes or until cooked. Chill, cut into ½-inch cubes. Boil pork skin until tender. Blanch liver. Place hot pork skin into food processor and blend until creamy. Add blood and hot broth slowly.

Fold cubed pork, liver, onion, and spices into blood mixture. Adjust salt to taste. Stuff into beef middle, tie well.

Blanch in 180°F water to an internal temperature of 170°F.

Rinse with warm water and slowly cool in running water. Chill well before using.

If smoke flavor is desired, smoke in cold smoke at 98°F for 6 hours.

HEADCHEESE

Yield: 5 lb.

Ingredients

Boneless pig ears	2 lb.
Boneless pig snouts	3 lb.
Brine	2 gal.
Unsalted stock	up to 3 gal.
Bouquet garni	1
Onion pique (onion studded with clove and bay leaf)	1
Carrots	2
Crushed peppercorns	½ tsp.
Powdered unflavored gelatin	1 T per pt. of stock

Method

Soak meat in brine for about 3 hours. Rinse and place in a deep pan. Cover with unsalted stock, then add the bouquet garni, onion, carrots, and peppercorns. Bring to a boil and simmer until the meat is tender, approximately 1½ to 2 hours.

Remove the garniture and place meat in a strainer. Reserve the juice. Cool the meat a little and dice it into ½-inch cubes.

Press into a rectangular mold. Strain the stock, dissolve gelatin in the stock needed, and pour into mold to cover the meat.

Cool completely. Serve in thick slices.

Note: Diced pimentos, gherkins, and ham are sometimes added to this dish.

PRESSED PIG'S HEAD

(*Tête Pressée*)

Yield: 3½ lb.

Ingredients

Pig's head	12 lb.
Brine	2 gal.
Unsalted stock	to cover

(continued)

Charcuterie the Old-Fashioned Way. From left to right: Pig's Foot Zamboni, Split; Sliced Pressed Pig's Head; Sliced Pig Shoulder Zamboni; Marinated Okra, Pearl Onions, and Carrots; Ring of Sauerkraut Salad Topped with Jambon Persillée; Sliced Black Pudding; Sliced Headcheese; Marinated Turnip Ovals Decorated with Plum Tomatoes, Pumpkin Mousse, Baby Corn, and String Beans.

Pressed Pig's Head (continued)

Bouquet garni	1
Onion pique (onions studded with cloves and bay leaves)	2
Carrots, sliced	2
Peppercorns, crushed	½ tsp.
Shallots, chopped	4
Parsley, chopped	2 to 3 oz.
Butter	2 oz.

Method

Soak pig's head in brine for 24 hours. Rinse and place in a deep pan. Cover with unsalted stock; add the bouquet garni, the onions, the carrots, and the peppercorns.

Bring to a boil, and simmer until the meat is very tender, approximately 1½ to 2 hours.

Remove the meat, fat, tongue, and skin from the bones; discard the bones. Reserve the stock.

Spread a large napkin or piece of cheesecloth on the table, and arrange the meat and fat in a cylindrical shape on it. Put the ears on either side of the cylinder and the tongue in the center.

Sauté the shallots and parsley in butter spoon over the meat. Roll the meat in the cloth, and tie both ends carefully and tightly. Strain the stock over the roll and cool in the stock.

Slice thinly and serve with vinaigrette and sliced onion.

KISHKA A LA MESHEL

Yield: 2½ lb.

Ingredients

Matzo meal	12 oz.
Flour	4 oz.
Chicken fat	1 to 2 cups
Carrots, peeled and diced	2
Celery stalks, peeled and diced	2
Large onion, diced	1
Salt	1 tsp.
Egg, beaten	1
Chicken neck skin *or*	4 to 5
turkey neck skin	2 to 3
Chicken stock	to poach

Method

Mix matzo meal and flour. Add 1 cup chicken fat (hot) and knead into a dough. Sauté carrots, celery, and onions in remaining chicken fat and grind through a medium plate. Add to mixture. Season. Fold in beaten egg. Stuff mixture into necks, tie both ends, and poach in chicken stock at 160°F to an internal temperature of 170°F. Remove and chill. Cut on a bias into slices and sauté without fat in a skillet or griddle before serving.

ZAMBONI

Yield: 3 to 4 lb.

Ingredients

Pork shoulder with long leg	1 small, 8 to 10 lb.
Brine	to cover
Farmer's Sausage Mixture (see recipe, p. 253)	1 to 2 lb.

Method

Start skinning the shoulder carefully at the upper end of the shoulder. Remove by cutting and pulling all the skin to the first joint above the toes. Cut through joint without damaging the skin. Trim any excess skin and sew with a needle and thin butcher's twine into a 3- to 4-inch-diameter casing. Submerge in a brine for 24 hours. Remove, dry well, and stuff with Farmer's Sausage Mixture. Seal end carefully with a needle and twine. Poach in a strong stock at 170°F to an internal temperature of 160°F. Remove and cool, dry well, smoke for 3 to 4 hours. Refrigerate and slice for service.

STUFFED DERMA

Yield: 1½ lb.

Ingredients

Ground beef suet	½ lb.
Onion, finely chopped	1 small
Carrot, peeled and finely chopped	1
Celery stalk, peeled and finely chopped	1
Oatmeal	2 to 3 T
Salt	1 tsp. or to taste
White pepper	to taste
Garlic powder	½ tsp.
Eggs	1 to 2

Method

Place suet, onion, carrot, celery, oatmeal, salt, pepper, garlic powder, and eggs into a mixing bowl and mix well. If mixture seems too thin, add more oatmeal.

Stuff into a beef middle and tie. Poach at 170°F to an internal temperature of 145°F.

Chill, slice, and sauté until brown on both sides.

Note: This type of sausage can also be roasted.

Glossary

aitchbone. The hip or rump bone; also, the cut of meat (usually beef or pork) containing the bone.

à la. According to the style of, such as *à la Française* or according to the French way.

à la carte. Foods prepared to order: each dish priced separately.

al dente. Cooked just to the point of being done, especially pastas and fresh vegetables; cooked to retain crispness.

allumettes. Potatoes, carrots, and similar items cut into thin strips like matchsticks.

antipasto. Italian hors d'oeuvre. Assortment of appetizers.

appetizers. Beverages or assorted snacks served before a meal.

aspic. Term that applies to a way of arranging cold dishes. It consists of placing slices or fillets of meat, fish, or vegetables into molded jelly.

aspic jelly. A clarified, jellied stock that solidifies when cold. It can be flavored with such wines as port, sherry, marsala, madeira, champagnes, or white wine. It is used to coat foodstuffs or in the production of molds.

au naturel. Cooked simply.

bain-marie. A table having openings to hold containers of food over hot water in steam table. Double boiler can be used for same purpose with smaller amounts of food.

barding. To cover (for example, meat or game) with slices of bacon for cooking.

baste. To pour liquid or drippings over meat while cooking to hold moisture and provide flavor.

bean sprouts. Mung beans from China. Sprouts are used when tiny, tender, and green in making Chinese dishes; also as a salad ingredient.

beating. Regular lifting and stirring motion to bring mixture to a smooth texture. Often done to make mixture fluffy by incorporating air into it.

beignets. Fritters.

Belgian endive. A variety of chicory having leaves in stalk that are pale green to white; used raw as a salad, or braised.

bind. To cause to cohere, unite, or hold together, such as white sauce used to bind a croquette mixture.

blanch. To scald or parboil foods in boiling water or steam before cooking or freezing. Also, to dip in boiling water to facilitate the removal of skins from tomatoes, fruits, nuts.

blending. Thoroughly mixing two or more ingredients.

bouchée. Small meat patty or pastry shell filled with meat, poultry, or lobster. Sometimes filled with fruits.

bouquetière. A variety of vegetables in season arranged around a dish or platter of meat, poultry, or fish.

braise. To brown meat or vegetables in a small amount of fat and then cook covered in oven or on top of the range, adding liquid as needed to prevent scorching or burning.

brazier. Heavy-duty stewing pan with tightly fitting cover.

brine. Liquid of salt, nitrites, spices, and water used for pickling meats or fish.

brioche. A small pear-shaped roll of raised dough made with yeast, eggs, milk, butter, and flour. Very light. Sometimes filled for service as canapé.

brunoise. Cut in fine dice.

buffet. Display of ready-to-eat hot and cold foods. Often self-service from table or tables of assorted foods.

canapé. An appetizer prepared on a base such as bread, toast, or crackers.

capon. Castrated poultry noted for its tenderness and delicate flavor.

charcuterie. Cold cuts and meat dishes such as sausages. Also a delicatessen specializing in dressed meats and meat dishes.

chaud-froid. A jellied sauce used as a covering for meat, fish, or poultry; food covered with a chaud-froid sauce usually has been molded into shapes after cooking and is served cold. May be white, brown, green (asparagus), or red (tomatoes).

chef. Chief of the kitchen. Person in charge of food preparation.

ciseler. To shred finely; to score in the skin of fish or meat.

clarify. To make clear by adding a clarifying agent, which removes suspended particles, such as in the preparation of consommé.

cocotte. A small, shallow, individual baking dish, usually with one or two handles.

concasser. To chop coarsely.

coral. The cooked roe of a lobster.

corn. To salt lightly by placing in brine containing preservatives, sweetening, and sometimes spices. Usually for meat.

cornucopia. A receptacle shaped like a horn or cone. For a buffet may be filled with choice fruits. May be carved out of ice. Also, a pastry roll filled with whipped cream or meringue and nuts.

court bouillon. Fish stock, water, or other liquid in which fish is cooked, usually mixed with vinegar or wine, and savory herbs.

croquettes. Chopped or ground food usually held together with a thick sauce, shaped and rolled in breadcrumbs or cornmeal, and fried in a skillet in deep fat or oven-baked.

croustades. Baked forms or patty shells. Also hot patties filled with meat or liver paste.

croutons. Small pieces of fried or toasted bread used in soups, in garnishing, etc. Also made of thick layers of aspic.

deglaze. To moisten a roast pan or sauté pan with wine, vinegar, stock, or water in order to dissolve the caramelized drippings so that they may be incorporated into the sauce.

dice. To cut into small cubes.

egg albumen. The white of an egg.

egg wash. Egg yolk diluted with water or milk. Used to give color and gloss to yeast dough or pastry.

emulsification. The blending together of two incompatible liquids, such as oil and water. The blending is achieved by slowly adding droplets of one liquid to the other while beating constantly.

en Bordure. Bordered or ringed (as with rice or mashed potatoes) as a garnish.

en Croûte. In a crust.

farce. Stuffing, forcemeat.

farci. Stuffed.

fatback. Fresh pork fat with skin.

fennel. Vegetable resembling celery. It has a slight anise flavor.

fillet. A piece or slice of boneless lean meat or fish. To cut into fillets.

fleuron. Puff paste baked in a crescent shape used as a garnish.

forcemeat. Ground or emulsified meats and seasoning used for stuffing. *not always meat*

game. Edible wild animals such as bear, buffalo, deer, hare, opossum, squirrel, rabbit, and reindeer.

garnish. To embellish platter or tray or food item to be used in displays; to decorate. Also used as a noun, referring to a food-stuff being used as a garnish.

garnitures. French term for items used in garnishing: hard-cooked egg slices; timbales; aspic croutons; stuffed cherry tomatoes; filled fruits. *Accompaniment to entree*

gelatin. Colorless, tasteless, brittle substance made by boiling bones, hooves, and animal tissues. When granulated or powdered, gelatin is used to make jelly-like dishes such as aspics, desserts, molded salads, and mousses. Because gelatin has no flavor of its own, it makes a compatible ingredient for flavorful food combinations. *binds & solidifies*

gelée. Jelly or jellied.

glace de viande. A meat glaze from white or brown poultry stock or brown meat stock. Boiled down, it is reduced to a syrup that jells when cold. Used to add flavor to sauces and soups.

glaze. A liquid preparation (as sugar syrup, gelatin dissolved in meat stock) brushed over food (as meat, fish, pastry), which, after application, becomes firm and adds flavor and a glossy appearance.

gourmet. A connoisseur of food and/or wine, as well as the proper combination of dishes on menus; one with sensitive and discriminating tastes in food and wine.

hank. A measure for sausage casing, equal to 100 yards.

herb bouquet. Mixed herbs tied and used for seasoning.

herbs. Cultivated plants that are combined with foods to improve flavor. Some, such as parsley, basil, and chervil, can be used fresh. Most can also be used when dried.

hors d'oeuvre. Small appetizers or canapés served before a meal or as first course of a meal.

julienne. Potatoes cut in long slices, thinner than for french fries, and served very crisp. Also clear soup with thin strips of vegetables. Also poultry cut in narrow 1½-inch strips.

kibbe. Ground lamb and wheat baked in a cake.

Kirschwasser. A dry, colorless brandy made in Germany, France, and Switzerland. It is distilled from the fermented juices of the black Morello cherry and has a bitter almond flavor.

larding. Strips of salt pork inserted with a special larding needle through a good-sized piece of meat or fish that is to be roasted.

lardons. Strips of salt pork used for larding and as a garnish. Also, julienne of bacon.

leek. Mild form of onion with broad, long, succulent leaves. Used as a vegetable or an aromatic seasoning.

liaison. A binding agent for sauces; usually cream and egg yolks.

lox. Smoked salmon.

macedoine. Mixture usually of fruits or vegetables.

maraschino cherries. Large cherries preserved in true or imitation maraschino liqueur.

marzipan. A confection of crushed almonds or almond paste, sugar, and whites of eggs that may be shaped into various forms (fruits, vegetables).

masking. To cover completely, as with frosting or sauce (aspic or chaud-froid).

medallion, medaillon. A small, round, or oval serving of food, usually meat fillets.

melting. Making liquid by application of heat.

minced. Finely chopped.

mirepoix. Mixture consisting of 50 percent onion, 25 percent carrot, and 25 percent celery used to enhance the flavor of meat, fish, and shellfish dishes. It also is used for sauces, roasts, or baked meats.

mousseline. Fine forcemeats, served either hot or cold, made with whipped heavy cream. This term also is used to denote a sauce enriched with whipped cream (mayonnaise mousseline or hollandaise mousseline).

noisette. A small, rounded morsel of food, such as a small piece of lean meat or a small potato ball browned in butter.

oeufs (French). Eggs.

paillettes. Straws, often of pastry.

papillote. Cooked in parchment paper (or foil) to seal in flavors.

parboil. To boil until partially cooked.

parchment paper. A highly grease-resistant and water-resistant paper with a gelatinized surface, often used as a food wrapper.

Parmesan cheese. Italian cheese used for grating. Flavor is mild but pronounced; texture, hard.

pastry bag, pastry tube. A funnel-shaped container for holding soft food (mashed potatoes, whipped cream, cake frosting) from which the foods are forced through the pastry tube at the tip to make ornamental coatings or decorations.

paupiettes. Thin slices of poached or braised meat or fish rolled around forcemeat.

pilaf, pilau. Rice, usually combined with meat and vegetables, sautéed in oil, steamed in stock, and seasoned with any of several herbs (as saffron or curry).

piping. Forcing dough or decorating icing through a pastry tube in a narrow stream.

pimento, pimiento. Sweet red pepper, cooked and canned for use as a garnish for salads or casserole dishes. The source of paprika.

piquant. Spicy, highly seasoned. *sauce cocktail*

poaching. Cooking eggs, fish, etc., in water or fond that is just below boiling temperature.

profiteroles. Small balls of pâte à choux used as a garnish; usually hold savory filling.

prosciutto. Dry-cured, spiced ham.

pumpernickel. A sourdough bread; made with rye flour as a dark variety, and with a mixture of rye and wheat flours for the lighter types.

purée. Thick soup made of strained pulp of vegetables. May also refer to any vegetable or fruit pulp that has been mashed and sieved.

quenelles. Dumplings of forcemeat, flour, or semolina mixture cooked in boiling water or stock; used as a garnish for entrées and soups or may be served as a separate dish.

quiche. A pastry shell sprinkled with bits of fried bacon and grated cheese, filled with onion-flavored custard and baked.

rack. Market term for the unsplit rib section of veal or lamb.

ragout. Thick savory stew.

ramekin. Shallow china dish in which food may be baked and served.

ramequins (*see also ramekin*). Slices of bread covered with cheese and eggs and baked in a mold or shell.

ravier. An oval container. *mold*

reduce. To decrease volume by cooking or simmering.

rendering. Melting fat out of suet or other animal fats to free it from connective tissues.

rennin. An enzyme found in the lining of calves' stomachs, used in converting milk into junket or cheese.

rillettes. Highly seasoned, potted pork.

rissoles. Little turnovers of very thin puff paste with a filling of a highly seasoned mixture of ham or chicken or other delicate meat, chopped and moistened with white sauce. Dipped in egg and fried in deep fat.

romaine. Lettuce with deep green, straight leaves and marked flavor.

rôti. Roast.

roulade. A thin slice of meat rolled with or without stuffing and braised or roasted.

roux. Equal parts of fat and flour cooked; used to thicken sauces and gravies. Roux may be light-colored for light sauces; cooked until browned for darker sauces.

sachet. A small bag with selected herbs, used to season stock, soups, etc.; removed after cooking.

saddle. Market term for the unsplit loin of lamb, veal, or venison.

salami. Sausage of pork, beef, and seasonings. Dried. Usually contains garlic.

sauté. To cook quickly in a small amount of fat.

shallots. Onionlike plants with clustered bulbs that resemble garlic but are milder. Used for seasoning soups, stews, salads, etc.

simmer. To cook slowly just below the boiling point. Cooking time is longer than in poaching.

skewer. A long pin of wood or metal for fastening meat to keep it in desired shape while roasting; also used to hold small pieces of meat and vegetables for broiling.

skim. Using a skimmer or ladle to remove scum or grease accumulated on top of a soup, sauce, or stock.

smorgasbord. Swedish appetizers or full meals arranged on a table like a buffet.

steeping. To soak in liquid below boiling point, off heat, to extract flavor or color, as for tea.

stock. The liquid in which meat, poultry, fish, or vegetables have been cooked. Brown or white.

strand. The natural length of intestine, used as a measure for sausage casing.

tallow. A waxy substance, such as paraffin, beeswax, or beef fat, used in making displays for buffets.

template. A pattern or guide to be followed in making, for example, an ice sculpture.

timbales. From the arabic word *thabac*, meaning drum. A small, round metal container used for cooking vegetables and other foodstuffs, with or without a crust.

tournedos. A small fillet of beef, usually cut from the tip of the tenderloin and encircled by a strip of suet, salt pork, or bacon for quick cooking.

trussing. To skewer or to tie wings and legs of poultry before roasting.

try out. To cook fat until oil is out. Render.

turban. Style of arranging foods in a spiral on a dish. May also refer to certain forcemeat preparations that are cooked in a border mold, such as Turbany sole, chicken, or pheasant.

venison. Deer or reindeer meat.

vinaigrette. A sauce made of vinegar, oil, onions, parsley, and herbs.

vol-au-vent. Case made of puff pastry in which meat or poultry is served; usually covered with a crust lid.

water bath. A vessel containing water, usually hot, over or in which food is processed. Also called a bain-marie.

whipping. Beating rapidly to increase volume by mixing in air.

zest. Piece of peel or of thin, oily outer skin of an orange or lemon; used to flavor.

Pate - seasoned forcemeat (vegetable, seafood, ...)

Pate de Fois Gras → 75% goose liver

Pate Maison → House Pate

Pate de Jour → Pate of the day

Piece Montee → smallest piece on a buffet (CENTER)

Grosse Piece → largest " " " "

Chemise → To Coat

Index